Greenhill Books

BORN OF THE DESERT

BORN OF THE DESERT

With the SAS in North Africa

by Malcolm James

[Malcolm James Pleydell]

Greenhill Books, London
Stackpole Books, Pennsylvania

This edition of *Born of the Desert*
first published 2001 by Greenhill Books, Lionel Leventhal Limited,
Park House, 1 Russell Gardens, London NW11 9NN
and
Stackpole Books, 5067 Ritter Road, Mechanicsburg, PA 17055, USA

British Library Cataloguing in Publication Data
James, Malcolm
Born of the desert: with the SAS in North Africa. – (Greenhill
military paperback)
1. Great Britain. Army. Special Air Service Regiment – History 2. World War,
1939–1945 – Campaigns – Africa, North 3. Desert warfare 4. World War,
1939–1945 – Personal narratives, British
I. Title
940.5'423

ISBN 1-85367-438-9

Library of Congress Cataloging-in-Publication Data available

Publishing History
Born of the Desert was first published in 1945 (Collins, London) and
reprinted in 1991 by Greenhill Books with the addition of photographs and
the author's Postscript. The 1991 edition is now reproduced in paperback,
complete and unabridged, with the addition of Notes to New Edition and two
appendices (Roll of Honour and Honours and Awards).

Printed and bound in Great Britain by Creative Print and Design (Wales),
Ebbw Vale

FOREWORD

BORN OF THE DESERT tells simply the experience and reminiscences of an Army Doctor during the twelve months he served with the 1st S.A.S. Regiment in the desert in 1942-43. It is not an official history of the S.A.S. Regiment, nor does it aim at giving a military account of the many operations that were carried out during this period. It is perhaps for this reason that Captain James has been able to bring to life in human incidents and stories the men who started this force, the " Special Air Service," and to make clear something of their aims and the spirit which prompted them.

The S.A.S. was formed to attack military targets, including airfields, behind the enemy lines. They operated in small parties in uniform and whether they arrived at their destination by sea, air or land was immaterial. A certain glamour is always attached to units of this sort, whose work may be compared with that of a submarine in the Royal Navy or of Mosquito aircraft in the Royal Air Force. It is, however, unfortunate and invidious to compare their life and duties with those of the ordinary infantry, the " P.B.I.," who have in this, as in all wars, had to bear the brunt of the fighting and the casualties. Each has its different role and different training and qualifications are required.

The spirit of adventurous individualism has always been a characteristic of this nation and one which has been handed down to us through generations. This, in spite of the apparent apathy and " spirit of safety first " of the pre-war years, is still very much alive. There are and always will be in this country and empire those whose finer qualities are brought out to the full when they are given individual responsibility, and it is these men who initiate, lead and make a success of a force like the S.A.S. The work of the S.A.S. called for initiative and an original approach, self-reliance, control, a strong sense of discipline and immensely quick thought and action.

The S.A.S. was formed in 1941 at a time when we were still on the defensive and struggling almost alone against an enemy superior to us in numbers, arms and equipment. In spite of this, most of us were always sublimely confident that we should win the war even if we did not know and could not have tried to say how and when we should do so.

The war in the desert was a strange one ; although only a comparatively small part of our armed forces was employed there and a still smaller proportion of the German Army, it stood for a great deal more. It was the only theatre where ground forces were actively fighting against the Germans and the life-line to India and the Empire depended on the defence of Egypt and Palestine. To those who were out there, the outcome seemed even more vital and it was right that this feeling should exist. The defeat of the Germans at El Alamein had an immense effect on morale both in the Army and at home and, although two and a half years of intensive fighting were to come, it seemed that the European War was nearly won.

Looking back, one is apt to forget the sand and the heat and the flies and, as in life generally, to remember only the better moments of this desert life. If there had to be war, it seemed better to fight in an area where the destruction of civilians and cities and all the horrors that war in a fully populated country implies did not enter into it. (Gestapo methods were almost unknown and warfare seemed cleaner.) There was, too, as was natural when we were all many thousands of miles from home and all that home meant, a different spirit and a closer bond between all ranks. In a unit like the S.A.S. this feeling was particularly noticeable and there are many illustrations and instances of it throughout this book.

But it is not only in time of war that this spirit of energetic and generous companionship is wanted. At home we are faced with the enormous problems caused by six years of war and to tackle these we do most urgently need the spirit kindled during the war —the courage, unselfishness, determination and co-operation shown by so many people in so many different ways.

Captain James says that he wondered, on joining the S.A.S., if he would find sincerity there, " for rightly or wrongly, it seemed to me that sincerity was the thing that mattered most." Any one who reads this book, although the names, the places and perhaps the whole atmosphere may mean little to them, will surely be

impressed by his sincerity and inspired by the courage and
initiative of the small force whose story he tells to ensure that
the sacrifice and sufferings of all these years are not wasted and
that the spirit generated is kept alive to help us to deal with the
problems of Peace.

July, 1945.

CONTENTS

PAGE

FOREWORD   5

INTRODUCTION—BIRTH OF A UNIT   13

CHAP.

1   FIRST IMPRESSIONS   29

2   EARLY TRAINING   42

3   ON PARACHUTING   54

4   BEHIND ROMMEL'S LINES   67

5   JOURNEY TO THE RENDEZVOUS   85

6   WE ATTACK FUKA AERODROME   101

7   GERMAN PRISONERS AND A RUM PARTY   129

8   LIFE AT THE RENDEZVOUS   138

9   RAID ON SIDI HANEISH   154

10   VIEWS OF A GERMAN DOCTOR   165

11   WE RETURN BY AIR   178

12   OBSERVATIONS ON CAIRO   186

13   WE TRAVEL SOUTH TO KUFRA   198

14   WE APPROACH BENGHAZI   225

15   WOUNDED MEN IN THE JEBEL   238

16   THE AMBUSH   250

17   OUR SAD WITHDRAWAL   260

18   RETURN TO KUFRA   272

19   LIFE IN THE SAND SEA   282

20   THE STORY TELLERS   289

21   THE GROWTH OF A UNIT   302

POSTSCRIPT   321

NOTES TO NEW EDITION   323

APPENDIX   332

ILLUSTRATIONS

Appearing between pages 96 and 97
Mike Sadler, M.M., with David Stirling
Soldiers brewing up tea
Digging a battle jeep out of the Sand Sea
Paddy Mayne, D.S.O.
Parachutist Sillitoe [Sillito]
Caravan route to Kharga Oasis
Cpl. Austin and Sgt. Hevans [Heavens]
Cook-house scene in Kufra Oasis: (left to right) 'Slim' Somerville,
'Paddy' Reilly, 'Darkie' Kendall, 'Grazzi' Shaw, 'Syd' Jackson,
J. Lambert, Cecil Cleverly
Bill Fraser, the author, and Jim Chambers
Paddy Mayne with members of his squadron
Mike Sadler, chief navigator to the SAS
Sjt. Bunfield
Sjt. Badger, M.M. and Sgt. Cooper, D.C.M.
Sjt. Lilley, M.M.
Author's Red Cross Jeep approaching Wadi Sura
Parachute training
Desert Oasis
The author

MAPS

PAGE

Area of Operations and Raids on Air-fields.
July-August, 1942   103

The Attack on Benghazi and Rendezvous in the Sand Sea.
September-October-November, 1942   221

Areas of Operations of A and B Squadrons. December 1942
and January, 1943   305

INTRODUCTION

BIRTH OF A UNIT

" Forsooth, brothers, fellowship is heaven, and lack of fellowship is hell : fellowship is life, and lack of fellowship is death : and the deeds that ye do upon the earth, it is for fellowship's sake that ye do them."—*The Dream of John Ball.*

WILLIAM MORRIS.

EARLY in the summer of 1941, David Stirling, a subaltern in the Middle East Guards Commando, first conceived the idea of the Special Air Service. His scheme was ambitious : firstly, he had to form the Unit ; then he had to ensure its success in the role of harassing the enemy's lines of communications in the Western Desert. In the latter capacity he knew that the country and the nature of the campaign would provide him with endless opportunities. For the desert war was a war of supply ; and it had been remarked that, with such a limitless battlefield, it was the paradise of the tactician and the very nightmare of the quarter-master. Behind the two opposing main forces lay a long coastal road, reaching out for mile after deserted mile over open, barren stretches, with only an occasional encampment or rest-house where the dusty, weary convoys might draw up for the night. Aerodromes and landing grounds were scattered sparsely along the route ; they consisted in the main of a flat piece of firm ground with a few tents scattered unevenly around.

These little colonies of troops which lined the main artery of supply were poorly guarded. As a regimental doctor my duties had not infrequently led me along that hot desert road in quest of further medical supplies for the aid post. As the driver and I jogged along in our open truck, I would keep a look out for the camps on either side ; they were landmarks, and they helped to vary the journey. Here was an airfield with a squadron of planes waiting to take off, their racing engines throwing out great storms of yellow dust against the trembling blue background of the sky.

13

Here was a workshop with dismembered vehicles in every stage of repair, while the half-naked mechanics went about their jobs with a thoroughness which came from long months of forced improvisation. Here was a divisional headquarters, and from the truck I could just make out the queue of men lining up for their midday meal. I was seldom stopped or questioned as I went about my business. Perhaps a military policeman might halt the truck and ask for my identity card ; possibly a sentry would wonder who I was as I drove over to the officers' mess ; but it was more often a polite salute than an officious inquiry that sped me on my way.

For in these camps one was conscious only of the fact that the enemy were fifty or a hundred miles away as the case might be, and accordingly one felt completely safe from any hostile land interference. The fact that there was a completely unguarded flank to the south and a long coastal flank to the north on which anybody might land with impunity, seldom if ever dawned on the intelligence. Men strolled in careless, unarmed confidence knowing that everything was quiet further forward ; at the appropriate moment they would " down tools " for a meal ; at night they would all settle down for a good rest. Presumably each man possessed a rifle ; but I doubt if many of them could have laid their hands on a weapon in less than a minute, and if it was dark they would not know what to shoot at. A solitary sentry in the desert was of little value to such a camp ; he might well be more dangerous to his fellows than to an enterprising marauder. These men were not in a state of readiness to fight ; they did not expect to fight, for they were a hundred miles behind the front line. Exactly the same applied to the aerodromes. The pilots flew their planes and fought in the air ; once they set their feet on solid ground they had finished with the war for the time being. Naturally they were unarmed as they sat drinking in the mess or made their way to their tents : the enemy was a hundred miles away.

But suppose for a minute that a German soldier were to load up a captured English lorry with sufficient supplies of petrol, food, and water, and then drive round the southern end of the opposing lines, and turn up north until he struck the same road along which I had been travelling. What was there to stop him from placing some small charges and explosives amongst those vehicles, or in the cockpits of those stationary aircraft? The fact that he was a foreigner? I doubt it. There were Czech, Polish and French troops amongst the Allied desert forces. His uniform? Never. One had only to view the assorted desert apparel of the Australians to realise how unconventional military attire could be. Why, even their road-police were seldom dressed in more than a slouch hat and the briefest pair of shorts, rolled well up the thighs in order to expose their brawny sinews to the sun. No, the reverse held good. For if this German spoke English he would be helped and directed on his way, whereas if a zealous sentry should happen to challenge him in the characteristically apologetic manner of the British, he could almost certainly produce a captured identity card.

Perhaps this sounds far-fetched and too easy ; but I can well remember returning in January of 1943 with a squadron of the Special Air Service from their raiding base which had been situated behind the enemy's lines. We were driving northwards along a small winding track that led to the coast road, when we found ourselves approaching an American landing ground. This was situated about three hundred miles from the fighting line at that time, and since we were coming up from the south, this was the first glimpse of Allied troops that we had had for some while. Aircraft and tents were clustered on either side of the track ; and we, a ruffianly, bearded, unkempt and ill-clothed mob, drove right through them with no other interference than an occasional questioning stare from an American who evidently appreciated his chewing gum.

" What price a few buckshee planes here, mate ? " shouted a member of our party, and one was obliged to agree. It is not difficult to picture the chaos and confusion that would have resulted if we had dropped a few explosives into the cockpits as we jogged past. Then we could have driven away quite quietly and a few minutes later there would have been aircraft blowing up all over the place.

If this was the case with ourselves, how much more so would it apply to the Italians? The Germans, perhaps, were a little more thorough. David Stirling considered the possibilities. There were three means of approach : overland, by driving round the southern end of the fighting lines ; from the sea with the aid of a collapsible boat launched from a submarine ; from the air by parachuting down in the region of the objective. The latter two methods would be influenced by the weather. They would entail a long walk and a difficult return journey, and hence were not as suitable as a land approach. Driving round to the target would mean a careful stocking and husbanding of petrol, food and water : the three essentials. Later on, when our raids had become a trial to the enemy, it also meant an almost perfect camouflage and concealment from aircraft which were out patrolling the enemy's southern flank.

Such operations would necessitate complete secrecy, and this would mean small parties or raiding forces. Large numbers of men could seldom conceal their intentions in the desert, where the country was so open and where the bases in Egypt were riddled with informers and agents. Furthermore, three men on an enemy aerodrome could probably do as much damage as thirty, and certainly would be more elusive in the hide-and-seek sort of warfare that followed.

Such operations, also, would need men finely trained and utterly reliable. There would have to be first-class navigators who could steer a course over several hundreds of miles, and bring the party to an exact point on the coastal road, or to the exact site of the aerodrome that was to be attacked. The drivers would need to be efficient in getting their trucks across the long drifts of loose, blown sand, in attending to all repairs, and in making themselves self-sufficient. Only with these capabilities could a patrol raid an objective at a given time on a given night, or arrive punctually at a rendezvous prior to an attack. Then the men would have to be familiar with the special forms of explosives which were required ; and although this would be a relatively simple matter, an engineer would be needed to make the bombs in sufficient quantities.

These were David Stirling's ideas, and I can imagine him explaining them in some mess or other while his fellow officers laughed and shook their heads, telling him not to get hold of these fancy notions but to stick to the real orthodox fighting.

Yet his ideas were not original. There was the Long Range Desert Group which had been active throughout the war, working on a similar principle but putting chief emphasis on reconnaissance and observation of the enemy's movements. David merely wished to add the element of surprise attacks.

His schemes were turned to actualities chiefly by the enthusiasm of Jock Lewis who was also a member of the Guards Commando. Although I never met Lewis, I had not been in the S.A.S. for long before I realised that he was the man who was responsible for its construction and organisation. An Australian by birth, he had decided to complete his education at Oxford, and from there he joined the Guards at the outbreak of war. Finding, as did a number of others, that regimental duties were not greatly attractive, he transferred to the Guards Commando ; and during those spring months of 1941 when that unit formed a part of the garrison of beleaguered Tobruk, he led as many as twenty-eight fighting patrols against the enemy. By all accounts he was a remarkable man, possessing, as he did, a terrific drive of character together with a natural sense of leadership. More than that, he expected others to do what he himself could do ; where he could lead them they must follow, for he was as severe on others as he was hard upon himself.

The idea of the Special Air Service brought Stirling and Lewis together ; the one a man who thought in terms of future possibilities, and the other so rigidly practical. They did not have to wait long for their plans to materialise ; for that summer the Guards Commando was disbanded, and Stirling, who was well known at headquarters, and a friend of General Auchinleck's, had soon interested the staff in his schemes, and received official sanction to raise this special force. He and Lewis picked what they considered to be the best of the Commando unit, and reinforced it with volunteers from the Scottish Commando, taking care as they did so to restrict the numbers of intake. They chose Kabrit for their training base, a headland situated on the western shore of the Bitter Lake near its junction with the Suez Canal, where a large airfield was situated close enough to assist in the parachute training of its members ; and it was here, almost on the lake shore, that the unit first pitched its tents, and began to consider its course of training. Such was the commencement of the Special Air Service ; a unit that was born of the desert ; that learned its early lessons from desert warfare ; that struck its first blows, knew its first reverses, and gained its first spectacular successes in this arid battlefield.

Since their chief objective was to get behind the enemy's lines, Stirling and Lewis decided that all operatives must learn how to parachute as soon as possible. But here they came up against their first difficulty, for it was no easy matter to get hold of the planes from which to jump. They had obtained permission to form the unit, it is true ; but who was going to lend them the aircraft, each one of which would have to be specially fitted up with strongpoints for the attachment of statachute lines ? It was with great difficulty that they overcame this obstacle, for little or no help came from England whose officials informed them that when they wanted parachute units in the Middle East they would send them there, or arrange for their training. It was a case of the superior teacher rebuking the impudent child. Accordingly the Special Air Service had to turn their efforts in other directions until, by fair means or foul, they managed to obtain the loan of an old Bombay aircraft on which they persuaded a friendly engineer to construct the strongpoints.

I believe there were four men who stepped into that plane as it stood waiting on Bagoush airfield one hot summer's morning : David Stirling, Jock Lewis and two sergeants. Blair Mayne was soon to join these pioneers. He had recently transferred to the unit from the Scottish Commando, and with him he brought a fiery reputation as a fighter that was based on actions in the Syrian campaign. Large in stature, and powerfully built—he had led the Irish pack in pre-war days—he possessed an uncommon amount of physical strength ; but what was more outstanding was his extraordinary gift of natural cunning in personal warfare, a quality that was to save his life, and the lives of those who were with him, on more than one occasion in the future.

These, then, were the first men of the Special Air Service to parachute ; there was no one to train them so they had to learn for themselves. To the best of their knowledge nobody had ever jumped out of a Bombay aircraft before, and when they landed on the gravel desert surface a thousand feet below, it did not take them long to find out why this was so. For the tail of the Bombay was set too low in relation to the fuselage to allow safe parachuting, and it had ripped great gashes in the silk canopies of some of the 'chutes as the men jumped out of the plane. This is but an example of the way the unit had to learn each point from practice; there was no experience on which to base their experiments, and it was only by good fortune that there wēre not mañy accidents to mar those early days.

Thus they exercised and toiled, always modifying, continually improving. It was in this respect that Jock Lewis was invaluable. He drew out plans and time-tables for the training. How should they best become fit so that this sort of warfare could be rewarded with tangible results? In England they had jumping platforms set at various heights from the ground, and by jumping from these a man could learn how to fall without injuring himself. Wasn't there some story that in England parachute troops were jumping from moving lorries? He tried the theories out, one after another. He jumped from a truck travelling at twenty miles an hour and did a forward roll. " All right," he cried out as he picked himself up, " that one's O.K.," and he put it down in the training syllabus. Then he jumped facing backwards from the truck travelling at the same speed, but in so doing he hurt himself. Accordingly the exercise was ruled out, for there was no object in causing more casualties than were necessary over the training itself.

This building up of a unit was hard work ; and in speaking of . it afterwards the men would tell me how every night they could see the light of a hurricane lamp dimly outlining Lewis's tent, while inside he sat at his camp table working away at fresh plans and schemes.

He cut down water on the march to a bare necessity—a water-bottle a day. March thirty miles in a night. Hide up during the day taking whatever cover was available. Never drink before midday ; save your water until the cool of the evening ; only rinse out your mouth with a small sip of water, swallow it, and put your bottle away ; never gulp at your water ; never lend your water to a friend, for this habit could breed more enemies than you imagined possible. Those were his rules of water discipline. Never let any one try to do something until you had done it first and proved it to be possible. That was his plan of leadership.

One result of Lewis's inventive labours at this time was the sticky bomb or, as we knew it, the Lewis bomb. This was a small portable form of explosive which resulted in a fire after it had blown up. It was especially devised so that a man might carry several of these bombs over a long distance without undue fatigue, and then he could leave them, like visiting cards, on whatever objects he wished to demolish. Fuses for these bombs were called " time-pencils " ; they worked on the principle of acid eroding through a metal wire, thus releasing a spring which resulted in the explosion. The acid was stored in a small glass phial which could easily be broken just before the bomb was placed on the target ; variations of wire thicknesses resulted in bombs with fuses of anything from half a minute to half an hour. Although they did not always work exactly to time, they were invaluable for their purpose ; and with the aid of an engineer, they were soon being constructed in adequate numbers.

Under Stirling's and Lewis's guidance the unit settled down slowly, and in time was joined by a small volunteer detachment of officers and men of the Fighting French Forces. For accommodation they shared the mess of H.M.S. *Saunders*, an adjoining naval camp, since as yet they had no proper catering arrangements of their own. Gradually the platforms and swings were constructed. Inclined rails were built to take the trolleys which now were used in place of trucks to jump from. The discipline was hard ; but practically enough, the unit was founded on a natural and selective leadership.

On November the nineteenth, 1941, General Auchinleck launched his winter attack against the enemy in the Western Desert. Two days prior to that event the Special Air Service were given their first opportunity to show their worth : they were asked to destroy the aircraft, sheds and other objectives in the Tmimi area. In high spirits the fifty-four men who were picked for the job clambered into three planes that had been loaned to them for the occasion. Sergeant Bennett told me about it one morning sometime later in his characteristically informal way. But story telling did not come readily to him, and in any case he had been in so many raids since then that every now and again he would get muddled up, and pause for a moment, and say, " No, that was the Bagoush raid in '42, wasn't it ? " or " Hold on a minute, sir, I've got it wrong again. That was the next raid we did," However, he sorted out his facts eventually, and this was his tale.

They got into their planes and left Kabrit in the early evening, flying to Bagoush airfield in order to refuel, and taking off again at about ten o'clock. Their course took them out to sea, and then they turned inland when they reached the gulf of Bomba. Apart from a certain amount of flak sent up at them as they crossed the coast, they received no attention from the enemy ; but the weather, which had been good when they started, deteriorated steadily throughout the flight and by now had become really foul. It was on account of this that the Air Force pilots lost their way and the men were given the orders to jump while the planes were over the wrong area. In the stormy blackness of that night, broken only by an occasional flash of lightning, the men jumped out of the planes into a wind that was blowing at half-gale strength. They drifted down fast, striking the ground heavily when they landed, and being dragged hard along the stony surface before they had any opportunity to find their feet. Little wonder, then, that they were widely scattered and separated, and had great difficulty in finding one another.

Sergeant Bennett was fortunate in only grazing himself when he landed. As he tried to struggle to his feet a fresh buffet of wind caught his 'chute, billowing it out and dragging him along once more. At last he managed to release the safety-box round his waist and rolled out of his harness. Then he got to his feet wondering what to do next. There was not a soul to be seen, nor the slightest sign of a land feature ; in the pitch blackness and the blustering wind, he told me, he might have been the only person in the desert that night. It was a full half-hour before he found any one else, for under these circumstances whistle-blowing and shouting were of little value in personal location. But at length nine of the men had joined one another, although of this number, two had been crippled by injuries in falling and were unable to walk. The remaining seven went out in different directions searching for the ammunition and supplies which had been dropped with them in parachute containers. They found only three of the sixteen containers which had been dropped, and from these they sorted out the explosives and ammunition they would need. When they had done this they made the two injured men comfortable, leaving them most of the food and water ; and then, after saying good-bye, they marched off on a north-easterly bearing which by rights should have taken them to the airfield. In the remaining hours of darkness they covered fifteen miles, and with a grey dawn lighting up the desolate scene of the open desert they began to search round for a hiding-place.

The weather continued to be stormy throughout the day, and at five-thirty that afternoon, just as it was getting dark, there was a sudden cloudburst. They had three blankets between the seven men and they lay there shivering, doubtless feeling very miserable in their isolation. The rain kept on during the night, beating down with the wind, driving into their faces as they trudged northwards once more, until daylight the next morning showed the water fairly cascading down the rough stony slopes of the small wadis. They were wet through ; but what was far worse was the depressing fact that their sticky bombs had been rendered quite useless. For this meant that they were no longer effectual as far as the raid was concerned. Accordingly they decided to march back to the prearranged rendezvous area where a patrol of the Long Range Desert Group had been detailed to stand by and pick them up.

For the next two days and nights they walked south, with occasional halts for resting and sleeping. At the end of that time they stopped, since they had covered more than the distance which had been given to them in their instructions. It should be borne in mind that these men did not know they had been dropped in the wrong place. Further one should realise that it required a considerable amount of courage and determination to decide to stay in one place like this. For their food supplies were dwindling, and if the weather turned dry their water would soon become another problem. Perhaps it might be compared to a person swimming out to sea and waiting, say half a mile out, not knowing whether he had sufficient strength to swim back to shore again ; only for these men the shore would be represented by the enemy held coastline.

They kept a good look-out the next day and saw nothing ; but soon after darkness had fallen they caught sight of a light low down on the horizon. After about half an hour it went

out, and thinking it to be a star, they did not investigate.
By now they were feeling "very tired," as Sergeant Bennett
expressed it.

On the following morning they noticed smoke where previously
they had seen the light. Their spirits rose, and they trudged
wearily across the intervening miles. It was the patrol of the
Long Range Desert Group which had arranged to come and pick
up the Special Air Service operatives after the raid. For the next
three days they all searched the area for the rest of the men ; but
of the fifty-four who started out, only twenty-one were picked up.
Realising that there was no object in remaining longer, they turned
south and drove down to the oasis of Siwa which, at this time, was
in British possession, and was being used by the L.R.D.G. as their
headquarters.

So this, their first raid, was a most complete and utter failure.
They had been dropped in the wrong area ; they had been
scattered all over the place by the storm ; their explosives had
been ruined by the rain. It was uncertain whether any of them
had ever reached the aerodrome. Several of the officers and men
had to be left where they had fallen. A few of them were in a
critical condition, and were almost certain to have died before
they were found by the enemy. Obviously, then, parachuting in
the desert was not worth it. The odds against were too high, and
the chances of success too low. They did, however, persist with
the parachute training ; for it was, as David Stirling said, " an
extra feather in their caps," a standby if need be, and it made a
good basis for judgment of character of the new volunteers who
were replacing the unit's losses. Only now they began to think
more in terms of a land approach towards their objective, and it
was at this stage of their development that their real friendship
with the Long Range Desert Group began. This latter unit, with
its long history of past successes, offered to provide the Special Air
Service with transport, and to navigate them to their targets. In
such a way did the two units come to work together in that happy
combination which was to cost the enemy so dear in the days
to come.

Of the ground training there is little to relate, except that at
some period they decided to put their theories to the test by
"raiding" Heliopolis aerodrome. I gather that this was done in

conjunction with the Air Force who knew the date of the mock
attack, and laid on a special defensive guard. The raiding parties
set out from Kabrit, marching the ninety odd miles across the
desert to Cairo under cover of darkness, lying up by day, and, by
using native conveyance when they came in handy, they experienced little difficulty in getting past the guards and on to the
airfield on the night in question. Gummed labels were employed
instead of time-bombs, and the next morning showed that a good
number of the aircraft, buildings, stores, sheds, etc. had been
effectively destroyed. It was said that there were distinct repre-
cussions over this matter, and that even a few of the stately homes
in G.H.Q., Cairo, experienced a slight tremor. Perhaps it led to
a better guarding of aerodromes, perhaps it may even have
influenced the organisation of the R.A.F. Regiment : only the
omnipotent can tell.

At the end of November, when Auchinleck's army was
advancing on Benghazi, several raiding parties left Kabrit and
flew to the oasis of Jalo, which lies about four hundred miles to
the south of Benghazi. Here they joined up with T patrol of the
L.R.D.G. who took the responsibility of navigation, and drove
a party led by Jock Lewis to within thirty miles of Agheila
airfield. From here the Special Air Service patrol marched
to the airfield· by night only to find that, whereas a considerable number of aircraft had previously been reported on
the field, it was now deserted. Feeling very depressed and
disappointed, they trudged back with their bombs unused. This
was the second failure.

But their feelings very soon changed when, at just about this
time Blair Mayne and a handful of men made their way on to
Tamet airfield, and blew up twenty-four aircraft and a petrol
dump in a very short space of time.. For not only did this success
justify their efforts but, what was almost more important, it meant
that their plans were feasible ; it proved that their training was
not in vain ; and strangely enough, it brought quite a fresh
element suddenly into being : the spirit of personal competition
amongst the operatives.

A few days later Jock Lewis set off with a few men in a
captured Italian lorry, accompanied by some trucks of an
L.R.D.G. patrol. Their object was to strafe the main road, the

road-house at Mersa Brega and generally to put the wind-up the enemy. This is how Sergeant Lilley tells the story :

" After four days travelling over the desert, with lots of digging and sweating—we were travelling in an Italian Lancia— we hit the main coast road about ten miles west of Mersa Brega, and then proceeded towards the Mersa Brega road-house, passing German and Italian convoys going in the opposite direction. On arrival at the road-house we found a lot of Lancias parked there, so Lieutenant Lewis parked our Lancia alongside them. The driver in the next Lancia to ours got out and asked Lieutenant Lewis for a light. Lieutenant Lewis told him we were English, and that he was a prisoner. The Italian thought this was a great joke, and walked off laughing, imagining that we were Germans until Mr. Lewis convinced him otherwise. In the meantime we had been trying to get our guns working, but they were jammed owing to the thick oil we were using. While we were doing this the Italians began to realise that something was wrong, and a minute later they opened up on us with everything they had. We managed to put bombs on the Lancias and round the building, and after a bit we got the guns going and shot the place up. Then we started moving off down the road again ; but before we left we mined the road, cutting off into the desert as soon as we had finished, and waiting to see the bombs go off. That night we got the prisoner drunk on rum and couldn't stop him singing till three o'clock in the morning."

They had only been back in Jalo a few days before Blair Mayne set off again with five men to raid Tamet aerodrome for the second time within a week. S patrol of the L.R.D.G. took them to within three miles of the drome. It was very dark with a fine drizzle blowing on the night wind. On reaching the airfield they split up into two parties of two and three men respectively ; then they scattered across the field placing their bombs in the cockpits, and on the wings of the planes. In this way they destroyed twenty-seven aircraft ; the first blew up with a roar while they were still on the drome, and the light of the blazing wreck showed them up as they tried to get away. Italian sentries saw them and challenged. " Freund," shouted Mayne in reply, but his accent could not have been convincing, for the sentries immediately opened fire. The operatives ran round and past them and got away into the open where they rejoined the trucks at 4.30 in the morning. On their way back to Jalo they met David Stirling also returning from a raid, but his luck had been out and he had little to show for his efforts.

Quite soon after this Jock Lewis was killed while returning from a raid on Nufilia landing ground. Sergeant Lilley was with him and writes :

" The Long Range Desert Group dropped us off about thirty-five miles from Nufilia aerodrome, so the five of us with Mr. Lewis in charge put on our packs containing bombs and rations, and set off for the drome. That night we slept out in the rain with one blanket, and the blanket was just one sheet of ice when we woke up in the morning. Mr. Lewis went out and found an empty bir (well) about half a mile from the drome, so we lay up in there for a day and kept a good watch on the place. At about one o'clock the next night we went on the drome and put a bomb on the first plane. Just as we were putting one on the second plane the first went off. We pushed on in search of more planes but they were dispersed too far apart and we could not find them. By this time the guards were surrounding the drome, but we heard them talking together in bunches so it was easy to crawl past them. We reached the L.R.D.G. again the next morning. After a meal we started on the return journey, and everything was going quite smoothly when suddenly we spotted a Messerschmitt 110 following our tracks. We loaded the guns and waited for him. He was only about twenty-five feet off the ground, and when he opened up we gave him everything we'd got ; but it did not make any difference to him ; he just kept at the same height strafing all the time. Mr. Lewis was shot through the leg, and died in about four minutes. Old boy Messerschmitt went back to fetch his pals, and we buried Mr. Lewis, one of the best officers ever to wear uniform. Ten minutes later the Stukas arrived and gave us hell. They got all the trucks in the space of three minutes, and then went gunning for the men for eight and a half hours. There wasn't one minute when we didn't have a Stuka above us.

" Just before dark a reconnaissance plane came over with four

Stukas. They must have seen the men sprawled out on the ground, and thought they were dead. The ground was as flat as a billiard table, but none of the men got shot. That was the last we saw of their planes for that trip. . . ."

The death of Jock Lewis was felt very keenly ; and later when I heard the men speaking of him, it was always with admiration, and with as much reverence as could be expressed in their rather gruff and unemotional voices. For these men were seldom impressed by what an officer said, or the way he spoke ; it was what he did that counted with them, and Jock Lewis was a man who always tried a thing out himself before he would allow any of the others to make the attempt. His loss was something that could never be replaced. But he had at any rate seen the unit's first successes ; and the work of his planning remained unchanged, and continued, and will continue, as long as the Special Air Service is in existence.

Despite this set-back the raids went on throughout December, 1942, and January of 1943. They were concentrated chiefly on aerodromes and road convoys, with the attacks being launched by night and the patrols getting as far away as possible before daylight the next morning. They were more than pinpricks. Within a week Blair Mayne and his patrol alone had destroyed more than fifty aircraft, while the road strafing slowed up the supplies to the enemy's front, and meant that the convoys had to be closely guarded. The Germans reacted to this by using aircraft to patrol the desert in order to catch our forces as they approached, or while they were withdrawing from an objective. This in turn restricted our movements chiefly to the hours of darkness, and demanded a high standard of navigation. By day the trucks were camouflaged perfectly, for there is no lesson which improves camouflage as well as a low level machine-gunning attack. On the other hand there were times when it was necessary to drive up by day and accept the risk, since an earlier night attack meant that the patrol would get further away from the target area before the next morning's light. It was always the day or two after an attack that was the most dangerous time : aircraft would be searching in all directions, following the tracks made by the vehicles in the soft sand and gravel, ever on the look-out for the

first movement on the ground that should betray human existence.
It was one thing to raid an objective successfully, and quite
another to depart undetected. There were numerous personal
adventures, and several cases where men had to make long forced
marches to get back to " base " after their transport had been
destroyed. One of the Special Air Service officers, Bill Fraser,
having destroyed thirty-seven planes, walked his patrol back to
British lines, making a wide circle south in order to get round the
fighting front. To relieve their thirst his men distilled some water
from the salt-marshes at El Agheila, using two water-bottles and
a piece of rubber tubing ; a slow tedious process but sufficiently
productive to be of value. They were exhausted when, eight days
later, they reached their own troops ; and I remember one of the
party telling me that, for many weeks after this experience, the
smell of cooking food was something he could not bear : he had
to eat something immediately to satisfy his lust.

By January of 1942 Rommel had gathered his forces together ;
and early one morning he launched the counter-offensive which
sent our troops reeling back to the Gazala line. The Special Air
Service took the occasion of making several attacks in the Benghazi
area. One raid destroyed fifteen aircraft on Berka airfield in the
middle of March ; but in the raids on the dockyards and the
railways south of the town, fortune was not with them ; and so
often it was luck that was the deciding factor. For a while the
fighting in the desert died down ; but then in May Rommel
attacked again, forcing the British back mile after stubborn mile
to El Alamein. It was at this time that I joined the Special Air
Service, and had the good fortune of getting to know some of
these men personally and seeing just how they went about
their work.

CHAPTER ONE

" Time but the impression deeper makes
As streams their channels deeper wear."
                                        ROBERT BURNS.

IT WOULD be interesting to know just what were the motives that
prompted men to join the Special Air Service : the reasons that
made a man in a company or battalion want to leave the friends
and associations he had made for something new and so entirely
uncertain.

I was thinking it over as I leaned back in the corner seat of an
Egyptian railway compartment and disinterestedly watched the
flat yellow landscape drift past. For my own part, I knew that I
had been most dreadfully bored at the hospital which I had just
left and that, I realised, was my chief reason for joining. Not
very heroic, perhaps, but then the life of a general duty officer in
a military hospital was, in all conscience, a pretty tedious affair.
In the main it consisted of writing notes in duplicate, sometimes
in triplicate, signing one piece of paper after another, attending
numerous meetings, seeing that the wards were kept clean for the
commanding officer's weekly inspection and humouring the
matron. I had been acquainted, too, with duties as a regimental
doctor, but even there I had found it to be more a case of fighting
ennui than battling with the enemy—it brought out the truth in
the old saying that war consisted of long periods of boredom
alternating with short spells of acute wind-up. But any sort of
variation to the life that I had been leading in a desert hospital
would prove acceptable ; at any rate that was the way it seemed
to me.

For a fighting man, of course, it would be different. This
change would give him a chance to prove himself and satisfy any
little doubts of the conscience. He knew he would not be sitting
around inactive for long intervals of time ; nor would he be

attending one lecture after another, or made to see that his
buttons sparkled and his webbing was kept spotless. Besides this
sort of warfare possessed a definite flavour of romance. It con-
jured up visions of dashing deeds which might become famous
overnight. It left out all the disappointments and the many
hardships which were to become so commonplace in our lives.

And that is always the way, with anticipation cheating reality
at every turn. The photographs of the desert accentuated all the
attractions and left out such things as the flies, the sweat, and the
dreadful night drives that at times made life a hideous nightmare.
Yes, these photographs made the war look like a jolly good game
of French v. English at school, while the wireless commentators
gave the impression of having just returned in blazers and flannels
from an enjoyable evening at the nets, and wasn't it a pity that
rain had stopped play.

But what of the countless hours when nothing happened at all,
when day followed night with tireless definition and when the
mail from home had fallen by the wayside? What of the little
things that really mattered and crowded in with such an imposing
insistence? These were the main constituents and the real stuff
of which the desert war was made. Not a picture of a plane on
fire as it dived earthwards ; not an impression of tanks going into
action with turrets down ; not a recollection of a gun crew
outlined by the flash of an explosion, nor the memory of a Red
Cross team giving a blood transfusion in the front line to a man
with a clean white bandage round his forehead. Oh, no, it was
the soul-destroying monotony. The cloudless sky which might
have been painted over your head for month after month ; the
way the sand would snake and hiss across the uneven hummocky
ground ; the thought of four long days till your next wash ; the
way the sweat dried on your body leaving little white sinuous
tracks ; the digging of a slit trench at every conceivable halt.
Waiting for the next meal ; driving into the leaguer each night ;
dispersing with the dawn ; standing to ; wondering what the
devil was getting your mate down these past few days. Tapping
the sand off your biscuits ; skimming it off your tea ; combing it
out of your hair ; picking it out of your ears. That was the
glamour which the desert gave to the ordinary soldier and which
so seldom was mentioned in the communique from Cairo.

And what of the Special Air Service ? Would that be a myth ? A chase for the rainbow's end ? An illusion that died in its infancy ? I wondered if I should find sincerity there ; for, rightly or wrongly, it seemed to me that sincerity was the thing that mattered most : the stamp which gave the coin its true value. But was I merely foolish over this ? And was I pursuing an unreal will o' the wisp ? I wondered.

My reflections were cut short as the train drew up noisily at the dirty little station platform. I began to collect my odds and ends together. Suddenly the carriage had been invaded by the din, the clamour and the stench of an Egyptian habitat. Perspiring natives jostled and shoved in ceaseless confusion—this was the Middle East at a single glance. I made my way towards the telephone in the station-master's apology for an office. After some delay I recognised the official tones of the A.D.M.S. No, he knew nothing of my arrival. What was the name again ? I was quite sure that I had come to the right place ? Did I possess (that golden key) a posting order ? I did ? Ah, well then, he would probably be informed through " the usual channels at a later date." Since I had got a posting order, he would send a car round and we could continue our conversation in his office.

As a matter of fact I found him to be very affable, since he had developed to a fine degree that practised air of being interested in the welfare of his subordinates. Well that, at any rate, was more than could be said for a large number of administrative officers.

" So you are going to join the S.A.S. ? " he said.

" Yes, sir."

" They are just down the road here—oh, a matter of some twenty miles or so," he paused to flick at some flies on his desk, " They practise parachuting, I'm told, but I haven't seen them yet. Too early in the morning for me ! Are you going to parachute ? "

" I suppose so," I admitted. I had never cared for the thought of parachuting. " I'll see what the form is. There is no glider work involved, I hope ? "

He looked up, rather surprised. " Not that I know of, but of course everything is very hush hush down there. We never get to know anything at all really, and although you are supposed to be under me I doubt if I shall be seeing much of you. They are always dashing in and out on raids. Cigarette? Yes," he went on after I had produced a light, " I expect they will keep you on the move all right. But what I *cannot* understand is why I never knew you were coming."

I did not mention that for my part it would have been strange if he had known of my posting. Never yet in the army had my arrival by official posting been expected by the authorities of the reception area, despite the fact that the whole affair took up quite a decent amount of paper work.

" Anyhow, I expect you will like the unit," he reflected. " There will be plenty of exercise and swimming in the Bitter Lake. Incidentally, I think they train in other forms of landing behind the enemy lines as well as parachuting."

I could almost feel my heart miss a beat. This, I thought, was rather more than I had bargained for. I had not heard of the nautical aspect of these raids and the very thought of it made me feel nervous.

" I think I shall try to avoid *that*," I remarked.

" Well, that's frank enough," he smiled. " Anyhow, see how you get on and let me know if you are in any difficulties." He opened the door and the white glare of the sand outside sent us both blinking and screwing up our eyes.

" Driver," he yelled. " Damn the fellow ! Where's he got to now ? " He might have been shouting for a truant dog at home. " Ah, *there* you are. Take this officer to the S.A.S.—next door to the Navy Camp at Kabrit. You know it ? "

" Yes, sir."

" All right then, and come straight back. You can have your food here."

" Yes, sir."

" Well, good-bye James," he held out a very clean hand, " I hope you enjoy yourself."

Decent old chap, I thought, as I climbed into the little Austin. Looked as if he took life nice and easily and did not get too interested in returns on inoculations and camp sanitation. Perhaps he had too many other fish to fry.

We went humming along the flat even road that skirted the

edge of the Bitter Lake. There were a few cargo ships standing well out from the lake side, and over on the far side I could see the white Sinai shore, shimmering in the heat haze. After a while we left the green cultivated area behind, and the hot air raced up to meet us as we followed the dark winding line of the asphalt road. Here and there we passed a camp with its tents lined out in toylike precision and little sunburned figures moving busily to and fro, while an occasional officer, distinguished by his sun-glasses, would turn a casual head to glance at our approach. I watched the driver with his face quite expressionless as he sat at the wheel.

" You like your job ? " I asked.

" Bit of duff, sir."

" Been out here long ? "

" Two years last March, sir."

" All well at home ? " One always felt rather like a member of some charitable organisation when you took any interest in the men's activities.

" Yes, sir." Perhaps he felt the same. I did not pursue the subject. Yet here, I thought, was just one type of English soldier —the chap who was content to remain in this sort of job for the duration of the war. In peace-time he would never have dreamed of doing a chauffeur's work yet now, in war, he was very well situated. Living at base, looking after a car, driving it around and getting about himself into the bargain—well, it *was* a bit of duff ! Probably he would not have exchanged it for anything. All of which went to show how relative were values in war-time.

We swung left, past the Kabrit aerodrome and headed straight towards the canal signalling station.

" It's somewhere along here, sir," he remarked unexpectedly. " Yes. There's H.M.S. *Saunders*. It must be next door."

H.M.S. *Saunders* was a very trim naval camp and in passing I noted with some amusement that you were not allowed to exceed ten knots an hour while driving in the camp area. We turned off the road just beyond it and bumped unevenly along the rough ground towards a group of tents. The white dust sprang up like a cloud behind us and then drifted slowly away.

" This is it, sir," he drew up with a jerk, and looking out I saw a little board propped up on top of the sand-bagged entrance to a tent. On it was written, " L DETACHMENT. S.A.S. REGIMENT."

" That must be the office," he remarked with a jerk of the thumb, and jumping out he began to lift off my baggage and equipment.

" Is that all, sir ? " he asked finally.

" Yes, thank you."

" Have to get back for grub, sir. Late if I don't get a rift on."

" O.K."

" Good-bye, sir."

" Good-bye."

I looked around. The place seemed deserted ; not a soul moving anywhere in the little cluster of tents. From time to time a puff of smoke rose from the lake's edge, and a second or two later there would be the dull boom of an explosion. Behind me was the great framework of the swings standing with skeletal gauntness against the powder-blue of the sky. In my ignorant stupidity I thought one had to jump from the platforms standing about twenty to thirty feet high. Then I saw some smaller platforms over to one side and derived a little consolation from their comparative diminution. Set away by itself was a boxing ring, while over on the other side the trolleys stood stationary at the foot of their inclined rails. Well, you certainly ought to get fit here, I said to myself, and it was a happy thought for there had been little physical exercise for some of us since leaving England.

Suddenly the flap of one of the tents flickered open and a wiry sergeant appeared, followed closely by a large alsatian. I approached him cautiously.

" Could I see the commanding officer ? " I asked.

" Major Stirling, sir ? " He looked me up and down. " He was in his tent a few minutes ago. Shall I take you over ? "

" Thank you."

He led the way to a small dug-in tent and down the sand-bagged steps to the entrance. Pushing back the flap he went inside, reappearing a few moments later.

" Major Stirling's inside, sir," he said, " will you go in ? "

It took me a little while to become accustomed to the darkness

inside the tent and I can recollect stumbling inside and giving
some sort of imitation of a smart salute. Somehow first impressions
of a new place remain very clearly in the memory, and I can still
see David Stirling getting up from the bare wooden table at which
he had been working and looking very surprised at my pseudo-
military approach.

"Captain James reporting for duty," I announced, or something equally foolish.

For a moment or two he appeared quite baffled, and then his
face lightened.

"Ah, *you're* James," he said, and it was my turn to look
surprised. "Yes," he went on glancing at my cap badge, "George
Jellicoe's been telling me about you. By Jove, this is marvellous
having our own doctor. This is real luxury!"

"I've got my posting order, sir," I said, and started to fumble
through my pockets.

"Posting order?" he did not seem to understand. "Oh,
that!" as I produced a crumpled piece of paper. "Give it to
Eric Parten, will you? He's our Adjutant, you know. By the
way, have you had any lunch? No? Well, what about going
over to the mess and having a drink, and then we can talk
things over. I expect George will be coming in soon. That's
him making all those horrible bangs over on the beach."

He sorted out a few papers on the table and then picked up
his cap. I noticed that he was not wearing his regimental Scots
Guards badge, but instead a dark blue cloth shield which bore a
crossed dagger for an emblem and underneath the words, "Who
Dares Wins." I was told later that this unit crest had been
designed by Sergeant Tate, one of the S.A.S. men.

As we were walking over to the mess, David started talking about Jellicoe. "He'll be glad you've come to-day,"
he said, "although I'm afraid he's leaving us and going
out on a party to-morrow. I've done everything I could to
stop him, but he would insist on going and I've just had to
give in."

"Will he be away long?" I asked as casually as I could and
without trying to appear inquisitive.

"About two weeks, I suppose, but I do wish he wasn't going.
I wanted him to stay here because Paddy Mayne and myself have

got to go off at the end of the week. You haven't met Paddy yet, have you ?"

I shook my head. " No, but I think I've heard about him."

" Oh, he's a grand chap—always up to something or other," he paused for a moment, " I do hope you will settle down here while we are away. I know it must seem awfully rude of us to push off like this just as you arrive."

For a moment I wanted to burst out laughing, and indeed it took me some little while to get used to David's seemingly airy and casual way of referring to operations. Somehow it sounded as if they were extremely sorry but they simply *had* to leave a newcomer in order to fulfil a rather dreary public engagement. Every now and then I had to give myself a mental nudge to realise that they were going out on secret raids, and that they would be risking their lives in some particularly daring and spectacular fashion. Then again, of course, his conversation would be, in part, a guardee manner of speaking ; for Guards officers, as I had come to know, took great pains to conceal their true emotions by adopting an especially flowery form of expression.

The naval mess on which we were billeted, so to speak, fed us extremely well and it was quite a revelation to see such good messing at such low prices. We had not been there long before George Jellicoe came in, mopping his brow and looking extremely warm ; and after a brief exchange of courtesies the conversation was occupied almost entirely by the technicalities and relative merits of different time fuses, bombs and explosives. He was incredibly eager to be off on his first raid and one could not but notice the nervous energy, the quick movements and restlessness that were so characteristic of him. Very dark and broadly built for his medium height, with prominent nose and jaw, he had already done well both in commando and battalion, and here he was with the S.A.S. in search of further adventures.

After lunch we both walked over to his tent where I began to interest myself in his collection of books. While I was thus employed four French officers stumbled down into the entrance. George got up to greet them. Obviously they had come in for a conference and were dubious about my presence, but a brief introduction set their minds at rest and soon they were all grouped round the table, unrolling different maps and pinning them down to the bare wood. Then they got down to it, and a fast buzz of conversation ensued, with every now and then the clear interruption of Jellicoe's slow insistent grammatical French. I turned back to my book thinking that this would be a good opportunity to learn the language, when all of a sudden I was startled into acute attention.

" Heraklion ! "

The name had stood out sharply in the middle of a patter of French conversation.

Heraklion ? But that was in Crete ! I must have misheard or misunderstood. But no, there it was again, and it was Jellicoe talking this time. Heraklion—Heraklion aerodrome !

I listened closely, pretending to read my book, while the voices rose and fell in steady cadence. One brief glance over my shoulder revealed the five of them bending over a map, pointing to the different name places and arguing over the various possibilities. A steady haze of cigarette smoke rose and drifted over their heads. Hardly believing my ears I could just make out enough to understand that they were going to board a Greek submarine on the following day, and a few days later they would be landing on Crete and raiding the Heraklion airfield. It can't be true, I thought, it just can't be true. This is something out of one of those absurd thrillers—it simply is not real. How could five men wander around Crete, attack an aerodrome and get away with it ? But the voices went on and a fresh map was produced as if to render a final proof and conviction.

Suddenly Jellicoe turned to me.

" I expect you have gathered where we are going," he said with that quick smile of his, " but don't let it go outside this tent. Now do you think you could fix us with a first-aid packet each— as small as possible and wrapped up in a waterproof covering ? You've got some fairly reasonable supplies at the medical bunk, I believe—do you know where it is ? "

He pointed it out from the tent entrance and I trudged across, my mind awhirl with the news. Don't tell anybody indeed ! Why, I had only been in the camp for a few hours and already I seemed to be involved—if you could call it so—in one of these raids which had given the unit such a mysterious name.

The medical supplies were not too bad, I discovered, as the

R.A.M.C. corporal who ran the medical inspection tent pointed
out to me. But there were no morphia tablets on stock, and these
had to be obtained later from the naval doctor at H.M.S. *Saunders*
by signing in triplicate. The packet of bandages, gauze, salt,
vaseline and morphia tablets, encased in a waterproof cover
obtained from the quartermaster stores, could be squeezed into a
trouser pocket without much difficulty. Field dressings they
carried separately. How much morphia to give them ? I think
they took eight tablets, or two grains, each, for previous experience
had shown me that these tablets were not as potent as I had
supposed. Anyhow, I thought, they were intelligent enough to
know how to use morphia properly ; for after all it was only the
" lay public " and the various administrative authorities who
considered these tablets to be so dangerous.

After tea we went for a swim at the headland where the
signalling station had been constructed. There was quite a stiff
breeze off the water and the little waves were lapping up against
the stone jetty. Neither Stirling nor Jellicoe were very adept in
the water, and the latter was coming in for some brisk leg-pulling,
with different forms of advice as to how he should improve his
swimming in the next few days. All of which passed quite easily
over his head with a rejoinder concerning the low percentage of
sailors who could swim, and the fact that a mile or two either way
would not cause *him* much worry !

The water was very salt and buoyant and not really invigorat-
ing so we did not stay in long. As we were dressing, David showed
me his wrist and asked if I could do anything about it. Clinically
it appeared to be a fractured scaphoid, so I inquired if it had been
X-rayed.

" Oh, yes," he replied. " They said there was a little bone
broken inside. Scaphoid ? Yes, that's what they said."

" Didn't they put it in plaster ? "

" Yes, they did ; but it was such a nuisance, and after a few
days it began to fray and crack—so in the end I cut it off with a
pair of scissors," he added with an apologetic smile.

" Well, there's only one thing to do, "I remarked, " it will
have to go back into plaster."

But this was not to his liking. " I can't afford the time,

Malcolm. You can't do anything with your arm encased in one of those plasters."

"Then it will probably mean an operation later on," I said, and at that he became interested at once. Would it be a quick one? Would he be in hospital for long? Would his wrist be strong afterwards? I'm afraid I was not very informative about the post-operative results, but with a final expression that it would be better in plaster, I felt that I had done the best I could with what looked like being a tricky case to treat.

That evening in the mess I met Eric Parten, the adjutant, who was as pleasant a person as you could wish to meet anywhere.

" Sorry we didn't have a carpet down and the flowers put out for your reception, Doc.," he said and with that, a broad grin, and an invitation to a drink he made you feel at home immediately. With him were Blair Mayne, or Paddy as I got to know him, and Peter Warr and Bernard Schott, our parachute instructors—for by now the unit had expanded sufficiently to have its own instructors and parachute packers.

I kept a good eye on Paddy throughout the evening. He was sitting on one of the parachute container cylinders, which served an excellent purpose as stools at the bar, smoking one cigarette after the other. He appeared to have little to say. Certainly nothing of the rather clever and witty nature that made Jellicoe's conversation so characteristic. No, he spoke very quietly with an Irish brogue, and altogether you didn't form many conclusions at the first meeting. It was the wings and D.S.O. ribbon on his breast pocket and his large size that remained chiefly in the memory.

The others, I recall, were busy with their talk of parachute training, of the unpleasant thrills connected with it, of some of the mishaps that had occurred.

Had any of the 'chutes failed to open? It was a subject that seemed to crop up repeatedly, and the story was told over and over again. Two 'chutes, they said, had failed to open quite recently. The second man had flinched from jumping out of the plane but eventually did so after having been prompted. Later, they thought he must have seen the first parachute fail to open. No, they could not have lost consciousness on the way down because the people on the ground had heard them screaming as they fell.

It was a dreadful story, I thought, and yet there seemed to be a sort of macabre relish in the telling of it. And in this, I may add, Paddy Mayne took no part.

Then there were all the navy chaps—for after all it was their mess ! —amongst whom Paddy had made many friends. They were a grand crowd, taken by and large, always interesting to talk to, very hospitable (they never made you feel you were lodgers), and full of high spirits. It was the exception rather than the rule to have a quiet evening in the mess, and if someone's trousers were not removed before the bar had closed you could be sure that there was something wrong somewhere. They abounded in practical jokes and certainly it was quite a job to keep yourself from being involved in a rough-house. For once the " old man " had retired to his " cabin " the mice began to play with a vengeance. And watching them I could not but compare this with the gloomy hospital life where " shop " and clandestine bridge had formed the chief substance of the evening's entertainment. How could one fail to be cheered by the change ?

And how pleasant it was to have a tent to yourself, for in the army privacy was more rare than fine gold. By jove, this is grand, I thougnt, as I got into my camp bed and looked across at the improvised wash-stand and the wooden board surmounted on trestles which I had managed to wangle from the quartermaster and which served as a table. On it I had stacked my few books and they looked very friendly and familiar in the dim light of the hurricane lamp. With a last look round I turned the wick down and watched the flame flicker up and down in diminishing crescents of yellow until finally it vanished in the blackness.

My thoughts ran riot. For all of a sudden I had met so many interesting people and my only hope was that they would be returning safe and sound from the raids. There was David Stirling : he was a baffling character all right. Whereas I had expected to meet some incredibly tough leader, here he was— pretty good-looking with his dark colouring—tall and slender, standing about six foot two, and seemingly far from strong. There was about him a charm which it would be impossible to describe and this, together with his personal modesty and his flattery of others, made him very difficult to deny. The reception which I had met was in no way different from that extended to the other ranks who joined the unit : it appeared to be they who were doing him a favour and not vice versa. Little wonder, then, that he exercised such a strong magnetic appeal over them. Then again it gave you a fine sense of encouragement to receive a welcome like this without any reservations or mind-you-toe-the-line sort of stuff. I recalled how in the course of the evening I had asked if I could do the parachute training, and the way his face had lit up. Why had I done it, I wondered, when as a rule I was so very cautious about any form of danger. Somehow it was the atmosphere in the mess and the firm conviction I had felt that it would be impossible to live with these chaps or enter into the unit, so to speak, if I did not go through the groundwork with them—the moral obligation was stronger than any military law. And also one had the feeling that if David Stirling could do it, then I could jolly well do it too, and anyway it would not be as dangerous as I had thought. George Jellicoe had recently grazed his face in trying to do a " forward roll " after he had landed. They were ragging him about it. Why, the whole thing was a glorious rag, and it left one wanting to mix into it as quickly as you possibly could. You felt you had to get to know these chaps : Stirling, Mayne, Jellicoe, and Bill Fraser with his M.C. ribbon and tartan kilt, who looked such a good fellow, and always had his daschund " Withers " (decked up in a naval coatee) following him in doggy manner, with deep and very soulful eyes.

Yes, I thought, this life looked almost too good to be true and, with a feeling of contented satisfaction, I turned over and fell asleep.

CHAPTER TWO

EARLY TRAINING

" A little work, a little play
To keep us going—and so, good-day !
Trilby. GEORGE DU MAURIER.

I DO NOT RECALL saying good-bye to George Jellicoe and the
French officers the next day ; but I was not sorry really for I had
never liked farewells, and you never knew what to say apart from
the routine expressions of good-luck and so on. It was usually the
case that when you had completed your handshaking and good-
byes and everything was all set to go, that you found the engine
would not start, or there was not enough petrol, or someone had
forgotten something and the odd minutes would be filled in with
foolish and formal repetitive remarks.

That morning, after a brief sick parade had been concluded,
I went out on to the dropping ground and waited expectantly to
see what parachuting really looked like. Jim Chambers had come
out with me as he, too, was a newcomer to the unit. He was a
stocky chap and, on first impression, seemed to be incredibly talkative about India, with such terms as " chota peg," and odd native
expressions scattered liberally throughout his vocabulary. We
were both starting our training course on the following day and
so we would be seeing a lot of each other. Looking back on it now
I can recall how later, when we had become extremely good
friends, I said to him, " You know when I first met you, I
thought you were the most talkative mug I had ever met," and
his replying, " Thanks, Doc, thanks the hell of a lot ! " and nearly
bringing the tent down with his laughter. Jim had a face that
was as honest as the day, and this was in keeping with his character
for he was as sincere as they are made. I never heard him say a
thing he did not mean, or ever adopt a hypocritical attitude, and
that is high praise indeed. He had come to the unit from an
Indian regiment and by his very genuine behaviour he soon
became *au fait* with the men.

We were both quite impressed with the parachuting. I had never realised how beautiful it could be to see ten men come swinging down, with the canopies of their parachutes a flowery white against the soft blue of the sky. At first there was the horrible moment of suspense as you saw the little figures come tumbling out of the plane and then, a second later, the 'chute would billow out and open in quiet peaceful reassurance. The men looked so minute and still as they floated down and it was only as they drew closer to earth that you appreciated the pendulum movement and the rapidity of their descent. Then as they came down, swinging heavily, it looked as if they must be injured by the fall until, with a heavy thud, they would hit the ground and somersault over backwards or forwards according to the line of the swing. To my surprise they all got up in obedience to the gruff command from the ground instructor's megaphone. One man, I remember, landed on his feet without falling so that his 'chute collapsed gently over his head—the whole thing rather giving him the effect of a bird alighting on a branch.

It was all very interesting and fascinating in its novelty and we returned to camp full of excited talk.

Our own training reminded me of the hefty sort of stuff that you see in the films. There were several of us in the " Officers' Class " together with a small group of French officers. These French officers were in charge of a small detachment of Frenchmen whom David had accepted into the unit. Their commanding officer had left with George Jellicoe to raid Crete, and it was unfortunate that he never returned since, by all accounts, he was an outstanding leader and maintained an iron discipline over the rest of them. The standard of their military training was extremely high, and in the operations to come this small force was to help us in a way that was out of all proportion to their size.

Here we were, then, lined up in two rows away from the tents, with a rather dour looking Lancashire sergeant sizing us up like sheep for the slaughter. He was a worthy man, this instructor, and I liked him by far the best of the bunch. Later he was commissioned and accompanied us on our Benghazi raid, only to break both his legs on a demonstration jump some while later. This accident was sheer bad luck, and in no way a reflection upon

his competence, for his 'chute failed to open properly and he came
down nearly twice as fast as any one else in that particular
" stick " of jumpers. But at the time of our training he seemed
almost too fit for some of us. He spoke French in a slow and
definite manner and, with his emphatic Northern dialect, he
could give, at times, the impression of mighty heavy sarcasm. He
had a way, too, of saying, " Now, gentlemen," that made us feel
incredibly small, and I have no doubt that his " messieurs " made
a similar impression on the French.

" Now, gentlemen," he remarked in just such a way, after we
had numbered off and taken up our positions, " We will start off
with the simple exercise of touching our toes." He looked round
at us and, in order to make quite sure that we all understood, he
showed us what to do.

Then " Touch your toes " he bellowed suddenly.

Rather surprised at the speed of this attack we bent down and
did as we were told.

" Gettup ! "—It was like the report of a rifle.

" Come on ! Come on ! Come on ! This is an exercise, not
an old women's washing parade. You touch the toes—so ! Up
and down ! Up and down ! " He showed us with a dreadful
precision and efficiency just what he expected of us. " Now,
gentlemen, are you *all* ready ? " There was no mistaking the note
in that voice. We might have been a class of tiny little children.

" Touch yer toes."

" Gettup !—Geddarn, gettup, geddarn." It was all one word
the way he said it, and we were shooting up and down like jack's-
in-boxes.

" Now, are you feeling better ? " he inquired solicitously.

We were not, but we understood what he was driving at. The
French were looking very puzzled indeed and perhaps a little
hurt. He made them fall in behind us so that they could take
their time from us.

" Right, gentlemen ! " we waited for it. " Run round the
boxing ring," he bellowed.

We chased round in a flurry of sand and dust and returned,
panting, to our positions.

" Run round again ! "

We obeyed his injunction and came back perspiring, to his

evident satisfaction. If this is going to be a long distance run, I thought, I'll take it easily.

"You, you and you, sir," he added ponderously, "Run round again."

We toiled round once more. It was not as easy as I had expected. After a brief rest we returned to our labours.

"Maintenant, nous sautons sur les pieds. Quand je dis ' Un ' vous sautez sur le pied gauche, et quand je dis ' Deux ' vous sautez sur le pied droit. Comme ca ! Vous comprenez ? "

We did ; and for the next five minutes we hopped busily from side to side kicking up a little cloud of dust around ourselves.

"Un—et deux, un-et deux, un-et deux ! " It was a sing-song metre. "A la droit—a la gauche. A la droit—a la gauche ! "

Slowly the sun arched up over our heads and on we went from one exercise to the next.

"On the backs down. Come on, come on ! Gettup, geddown ! Gettup, geddown ! On the hands down. One and two, Un et deux, Un et deux ! One man on another man's back. Come on, jump to it, jump to it ! Run round the boxing ring. Change positions. Run round again ! "

And so it went on for the better part of an hour.

"Right," he said finally (and the French promptly sprang to attention which showed how alert they had become). "Right, gentlemen, you may have a short break."

Some of us sat down in the warm sand while others walked over to their tents for a mug of water.

These training periods kept us at it throughout morning and evening ; in the afternoons we were expected to swim. One period would be devoted to the trolleys. These were small wooden platforms on wheels which we pushed down the inclined rails at a decent speed, accelerating as we ran. We took it in turns to stand on the trolley, both feet together, and when it had almost reached the bottom of the incline the individual concerned jumped off, landed with feet together and did a forward roll. This resembled a forward somersault except that you rolled over on one or other shoulder and did not break your fall with your hands. It was a comparatively easy and pleasant exercise, but not so enjoyable when you had to jump off backwards and do a backward roll. I never found it easy to jump backwards off either a moving trolley or a stationary platform—it was the sensation of not being able to look where you leaped that was so difficult to overcome.

The platforms were constructed at different heights from the ground, the top one being set at about twelve feet, and again the forward and backward rolls followed the landing. The object of these rolls was to prevent the full weight and strain from falling on the feet and ankles. By doing a roll when you landed from a parachute descent, you broke your fall and took your weight more evenly. The strain was no more severe than a hard rugger tackle, yet even so the number of sprained ankles and injured feet averaged about one a day.

Then there was another device known as " jumping through the hole " which took a bit of getting used to. It consisted of a square platform, set about eight to ten feet from the ground, in the centre of which was a circular hole. Attached to the under-surface of this hole was a piece of boarding about three feet in width. In the exercise you had to sit on the platform with your legs dangling over the rim of the aperture and on the command " Jump ! " you pushed off with your hands and fell, theoretically in the erect position, landing " easily on both your feet " as the instructor told us. I need hardly add that the majority of us landed neither easily nor on both our feet. It was the same old difficulty of not being able to look down through the hole as you jumped. No, you had to look straight ahead as if you were watching the instructor in the aircraft for the real jump. As a result you were always rather fearful of hitting your face on the wooden rim of the opposite side, and it was hard to stop yourself from flinching at the last moment. It was one of those exercises which looked absurdly easy until you had to do it. Later on we practised jumping through a similar aperture set in the fuselage of an aircraft which had been mounted at about the same height from the ground. Only this time we were wearing dummy parachutes on our backs and whereas previously we had been afraid of hitting our faces on the opposite side of the aperture, now we knew that if we did not jump far enough out the pack on our back would catch the aperture rim behind us and somer-sault us forward. So, whether you jumped too far or not far enough, you could reckon on getting a good smack in the face on the opposite side of the aperture. I am afraid that most of us jumped with downcast eyes and so avoided these misfortunes.

The period were broken up with vigorous games of a competitive nature which served to dispel any tendency towards monotony and there were occasional hours put in at roadwork, exercises with heavy logs, close combat and so on. As the reader may well imagine, we were pretty stiff after a few days of this training, a fact which afforded the keenest pleasure to the naval ratings of H.M.S. *Saunders*. When the classes broke up for lunch or " grub up " as the case might be, we would stagger off like a crowd of old pensioners, pursued by catcalls, jeers and ribald remarks.

" Yahoo, boys," they yelled, " here come the paratripes—Germans beware ! " or " Up with the paratroops. Why should England tremble ! " These gibes and falsetto laughter pursued us as we hobbled off for a welcome drink.

In the evening we sometimes played basket-ball on a small sandy pitch that had been laid out for this purpose. The only drawback to this was the fact that few of us knew how to play the game, whereas the French were obviously quite expert and had played it from early infancy. Useless to point out the rule that you were not supposed to run with the ball to an enthusiastic rugger player like Jim Chambers ! For the sake of simplicity and convenience we generally played French *v.* English, and within a few moments of the starting whistle the field of play had become quite obscured by a yellow cloud of dust. This cloud or pillar of dust moved rapidly up and down the pitch, stopping at frequent intervals for a sort of "scrum down," and a spectator seldom saw the ball but simply a group of threshing arms and legs as the battle ebbed to and fro. Cries of " Take it with your feet—feet, feet " varied with the rapid ejaculations of " Ici Jacques—A moi, A moi." and " On your right, Jim. Pass, man, pass ! " with vigorous and emphatic protests of " Non. Non ! Ce n'est pas vrai ! " accompanied by quick deprecatory gestures to the referee. At such a juncture the whistle would blow and, when the sand had cleared a little, various bodies would pick themselves up from off one another. Jim Chambers and myself, I fear, were frequent culprits and usually pulled ourselves out of the scrum from somewhere near the bottom. There followed a few explanatory rules about the game, during which we blinked at each other with yellow powdered faces and wiped our grazed knees, and then we were off again. I don't think we won many of these games, but we certainly put a fair amount of energy into them. I would like to have seen Paddy Mayne leading our forwards !

On the second week we went on to training with " swings " and ground parachute control. The supporting structure of the swings looked like a huge and vast meccano set. The swing was made of wire instead of rope, and parachute harness with the lower part of the rigging lines replaced the usual wooden bench on which to sit. One platform was allotted to each swing and this stood about 20-30 feet high and was mounted by a narrow ladder attached to the supporting framework. The centre piece of the platform could slide out, so that, when a person was standing on the edge of it, one or two other men standing on the side pieces of the platform could fix the parachute harness round his shoulders and thighs. If you had a poor head for heights there was little amusement in perching on the edge of the centre piece ; moreover you were obliged to lean forward over the edge since the wire swings were only just long enough to reach you. When the harness had been fitted, and the straps clipped in to the release box which was situated over the stomach, you prepared to jump at the given command. Obviously if the wire swing had been loose you would have fallen vertically until the slack had played out and then have been brought up with a severe jerk. As it was you swung off in a large arc, and the men left up on the platform hastily pulled in the centre piece so that you should not strike it on your back swing. While you were swinging in the air you grasped the rigging lines over your head and by twisting and crossing them you could practise right and left turns. As the pendulum swing slowed down, you freed yourself from your straps by adjusting the release box and then dropped out of the harness. A forward, sideways, or backward roll completed the exercise.

Ground training in parachute control consisted simply in practising measures to avoid being dragged along the ground. One man would get strapped up in his harness and three or four others would hold him back while the breeze billowed out his 'chute, and immediately the signal was given they would let him go. His object was then to run round on one side of his chute which he tried to collapse by pulling on the opposite set of rigging lines. The only difficulty of the exercise lay in whether you could run faster than your 'chute was travelling, for it would be blowing along the ground like a huge sail at a speed dependent upon the wind velocity. Unfortunately in the desert the wind could spring up in gusty squalls without a moment's notice and it was entirely due to this fact that, on a later occasion when I was doing some further training, one of the officers in the class was suddenly killed by being dragged into the superstructure of an aircraft fuselage. One moment it had been huge fun and we had all been ragging away—the next it had been a ghastly tragedy.

These weeks of training were very enjoyable for soon the stiffness wore off and we became bronzed and very fit.

In every class there is, I suppose, a laggard who helps to afford comic relief, and in ours it was a little Frenchman called Henri—or just plain Henry or 'Enry to us. He was an awfully nice chap and took the work so seriously, mainly perhaps because he was the duffer. The very fact that he had come to be in such a unit was just one more of those strange peculiarities that you met in the war. Whatever had made him join, I wondered, for in peace-time he had been working in a quiet diplomatic job, and somehow he seemed so out of place here. Yet all the more credit to him, by far, for being able to tackle it ; yes, and to succeed. For he was always in difficulties over the forward and backward rolls and finished up in the most grotesque positions. Exercises on the horse found him facing in any direction but the correct one, with his arms and legs all akimbo. On the mat somehow he seemed to end up sprawled across on his tummy like an energetic little frog. Yes, *he* was the one who would be out of step, the man who raised the laugh, the one to whom the others would turn for a joke if they found the training a trifle tedious.

Poor Henri ! I can see him now getting up from some exercise or other and wiping the sand out of his eyes while the rest of the French gave him humorous encouragement. I can see him sitting on the platform with his legs dangling over the aperture, and flinching from the jump at the last minute. I can remember the way he used to blink his eyes fast to keep away the hot pricking tears, and the way he shook his head as the rest of them laughed up at him from the ground below.

" Non. Non," he would say, shaking his head, " Ce n'est pas drôle, c'est formidable ! " But he jumped down all right.

And on the swings I feel sure he must have felt far worse than I did. It wasn't very nice standing up there on the platform. Two others would strap him up in the harness and there he would perch, with many a chaplinesque gesture to preserve his balance, peering down at us with his deep brown eyes.

" Un ! Deux ! Trois ! " the French would cry, and he would get all set, grasping the rigging lines very tight, and preparing to launch himself forth into the air. He would look out and across the Bitter Lake to the far Sinai shore and concentrate ferociously.

" Sautez ! " they cried.

Poor Henri ! It was difficult to understand how any one could come so near to jumping off that platform without actually doing so. He would sway this way and that and yet just manage to keep his balance. Then he would frown down at us.

" Non," he would say, " c'est *tres* formidable."

I'm afraid that all these exercises were " très formidable " for Henri. But eventually he surmounted each one in turn and when he did jump from the platform with a quick, timid, bird-like movement, and after he had swung to and fro, curled up in a little ball, and alighted in his own ungraceful manner, ah, then, that was the moment of rejoicing ! He smiled round at us with such happiness in his eyes. For he could do it the same as the others : he could keep up with the best.

And at basket-ball, too, he was always the one who picked himself last out of the scrum, shaking his head and rubbing the sand out of his eyes.

I remember how when we came on to the actual jumping, the instructor put him No. 10, the last in our " stick," so that if he baulked he would not put any one else off. But did he baulk ? Looking up from the ground below we saw number nine come tumbling out into the air. And number ten—where was No. 10 ? And then he came out, quickly and all of a sudden, and his chute opened white and peacefully over his head. But of course he was the one who was injured. For in jumping he had struck his face on the opposite side of the aperture and broken his nose. There was blood on his face when he landed and his nose soon started to become swollen. But he was very happy and joyful, for he had jumped with the rest of us.

"Non ce n'est rien, docteur," he said, "ce n'est rien."

I remember too, how some months later when we were on the Benghazi raid a casualty was brought to me one night. "One of the French," they said as they lowered him hammockwise in a blanket from one of the lorries. He looked pale and peaceful that night, wounded so seriously as to be far beyond any help of mine, with just his hands opening and closing like those of a child. He died very quietly. For him perhaps life had been "formidable" but, as is so often the case, it was a man of such a stamp who had shown the highest fortitude. For he had overcome more difficult obstacles and triumphed over greater moral hardships than we could ever know.

And so our training continued from one hot sunny day to the next and any tendency to monotony would quickly be dispelled by a period of boxing or wrestling. I enjoyed boxing with Jim Chambers although he was far better than I was. "Well done, Doc," he would say on the rare occasions that I managed to hit him, and I would see a healthy grin spread over his face and knew that I was in for trouble. He was one of those chaps you never seemed to be able to hit properly, all shoulders and gloves, and just as you thought you were going to land a quick one, out would shoot a sudden punch and leave you with a sore nose and watering eyes. At both these sports we excelled over the French— they appeared to have no conception at all of how to box.

As a rule we retired early at night, weary and with the contented feeling that we had earned our healthy sleep.

The evenings in the mess seemed quieter I thought after David Stirling and Paddy Mayne went out raiding. I can only remember speaking to Paddy once before he left, and that was on the day of his departure when our ways happened to cross. "Well, good luck," I said after we had exchanged a few remarks, to which he replied by saying he thought there should be some "good killing." As I walked over to the medical tent I wondered if I could ever think of "good killing" and felt rather weak-minded and unwarlike in my inability to do so. But still, I told myself, if it had been my job to kill I dare say I would have enjoyed it as well as any one. Certainly there were times when I wanted so desperately to have the opportunity, but I know I should have regretted it soon afterwards. It would only have been enjoyable in a fit of temper.

In this connection I can remember a French officer describing a raid on which he had accompanied David Stirling. He was sitting on the bar dangling his legs over the side and talking in his fast enthusiastic way.

" Ah, zat Major Stirling," he remarked when he had come to the end of his story, " 'e is a fonny one. While we was shooting 'e turns to me and 'e says, ' I like shootin' zese Italians, don't you ? ' " He shook his head in obvious admiration, and then laughed round at us. " And all ze time 'e look so gentle and so kind ! "

The French added a certain amount of colour and vivacity to our life : they would be so serious one minute and so childishly delightful the next. But on the whole I preferred Eric Parten's sleepy sort of humour and good-natured banter. He and Bobby Dodds, one of our old operatives who had recently transferred to the training side, made a very amusing couple with their coined American expressions and their " don't gimme dat " sort of stuff. Dodds, with his huge sweeping moustaches, had travelled round the world quite a bit and always had some sort of story to tell. But at this particular time he was not quite as lively as was his wont, for he had recently landed heavily on his tail end in a practise jump and consequently was very cautious in his movements.

Sometimes Eric Parent used to look at me very thoughtfully and then, as if he had just woken up, would say, " Tell me, Doc," and everybody would draw closer to hear this weighty question, " Tell me, Doc, what were you in civvy street ? " It was an old, old joke of his but you always had to laugh, and if Bobby Dodds was feeling up to it, he would climb a tent pole and laugh away up at the top as if he had only just seen the joke.

And so the time seemed to fly past until we were counting the days to our first real parachute jump. Now it was four days, now three, and now it was only two : until at last we were saying, " This time to-morrow, chaps "—you know the sort of thing. We looked forward to it with a sort of half-fearful anticipation ; and that last night I can remember going early to bed and lying awake thinking, " I ought to have more wind-up than this. I'm sure it's going to be grim. I wonder how I shall sleep to-night," and so on. Beneath my camp bed (of which I had grown very fond) were my parachute boots ; and scattered round the tent were the helmet, overalls, gauntlets, knee and ankle pads which we had drawn from the quartermaster's tent during the day. Outside the sand was gleaming a milky white in the light of a waning moon. It all looked so peaceful and serene.

And then, quite disjointedly, I wondered if to-night David Stirling and Paddy Mayne would be stalking round sentries and looking for " good things to put bombs on.. . ."

CHAPTER THREE

ON PARACHUTING

" I'm very brave generally," he went on in a low voice : " Only
to-day I happen to have a headache."
>   *Alice Through the Looking-Glass.* LEWIS CARROLL.

IT WAS EARLY when my batman called me the next morning, and
outside the sky was steadily growing lighter. I jumped out of bed,
wondering what sort of a breeze was blowing, and heaved a deep
sigh of relief as I felt it very faint and coming off the Bitter Lake.
" How are you feeling, Jim," I called out as I saw him poke
a yawning head out of his tent. He blinked round at the sky.
" Just the job ! " he said and disappeared from sight ; a moment
later a busy sound of splashing and towelling came from his
direction. He was one of the few people I met who really seemed
to enjoy parachuting and he put his whole heart into it. One of
his worries, I remember, was whether there was any future in it
for the regular army after the war !
That morning I seemed to be all fingers and thumbs as I
strove to pull my knee and ankle pads into position, and my
hands, I remember, were very clumsy and helpless as I tied up
my bootlaces. Feeling rather foolish in this strange attire, I
walked over to the packing sheds to collect my parachute. There
was no need to worry about the wind-up now, I thought, for I
had got the before breakfast funk with a vengeance. It was all
this waiting about that did it. We waited to collect our 'chutes.
We waited for the lorries to take us over the road to the airfield.
We waited dismally for two awful hours until it was our turn to
jump. I became surly and irritable as I always did when I was
frightened, and I found that I was unable to share in the forced
jokes which were circulating around, and the overloud laughter
of their response.
Most of us were chewing gum and smoking one cigarette after
another. Someone complained of not having had any breakfast.

" Why the —— hell are you thinking of breakfast when in a few minutes you will be jumping 1000 feet into sweet nothing," came the rather amusing rejoinder. It would not have been so bad if we *had* jumped in a few minutes but our particular stick was the last but one, and the two-hour wait was pretty grim. Some of us sat down on the sand, some walked around kicking listlessly at the stones, while others lay down and pretended to go to sleep.

The sun was just coming up, and over at the far end of the aerodrome a plane suddenly sprang into life with a shattering roar of its engines. It taxied slowly over towards us.

" All right, Group A, fall in," shouted one of the instructors. We watched them form up in two rows looking strange and deformed in their headgear and harness. Their hands were hanging limply by their sides, and their faces were quite set and expressionless as they chewed away at their gum. The instructor walked down the lines inspecting each one in turn and giving their release boxes a firm knock with his fist to make quite certain that they were adjusted correctly.

The plane drew up alongside, shuddering with the vibration of the airscrews. We could see the pilot looking down at us from his cabin. Perhaps, I thought, he would be glad when this rather monotonous job was over. Then came the order, " Ranks, right and left turn—Quick march."

Slowly they filed off into the plane, leaning foward as they did so against the wind of the port airscrew and shielding their eyes from the fine dust it threw up. One by one they climbed up the ladder and disappeared from sight into the nose of the machine, although we could just get a rather hazy glimpse of them through the dusty windows in the fuselage.

Then one of the ground crew pulled the ladder away, the door was closed, the engines roared up afresh, died down, roared up again and the plane began to taxi away. We watched it grow smaller as it ran evenly along the runway and then lifted heavily over the buildings at the far end. We could see it alter course and circle round the dropping ground about a mile away—we could just make out the little 'chutes as they came floating down in the still morning air. I glanced at the wind-sock. With any luck, I reckoned, it should keep calm for a little while yet.

About a quarter of an hour later the plane was back, coming

in for a three-point landing with the tyres hardly making a sound as they touched the tarmac.

"Group B—are you all ready, Group B." We were in Group F. God, how slowly the time passed ! Why couldn't we go next and get it over with ? Why couldn't we go next ? Oh, why the devil couldn't we ? There was a persistent repetitive voice in my ear. And then the feeling of slight consolation that it was not our turn yet. No need to get the wind up now. Plenty of time for that later on ! We could smoke a cigarette : that helped to steady things down a bit. As the minutes dragged past I grew to hate that plane with its shattering, noisy roar, and the silly little face of the pilot looking down at us each time as if he was analysing our every emotion. I grew to hate the banter of the instructors and their stupid efforts to cheer us up.

But at last it was our turn and we clambered slowly to our feet and formed up. An instructor looked us over closely, patting at our harness and banging at our release boxes.

I never quite understood how the straps were fastened in the release box. I simply realised that one's life was dependant upon its security, and that if anything went wrong with it, then you had had it so to speak. For it was the means of keeping you and the 'chute in one piece, and so I worshipped it with awe and due reverence. By this time we had all grown to like our Lancashire instructor and I remember how grateful I felt that he was not behaving with the irritating jocularity that the others seemed to feel the occasion demanded. " Take my course in easy self-confidence," one had remarked loudly, " and be a bloody nuisance to everybody." Very funny no doubt, but this was not the time for the ready appreciation of light humour. I fear that it only made me, for one, the more surly and ill-tempered.

We climbed up the ladder, past the pilot's cockpit and into the forward end of the fuselage. There we stood, crammed together in the vibrating plane while the engines revved up ; and then at last we were away and looking down I could see the hangers and buildings flash past below. We gained height as we circled over the Bitter Lake before heading off towards the dropping ground. The instructor pushed past us and laid a small wooden plank across the aperture in the floor of the fuselage. Those of us with odd numbers stepped warily across it, grasping firmly to the rope that acted as a rail. It was not as bad as I had expected ! That left us with five men on each side of the aperture. We sat down on our haunches and waited while the instructor went round fixing our statachute lines to the various strong points in the plane. These strong points were reinforced portions which could take the strain of a man's weight as he fell and, in so doing, would release the attachment to the parachute canopy which thereupon opened automatically.

This device of attachment to strong points appeared incredibly archaic, I thought. There was definitely a smack of Heath Robinson about it, and I must confess it was with a certain amount of misgiving that I watched the buckle of my statachute being attached to the plane with a gadget that looked like a safety pin and a little bit of string. However it seemed to work all right, and there was little object in worrying about it at this late stage of the proceedings.

In truth I was feeling dreadful. One look through the aperture at the ground, which seemed to be crawling literally miles below, had turned my body to water. I felt as weak as a baby. What the hell had made me go in for this, I wondered, as I gazed round dismally at the grim set faces of my companions.

Time passed, horrible and slow, and we sat there waiting—always waiting.

" Get ready and watch for the light ! "

The voice of the instructor came to us, thin and weak against the roar of the engines. We turned our heads and watched the little bulb, our bodies and minds numb with fear. Suddenly it flickered and shone a dark ruby red.

" Action Stations ! "

Feeling rather as if I was forced to watch some dreadful play, and with the strange unreality of a dream, I saw Jim Chambers swivel his body round so that his legs were dangling over the aperture.

Number two, with his back towards me, got ready to swing his legs over as soon as number one had jumped. The instructor was leaning forward with his clenched fist held up in the air.

" One ! " he shouted. " Two ! " he shouted again. It all happened very quickly. Their bodies rose suddenly into the air, hung for a fraction of a second, and then fell away through the aperture and out of sight. There was an unpleasant rattling sound as the statachute lines wreathed out into tautness and lay slung over the side of the aperture. I prayed that I might not get tangled up in the statachute lines as I jumped out : I seemed to remember that someone had been talking about that sort of accident in the mess one night.

The instructor was leaning over the aperture and watched the bodies fall away. " Bloody awful ! " he remarked as he straightened himself up. " Now, are you ready, numbers three and four."

I sidled over to the place so recently vacated and took a little peep down in order to brace myself for the test. The plane dipped and banked in the air currents and we sat there waiting. Then the engines cut down more quietly and our speed fell away.

" Action stations ! " Now for it—at last. The red light pricked up into life.

" One ! "

My opposite number jumped up as if to reach me and then dropped away. I swung round into position.

" Two ! " I heard the shout, and suddenly everything went blank, there was a loud roaring in my ears and a buffet of wind in my face. Then I seemed to wake from a noisy dream into a beautiful quietness. Looking up I saw my chute had opened huge and vast over my head. The consolation was wonderful, and the silence, ah God, the peaceful silence. Looking down I was surprised to see the ground spinning round slowly, first one way then the other, until I realised it was I who was spinning in the air. How foolish of me ! I felt like laughing with relief and took a closer look. I could make out the trucks now, and the tiny little dots of the men below, and the white letter T which was laid down on the ground to show us the direction of the wind. One more look round and I grasped the rigging lines more firmly ; below me and to one side I could see my opposite number, number one, floating earthwards.

A small voice came up from the ground. " Feet together, number two ! Feet together ! "

Suddenly it dawned on me that it was myself they were shouting at, and I banged my ankles close together. The ground was coming up faster now and I could see that I was swinging quite heavily. The dots were becoming figures and the figures were growing into people. I was going to hit the ground soon. Now, on the forward swing ! No, I had missed. Damn ! It would be on the back swing. No, wrong again ! And then I fell with a bang, not caring a tinker's curse for forward and backward rolls, and lay for a moment feeling weak with gratitude to the Almighty. I wasn't hurt, I realised, as I stretched out my legs ; it had not been such a bad landing after all.

" Are you all right, number two ? " The voice over the megaphone sounded angry. I got up, waved a hand and ran cheerfully round my 'chute. It was fortunate that the breeze was so light or I would have been dragged as I lay there in happy contemplation.

One of the instructors walked over to me and proffered a cigarette. I took it with trembling hands. " Nice work, Doc," he remarked, " how did you like it ? "

" Bloody awful ! " I replied as firmly as I could. " Bloody awful ! And the waiting was just bloody." I seemed to be unable to express myself any more fluently. He looked a little surprised and then said, " Well, that's honest at any rate, most people try to make out that they enjoy it."

He was right, I found, as I handed my 'chute and harness in to the loading truck. Every one seemed to be vying with each other in their loud applause of parachuting.

" Wasn't it grand ? "

" Wizard feeling when you landed, what ? "

" Did you feel your parachute open ? I did ! "

And so it went on, and little Henri with his broken nose passed almost unnoticed. Yet none of them did more than the scheduled five jumps, I noticed, even though they did enjoy parachuting so much—and there were plenty of opportunities later on if they had wanted to make use of them.

Jim Chambers was the only one who jumped whenever he could, and preferably from a different type of aircraft for the sake of experience.

As we were walking back to the mess our Lancashire instructor, Sculthorpe, came over to meet us.

He looked at me with his slow, lingering stare, " What

happened to you, doctor?" he asked. "You hit your head on the plane as you jumped and fell out like a sack of old potatoes. Were you stunned?"

As a matter of fact I had no idea of what had happened, but apart from a headache and a sore chin I was not feeling any the worse. Anyhow, I thought, as I threw my overalls and gloves on to my camp bed, I was glad that I had jumped too far and had not appeared frightened of getting out. Such are our own peculiar little vanities! At the same time I made up my mind not to repeat the performance if I could help it on the following day! On this occasion we were jumping at 800 feet, 200 feet lower and consequently with a shorter time of descent in the air. The waiting was just as bad, but I think I almost enjoyed the drop. (Or was it the contrast to the first jump?) I'm afraid, too, that I looked down as I pushed off and made no mistake about hitting my head on the opposite side.

Perhaps, if we had continued with our parachuting, I would not have disliked it so much; but our position in the desert had been steadily deteriorating, and now the Air Force called for every single plane that could fly to be put into active bombing operations. Consequently our aircraft was taken from us and our parachuting ceased for the time being.

For now the Allied forces were pulling back from Matruh, now from Bagoush, from Bagoush to Fuka and from Fuka to El Daba. It was galling to sit back there and not be able to do anything about it. There were warnings of spies and parachute troops in the Canal zone. The navy began to leave Alexandria, and there was something very tragic in seeing their warships steaming down the Bitter Lake towards Suez. It brought home the real gravity of the situation with a most unpleasant jar to watch the destroyers and cruisers and transports, one after another, move slowly southward and out of sight down the canal. We waved to them from our bathing beach and there was something infinitely sad in the way they waved back. It made us feel as if we were being left behind and, what was worse, with nothing in particular to do. On the road we would pass long convoys of nurses and South African girls being evacuated from the delta zone. What could we do? Absolutely nothing until David Stirling came back, and there was an abject futility in our idleness. Nevertheless we carried on with our training in the hopes that soon a more active life would follow.

In the mess of an evening, however, our spirits began to perk up. We stood round the wireless set, sipping at our John Collins's, and all eager for the latest news. Our two officer parachute-instructors would come in with excited " gen " they had just gleaned from the ops. room at the aerodrome. Mersa Matruh they said was obscured by a pillar of smoke, large oil dumps were ablaze at Bagoush ; now the bombing line was just west of Fuka, and now it had moved eastwards towards El Daba. By following our own bombing line as it withdrew towards Alamein, we kept slightly ahead of the official news.

These officer-instructors were amusing chaps, both of them, and after we had shaken our heads over the depressing situation in the Western Desert and given vent to our feelings on the subject, our natural good spirits started to return once more.

There was Peter Warr who instructed chiefly as a dispatcher from aircraft, and who seemed to be very impressed with the fact that I had " knocked myself out " as I made my first jump. I believe his estimate of me rose immediately ! He was quite a good talker and, with a certain sense of exaggeration, he could tell a tale as well as any, grasping a glass of lime juice in one hand (for he neither drank nor smoked) and giving descriptive emphasis with the other. He was thin, wiry, and always on the move with a suppressed nervous energy. Needless to add that he was almost invariably involved in a rough-house and as likely as not had been the originator of the fray. He used to fly a bit, too, and he was very proud of this—perhaps because he was not highly skilled in it—and the fact that he was not allowed to land or take off was a constant source of irritation to him.

I can remember one evening when we had a boxing tournament in full swing, how a Wellington came zooming low over the ring and then banked sharply as it crossed over the Bitter Lake. No need to ask who was at the controls !

He came into the mess about an hour later. " Did you see that Wimpey," he cried with his eyes alight and his hair ruffled. " Did you see that vertical turn over the lake. Know who was piloting ? Me, boys, it was me," and he moved restlessly round the tent, kicking at the legs of the chairs, and picking up a paper only to throw it down again.

His driving was of a similar nature, fast and very erratic ; and it seemed as if he drove with the object in mind of putting the wind-up his passengers, for he was not satisfied until someone had protested about the speed. If he could frighten someone, then he was well satisfied for he felt that they thought he was a dare-devil. Perhaps I am being too analytical, but that is how it struck me, and anyhow it is by no means an uncommon trait of character.

He made a good instructor ; very keen at his job and always on the look-out for fresh methods and modifications. But his French was not his strong point and I am afraid the French students were the bane of his unquiet form of life. There was a story of him in this connection, for, one day, it appeared that he had gone up to dispatch some of them. It was perfect weather for dropping, warm and airless, and everything seemed to be in fine trim. The French were rigged up correctly and had clambered into the plane without fuss or bother, so away they all went. When, however, they reached the dropping ground they discovered that the ground staff were not yet ready, so they flew up towards the main Suez road and round in a big circle to fill in the spare time.

Warr wanted to make quite sure that the French would understand him when the moment came to dispatch them, so he decided to hold a little rehearsal.

" Attention, messieurs ! " he shouted over the roar and rattle of the engines, " maintenant nous avons un petit demonstration," he paused to note the effect of his words, and then went on, " quand je dis ' Action,' il faut que vous êtes prêt. Eh, bien ! " He thought hard for a moment, " Quand je dis ' Un ! '—donc vous," he tapped number one on the shoulder, " Vous sautez. Et quand je dis ' Deux ! ' donc vous," he pointed across the aperture at number two, " Vous sautez aussi. Vous comprenez? C'est seulement un demonstration en preparation."

They nodded in emphatic agreement, and Warr congratulated himself on his fluent ability as a bilingual instructor.

" Action ! " he shouted. The two Frenchmen swung them-selves into position.

" C'est bien," he yelled, " c'est tres bien, et maintenant *si* je dis ' Un ! ' "

But he got no further for, with a great cry of " Pour la patrie ! " number one threw himself vigorously from the floorboards and vanished from sight.

" Hi ! " shouted Warr in bewilderment. Obedient to the call number two quickly followed the example of his opposite number. Warr looked wildly round the plane, " Cessez ! " he cried aghast, " Cessez, messieurs ! "

The remaining French looked up at him in surprise. Whatever had gone wrong now was the question writ large on every face. This instructor was a very strange man, surely ! Why did he look so worried and harassed when their comrades had performed their duty so nobly ?

In the meantime the two French parachutists had descended neatly into a stores depot where, since our military situation was so grave at this time, a little posse of Indian guards were waiting to pounce upon them with fixed bayonets. Protesting volubly and incoherently they were marched off in very quick time to the guard-room where they were allowed to cool their ardour and their heels for a while.

All this, of course, came back on Peter Warr when he endeavoured to liberate them, and it did not do to talk to him about French trainees for some considerable time. From then onwards he insisted on his pupils knowing a little elementary English !

Our other instructor, Bernard Schott by name, was an altogether different type of person. Robust, good-natured and always helpful, he could usually be found expending much energy over little things, and with a keen desire to make a mountain out of a molehill if it was humanly possible.

There was a story in connection with him, too—woven, it appeared, around his rather picturesque imagination. For on one moonless night, they told me, when it was as black as pitch, he was out on the landing ground as training instructor. He had everything ready for the dropping. The trucks had been run well clear of the landing area, the T-piece was lit up, and all the details were complete. Soon they heard the drone of the approaching aircraft and as it came closer they could make out the green and red lights on port and starboard wing.

"Get ready everybody," Schott cried out to the others. "They are coming down now. Ah! Here they come! Now, number one," he shouted up into the darkness, "that's very good, very good indeed—keep like that. Number two, keep those feet and knees together, number two—that's better! Well done! Now, number three—you are in a good position but you will have to do a half-right turn. Confound the fellow! Why can't he do what he's told. Reach out with your feet, number four. Position good on the whole, but reach out more with your feet."

The others looked at Schott and then followed his penetrating gaze into the starry heavens above, but for the life of them they could not pick out a single thing save the lights of the receding plane.

Schott followed the descent of the parachutists right down to the ground. "Now, are you all right, number one?" he blared out through the megaphone.

No reply.

"Number one, are you all right?"

Deathly silence in the blackness.

"Go and find what has happened to him, Smith." Thus instructed, Smith wandered vaguely out into the desert, calling "Number one? Number one?" in a rather self-conscious sort of way.

"Now, Number two, are *you* all right?"

Again that utter silence.

At this stage the corporal with him thought it was time that he interposed.

"Excuse me, sir," he said, "but wasn't that the plane's trial run?"

"Oh, don't be so silly," replied Schott abruptly at this obvious piece of stupidity.

"But I think it was, sir," persisted the corporal. "Look, sir, here comes the plane again."

Schott looked up and there it was, coming in for a straight run over the T-piece. This time they could all see the pale outline of the parachutes against the dark background of the sky. "Ah, yes," he said, "that's right. Now feet together, number one—that's good! Now hold it! Number two, bring your knees up a little bit more. Knees up, number two . . . ."

I do not know on what, if any, basis of truth these stories were founded; but you would hear them of an evening when the drinks were beginning to circulate, and it was most amusing to see Peter Warr telling the latter story. He would clear a little circle for himself and pull someone out to act the part of the corporal. Then he would cup his hands to his mouth and, staring up at the smoky gloom of the tent roof above, he would act the part of Bernard Schott in a most lively and comical manner, turning round every now and then to tick the " corporal " off for his impudent interruptions. It was all very funny to watch, the more so since old Bernard Schott himself would be there observing the act with a " wait till it's my turn " sort of look on his face, and as soon as the pantomime was over and the laughter had subsided, he would embark upon his story of Peter Warr. It was a regular tit for tat and one must admit that it was the actors that lent so much humour to the scenes.

Grouped round the bar on these occasions would be our two dentists, quite inseparable, and enjoying themselves hugely. Then there was Bill Fraser, looking very clean and with old Withers seated pensively beside him. And over in the far corner, there were Eric Parten with his sleepy, humorous smile, and Bobby Dodds with his great gift of being happy. Near them would be Jim Chambers waiting to give his own especial party piece. This consisted of a recitation in which we all must join with " Boo's " or " Hurrahs " as the occasion demanded. He would stand there with his feet apart, one hand on his hip and a glass of beer in the other, looking very sunburnt and the picture of good health.

" I'm going to open a house," he would yell.

" Boo ! " we shouted in unison.

" But it's a public house ! " he shouted back at us.

" Hurrah ! " we nearly went mad with excitement !

" It won't be open on *one* day of the week."

" Boo ! "

" But on *every* day ! "

" Hurrah ! "

And so it went on ; and all the time, behind the bar itself, was Corporal Leitch—a Scotsman if ever there was one—watching each one of us carefully with his bright blue eyes, taking us all in and summing us all up. There were not many things that escaped *his* notice, but every now and then you might see his head disappear behind the bar and then, a moment later, up he would bob again with only a little lick of the lips to betray his closely kept secret. Then he would gaze round upon us once more, for all the world as if butter would not melt in his mouth.

Yes, these were grand and boisterous evenings, full of life and filled to capacity with the rough joy of living. To-morrow? Well, perhaps the news would be bad again. But this was the day, and this was the hour to grasp and save and cherish. And as we walked back to our tents and felt the night breeze play on our faces and heard the little slapping of the lake water on the shore, I think that we all realised the extent of our happiness and knew that it could not be lasting. For things that last grow stale too soon, and joys are all the greater for their unexpected capture.

CHAPTER FOUR

BEHIND ROMMEL'S LINES

" Adventures are to the adventurous."
Coningsby. DISRAELI.

" Now is the hour, Aeneas, for the dauntless spirit—now for the stout heart."
Aeneid. VIRGIL

ONE EVENING we walked over to the sergeants' mess, Jim Chambers and I, picking our way between the tents and carefully avoiding the guy ropes and pegs. Their mess consisted of two tents set together at right angles to one another. At the end of one limb of this letter L was a wooden bar at which the sergeants seemed to take turns to do service, while at the end of the other limb was an old rickety piano ; and as we drew closer we could hear them singing, their voices sounding clear in the night air and made musical by the distance. We seldom received special invitations to the sergeants' mess, but instead there was always an open invitation and they made us welcome at once. The atmosphere in there reminded me of the notice, " Abandon rank all ye who enter here " which was hung up outside the bar of the Rhodesian Club in Cairo ; a notice, I used to think, that helped to put you at your ease straightaway.

This evening, I remember, as we entered rather shyly and made our way very quietly towards the bar, we were almost pounced upon and, before we knew where we were, we both held a large glass of beer in our hands while two full bottles stood on the bar nearby. It took us a little while to become acclimatised to our surroundings for the place was simply brimming over with vitality and good spirits. And all the time over the jumble of voices and the sound of noisy laughter, came the notes of the old worn piano and the vigorous singing. A few hurricane lamps shone down warmly on to the scene below while cloudy spirals of blue smoke went wreathing up into the darkness of the tent roof above and, as I remember, you could hardly see across the bar to the men on the other side. I stood back and tried to get the real feeling of the place, the sound of the glasses rattling and clinking on the counter, the red glow of the cigarettes and the little irregular processions of men and drinks to and from the jingling piano.

Sgt. Rose greeted us with a mock bow and a characteristic shake of his head. His thick hair kept falling in a heavy sweep over one eye and you could always distinguish him at a distance by the way he would shake it back impatiently every now and then. There was little restraint about him and from the lively way in which he and Jim Chambers got going, you might have thought they had known each other for years.

Sgt. Rose and one or two others had not long returned from Siwa oasis after having accompanied David Stirling on his last operation. Benghazi, we gathered, had been their objective, and of course this adventure made a very strong bait for Jim Chambers and he was not letting Rose go until he had got hold of the right idea and the technique of these raids. I could hear Jim questioning him as he dragged out the story, little by little, piece by piece, and this was roughly the way it went.

" No," Sgt. Rose was saying, " it was a lousy journey to Siwa all right. Talk about bumping ! I reckon most of our chaps wished they hadn't had any breakfast that morning. But we had an escort of fighters part of the way. Oh, yes, they must have reckoned we were important. No doubt about that ! " He laughed boyishly, " Well, we had no accidents—no enemy planes or anything, and when we got to Siwa we were met by the L.R.D.G.—you know them, don't you ? Yes, Long Range Desert Group, that's right. They're a good lot, believe me, and quite a few of our boys are pretty pally with them, see. We spent a few days with 'em, bathing and lazing about the place. What ? Oh, yes, there's bathing there all right. They've got a lot of Roman baths there in amongst the palm trees. Very nice too ! Wasn't it Cleopatra had a hide-out down there ? Makes you wonder what they did about the flies in those days, 'cos there's bags of 'em knocking about, you know ! Still, that's chiefly in the wog part of the oasis.

" Well, a few days later we got going. Major Stirling tells us we are going to have a shot at some of the destroyers and ships in Benghazi harbour and see if we couldn't blow 'em up. We'd got a couple of collapsible rubber boats with us, see—those fol-boat things you can launch off a submarine. What? You haven't seen one? Oh, there's quite a few in the camp. Well, as I say, we'd got these boats with us so all we had to do was inflate them when we reached the docks and then paddle round the harbour sticking our explosives on as many ships as we could. We hadn't tried blowing up ships before, you see, so we were quite excited to find out what would happen.

"There were six of us in the party, all told : Major Stirling, of course ; Captain Maclean who speaks Italian pretty well ; Mr. Alston, who knows his way round Benghazi from past experience ; and Captain Churchill—you know, Winston Churchill's son—was there to see the fun ; then Cooper and myself made up the party. Six in all, that's right, and we were driving along in a Ford staff car which had been made to look like a Jerry and had got the German recognition sign on it.

"Well, we set off with one of the L.R.D.G. patrols, and they did the navigating for us and took us as far as the hilly Jebel country to the south-east of Benghazi. We spent the night with them there, lay up the following day, see, and pushed off soon after it had got dark. Everything seemed to be going quite smoothly—we got on to the road O.K.—when suddenly our wheels started to make a dreadful screaming sound. Major Stirling was driving, I remember. You've never driven with him I suppose, have you? No? Well, if you'll excuse me, sir, that's a pleasure to come. One hand on the wheel, you know, puffing away quietly at his pipe, and looking at the scenery all around— though you couldn't see anything on this particular night 'cos it was as black as pitch—and all the time he's doing a cool sixty, for all the world as if he's out for a run down the Great North Road. You can imagine him—can't you, sir?—driving into Benghazi like that. Twice he stopped the car and got me to crawl underneath to find out what was making the screaming noise : I saw what it was the second time—wheels out of line ; but we hadn't got a moment to spare, and on we went.

"About five minutes later we came to a road block with an Italian sentry on guard, so we had to halt. Captain Maclean spoke to him sharply in Italian while Cooper and I got our knives out ready for a spot of bother ; he wasn't very inquisitive though and we got through without any trouble. But our wheels were making a terrible noise ; honestly doc, it was awful, and to make matters worse the air-raid sirens started up just as we entered Benghazi. Seemed as if it was specially on our account, and, what's more, just as we were coming into the main road two Boche cars came tearing out of an opening four hundred yards behind. Major Stirling stepped on the gas then, all right, and Captain Alston at the back was leaning forward and directing him. ' Second on the right,' he shouted out, ' that's right. No. You've passed it. Blast ! Go on. Go on, take the next turning instead.'

" We were simply scorching along, whipping round corners on two wheels, and all the time making enough noise to raise the dead. At last we pulled up in a little bombed-out cul-de-sac and jumped out into the road. ' Blow up the car,' said Major Stirling, ' we've got to get out of here on foot.'

" So Cooper and I got the charge ready and shoved it on the car ; then we all legged it hard. After about ten minutes we stopped. It was deathly silent. Not a murmur. ' That's funny we said, ' it looks as if we must have shaken off the Jerries,' and back we went to the car and took out the charge. I didn't waste any time in chucking away the detonator, I can tell you ! It landed on the other side of a wall and went off with a bang. Phew ! "

Sgt. Rose drew his hand across his forehead as if to wipe away the imaginary beads of perspiration and gave us a broad grin. Then he picked up his glass and took a good gulp at his beer. " Well," he went on, " Major Stirling told me that I was to stay and put the car right and that Churchill was to keep watch, while the rest of 'em went off with one of the fol-boats and explosives. Mr. Alston guided them down to the harbour and then came back to join us. Now the funny thing about this was that no sooner had they got down to the harbour than they found they hadn't got the ignitor, so Major Stirling started off back to the car to get it. That left just the two of them together—Captain Maclean and Cooper ; and they set to work to blow up the boat. After pumping away like mad for a bit they realised the boat had got a puncture which didn't please them at all. So back they came to the car for the second boat. Well, now, they must have come back a different way, see, 'cos when Major Stirling walked back to the docks again he found there wasn't anybody there—only the deserted boat, and he didn't think it looked at all healthy so back *he* came to the car. In the meantime Captain Maclean and Cooper had taken the other boat and returned to the harbour. You should have seen Major Stirling's face when I told him they had only just left ! Well, it was funny—wasn't it, sir ? Playing hide and seek round Benghazi in the middle of the night.

" Anyhow they all found each other at last down by the dock-gates ; only by this time a group of Italian sentries had crowded round the fol-boat that had been left behind and they were examining it and fairly shouting their heads off about it. Captain Maclean was furious. He strode up to them and demanded to see their guard commander at once ; and when their commander did turn up from somewhere, obviously half-asleep still, Captain Maclean gave him a good rocket because his sentries had allowed Cooper and Major Stirling to pass in and out of the dock-gates unchallenged. This shook them all up quite a lot, and while they were still sheepish and subdued, Maclean picked up the boat and the three of them came back to the car.

" Now you can imagine, doc, that while all this was going on I hadn't exactly been having a rest cure. There I was, lying under the car and trying to mend the axle by the light of a torch, while every few minutes Itis, and soldiers, and other odd people were strolling past. Phew ! It wasn't very amusing, you know ! Then suddenly Cooper and Captain Maclean had come looming out of the darkness asking me where Major Stirling had got to. ' I don't know,' I told them, ' he set off to join you when I last saw him.' And a little while later Major Stirling had turned up and wanted to know where the others were. I don't mind telling you, sir, I really began to wonder if I wouldn't be going nutty before the night was out.

" Still, they all got back at last. ' No go,' they said, which was rather disheartening ; but what was worse was the way it was beginning to get light. We realised we hadn't got time to get away from the town so we drove the car out of its cul-de-sac—it was running quietly now—and started searching round for somewhere to hide it. After a bit we found an old garage in a half-bombed house and with a lot of manœuvring we managed to back it in and shut the doors."

Suddenly Sergeant Rose laughed. " You know, I can't help being amused by that bit of the story," he said, " 'cos while we were cautiously edging the car into the garage, there was an Italian guard marching straight past us down the road. Still, a miss is as good as a mile, I suppose.

" Well, we crept upstairs into the room over the garage and there we decided to stay for the day. But I reckon the Germans knew about us all right, and knew we were still in the town, what's more. Why ? Well, there were aircraft flying low over the town all day and every now and then we heard sounds of firing. Ugly, it was, and that's a fact. It's pretty deadly, you know, sir, just sticking in a room and waiting for something to happen—preys on your mind after a bit so that you have to start forcing yourself to think about other things, such as what were you doing this time last year ; or you try to think about the best films you saw before you left England, say. And then you find your mind wandering round to what you'll be doing this time to-morrow, whether you'll be eating sphagetti or baked beans, and you say to yourself this time to-morrow, think of me and how I'm feeling now, although you know you will have forgotten by then.

" You see we hadn't got anything to do. We could only sit down on the floor with one of us keeping watch at the window, and hope for the best. By and by the sun came up and threw a great long patch of light on to one wall. Then, as the day went on, that patch of sunlight crept slowly across the wooden boards and I can still remember the way I watched it and wondered ' How long will it be before it reaches that plank with a crack in it ? ' and ' What's the betting that I am still here by the time it has reached the far corner ? ' Yes, I can picture that bare room now, with us sitting about on the floor and the patch of sunlight creeping ever so slowly across the boards. It got very hot in there and we had next to nothing to eat or drink. Looking through the dusty window I could see an old woman cooking her dinner in the downstairs room of the house next door. Dirty and grubby she looked, I thought, but how tempting her food seemed that morning ! I watched her moving from the stove to the table and then back

again, and all the time with the flies hovering round close waiting
to have a go at the food.

"Outside there were plenty of people walking up and down
the street, and round about midday we thought we heard someone
crawling over the roof. Darn me! That was a bad feeling and no
mistake. We all got ready for trouble, craning our necks up and
watching the ceiling like a pack of animals waiting to be fed, and
wondering all the time what the deuce was going to happen next.
After a while the noise stopped and we began to ease back a bit,
sort of half-waiting for something to happen and half-expecting
it, and yet half-hopeful if you see what I mean. We never found
out what it was but it made us sweat a bit I don't mind admitting.

"So the afternoon dragged by and nothing happened. Then
about half-past four—yes, that was about it 'cos I remember
looking at my watch—we suddenly heard someone open the door
downstairs and come in. Honestly, I shall never forget that
feeling inside me as I listened to his boots come stumping up the
wooden stairs. It seemed to last for ages and all the while the
sound of his steps came nearer and nearer. Then he came along
the passage and stopped outside the door. We could hear him
breathing hard after coming up the stairs, and we sat there watching, absolutely quiet, and our eyes glued on the door handle. We
saw it turn slowly and then the door was thrown open.

"Well, I don't know who got the bigger surprise—him or us—
'cos we all seemed to be mesmerised somehow, and we just sat
gaping at him. And he was a dirty Iti sailor who appeared
to have had too much drink and didn't properly know where
he was. He took one long look at us with his eyes staring almost
out of his head and his jaw dropped open, and then with a sort
of little yelp he turned round and shot down the stairs and out
into the street with the devil of a clatter."

Sergeant Rose paused for a moment to empty his glass and
light a fresh cigarette. "But nothing happened," he went on,
"fortunately for us. We stuck there throughout the evening, and
between you and me, it was just about the longest day I've ever
known. Round about 9.30, when it was really dark, we went
downstairs to the car, opened the garage doors and drove down
to a different part of the docks. The sentries were much more
awake, though, this time, and there seemed to be twice as many

as previously. What's more it looked as if fresh wiring had been put up. From where we were, we could see a couple of ships blazing away hard, so Captain Maclean called out to one of the sentries asking him how they had caught on fire. I wish you could have seen his face, sir. 'Bastard Inglisi,' he shouted back at us and spat into the water. We laughed like hell to ourselves, but what with the glare from the burning ships being reflected off the water and dockyards, and what with all the extra sentries about, we could see we hadn't got a cat's chance of blowing anything up.

" So we turned round and started to drive back down the main street, when all of a sudden the car started screeching again. Major Stirling drew up by the pavement. ' Rose,' he said, ' Have another go.' Down I got under the car and Cooper crawled under with me to lend a hand, but by this time we were so jumpy that we were calling each other all the names under heaven and quite a few more besides. After a bit we thought we'd mended it and off we went again, only we had hardly gone a hundred yards before the confounded din started again. Once more we stopped and tried to mend it, but our luck was out. Blast the car, we said eventually and away we shot as fast as we could. Back through the road block—Cooper and I with knives ready—but Captain Maclean had the sentry well under control and we were soon off the road and into the Jebel country.

" And that, gentlemen," said Sergeant Rose with another mock bow, " was that. A jolly game of hide and seek in Benghazi. When we got back to Siwa the fitter took a look at the car and told us we would need a new axle as ours was bent. However I fixed that up all right when we got to Alexandria and then in our drive back along the desert road to Cairo "—his voice became serious for the first time—" we had our only tragedy."

" Major Stirling had met Arthur Morton—the *Daily Telegraph* reporter—in Alex. and we were giving him a lift to Cairo, when by a bad stroke of luck we hit a truck and he was killed. It all happened so quickly, you know the way these accidents do, and when we came to pick ourselves up we found we had all been injured in some way or other except for Major Stirling who had just sprained his wrist. He seems to bear some sort of charm, there's no doubt about that. Still, the rest of us weren't hurt too badly, and anyway life is very short." He paused for a moment and then grinned in his boyish way, " I bet there'll be some fun all right on this present ride ; I'd love to see Major Stirling and Captain Mayne get going together."

For a while, we did not know quite what to say except that I remember Jim persistently cross-questioned him on this bit or that, and kept muttering, " I say ! " " By jove ! " and " Jolly good show ! " or " That must have been grim ! " for there were still a number of early youthful expressions in his vocabulary. And Sergeant Rose seemed to think the whole adventure was much of a routine in some respects, for he was an old operative and had been with the unit since it was formed, although from his very boyish appearance and looks you might never have thought it. He could sing, too—there was no doubt about that ! For he had by far the best voice in the mess and all the rowdiness and noise would sink down to a mere murmur once he had started to sing. Yes, there was a softness and a sentiment in that voice that somehow made you feel homesick—I don't quite know why, but it did. . . .

" By Jove," said Jim as we made our way back to our lines, " that's the real thing all right, isn't it—the raid, I mean. I wonder what the dickens they are doing now ! "

And thinking it over in my tent as I tried to keep the hurricane lamp from smoking, it occurred to me that a lot of these chaps were going to find it very difficult to settle down again after the war to the quiet life of peace-time. Take Sergeant Rose, for instance, who had been looking after a branch of Woolworths' before the war. From there to the Guards, from the Guards to the Commandos, and from there again to the S.A.S. There was something about the excitement of this life that so evidently satisfied some integral part of one's make up and fulfilled a latent longing. Could that longing, once allowed a free rein, be curbed and suppressed again ? What would a solicitor's life seem like to Paddy Mayne compared with the joy of comradeship and the thrill of destroying enemy planes ? What would routine medicine, with its inevitable sequelae of social intercourse and bedside manner stuff, be like after the life of a unit medical officer in the Western Desert.

How long would it take for us to settle down ? I wondered ; and then, of a sudden, I thought how foolish it was for me to be-considering these things when even now the enemy was standing at the gates of Alexandria, when the whole fate of the Middle East trembled and hung in the balance, and the very thought of peace seemed so infinitely remote.

When these chaps came back from a raid you were always so glad to see them again, even if you did not know them very well, and, in your English fashion, you tried to hide your gratification and relief with trite observations and rather superficial remarks. " Have a nice time ? " You would ask or, " That must have been fun ! " you would remark when you knew in your heart of hearts that really it must have been utterly bloody. And that was rather how I felt when I walked into the mess early one evening and saw Paddy Mayne talking with Corporal Leitch. (Sometimes I used to wonder if Corporal Leitch did not know more about us than we knew about each other, for he always had to stay up to see us to bed of a night. And later, when he had taken to parachuting and become a first-rate operative, he was one of the oldest and steadiest of the hands.) Paddy, I remember, was sitting by the bar with one huge thigh crossed over the other, his head sunk low between his heavy shoulders and a cigarette between his thick fingers. As I hung up my cap by the mess entrance I could hear Corporal Leitch's rolling r's and Scot's speech without any difficulty, but it was quite impossible to make out anything that Paddy was saying, for he spoke so quietly. I walked over to the letter rack, but my letters had not yet come through to my new address, and feeling a little disconsolate I wandered over towards the bar. Paddy turned round.

" Good evening, doctor," he remarked civilly, " will you have a drink ? "

" Thank you very much," I replied, " I'd like a John Collins."

" A Jun Cullins, surr—vurry gud ! " Corporal Leitch busied himself behind the bar, and over one of his expert concoctions I asked Paddy what sort of luck he had had.

" Och," he said, " nothing much. We got an oil dump and one or two things but nothing very exciting. Still, it was quite a good crack ! "

I kept quiet for a bit, not wishing to appear inquisitive and wondering whether it was " the done thing " to start questioning people about raids as soon as they had returned. Perhaps it was better, I thought, to try and imitate his quiet conversational manner which somehow fitted in so strangely with his great size and dashing exploits.

" Good shooting ? " I asked, rather as if we might have been discussing an afternoon at the ranges.

At that he did look a bit surprised for a moment, but then he just shook his head. " No. A bit here and there. Nothing close."

And I do not suppose I should have got much further, as I think we were just going on to talk about parachuting when some of the others arrived, and there was no peace for Paddy for quite a while after that. He was simply bombarded with questions, and I could not help but feeling a bit sorry for him when newcomers came along and started off with the same old questions over again. There was no consecutive story from what I could make out : it was just a jumble of questions and answers and you had to fit it together for yourself and make the best you could out of the disjointed remarks and descriptions.

It appeared that soon after David Stirling had returned to Siwa oasis, he had set out again in the " blitz buggy " with Paddy Mayne, Sergeant Cooper and a Palestinian refugee called Karl. Karl was a good man to have around, and I remember him telling me later how once he had called in at Derna on one of these raids, he and another Palestinian, and together they had gone into the German counterpart of the N.A.A.F.I. there and obtained an extremely good meal. So Karl knew his way around with the Germans all right, and he must have had a fairly cool head into the bargain. Well, these four had proceeded along the same course as on the previous raid to the Jebel country that lies to the south of Benghazi and, after a short rest, they set off by night on the main road leading into the town.

Paddy was driving with Karl beside him, while Sergeant Cooper and David Stirling were sitting in the back. Now Paddy used to drive very fast indeed, as I found out later on, but since he was also very competent there was never anything to worry about in that respect. On this particular night, as he was speeding along, he came round a bend only to find a road block a short distance ahead. This consisted of a heavy wooden barrier stretched across the road with a red lamp placed below it to serve as a warning and, at the speed at which they were travelling, Paddy had only just sufficient room in which to pull up. There was a German guard at this road block, about eight men in all, with a German sergeant in charge. No sooner had the car been halted than a light was switched on it and the guard turned out. The German sergeant shouted out, asking who they were, to which Karl replied to the effect that Colonel Muller in the back (David Stirling !) and three others—he rattled off the names—were returning from the front line and consequently did not know the password. Under these circumstances would the sergeant kindly allow them to pass immediately as Colonel Muller was tired and wanted a good night's rest. The German digested this information in silence for the next few moments but plainly he was suspicious about something. Perhaps old Karl was rather overdoing things, I don't know, but anyhow the sergeant decided to pick up his lantern and come and take a closer look. He started to walk over towards the car.

" To hell with this ! " said David. " Put her into reverse Paddy and let's get out of here. We'll go in another way."

Paddy slammed the gear into reverse and started to back round when suddenly the guard brought up their rifles and covered the car at almost point-blank range. He shoved the gear lever back into neutral. Things began to look a bit sticky.

The German sergeant walked up to the car and holding up the lantern looked down at Paddy as he sat in the driver's seat. " Now, who are you ? " he demanded.

The brief silence that followed the question was broken by a sharp click, and all of a sudden the sergeant found he was staring down into the nozzle of a revolver. Nothing had been said, no answer was given. There was Paddy holding the revolver in his lap, and pointing it straight up into the German's face ; the safety catch was off. The guard standing further down the road were unable to see what was taking place inside the car, but their rifles were up and they were ready to fire as soon as the order was given. It must have made a very strange little scene, with every one remaining perfectly still for a few seconds and with only the lantern to give it illumination. But it was up to the German to make the next move, and in those few seconds he decided quickly

that life was too good a thing to throw away in such a manner !
Without moving he shouted to the guard to lower their rifles
and pull up the road barrier. When this had been done
Paddy, still holding his revolver, put the car into gear with his
free hand and accelerated away past the raised barrier and
down the road.

Eventually they reached the outskirts of the town and, parking
the car in a secluded place beneath some trees, they set out in
search of suitable targets. But things seemed quiet that night
and they could not find anything very big—an oil dump, cars,
trucks, lorries, telegraph poles : they fell back on the usual sort
of stuff and then returned to their own car to make their exit
by a different road. On their way out they passed a road-house
which they shot up pretty thoroughly. Whether it was the sound
of this shooting or whether it was a phone message from the
German sergeant, they did not know, but soon afterwards the
two in the back seat reported that they were being chased by what
looked like armoured cars. So they accelerated into the open,
turning off the road into the rough country, and by zigzagging
from side to side they soon shook off their pursuers. Then, finding
themselves alone, they headed straight for the escarpment and
the Jebel beyond. But they had great difficulty in getting up the
rough steep slopes of the escarpment as any one who knows that
region may well imagine, and it was only after a lot of pushing
and sweating that they got to the top just as it began to grow
light. Then on they went to the rendezvous area that they had
arranged previously with the Long Range Desert Group, and it
was at this time that they very nearly came to grief.

' Sitting in the back seat Sgt. Cooper heard a sharp crack inside
the car, and looking down he realised that the time-pencil on one
of the bombs which they had kept in reserve, had gone off. He
could not see which bomb it was, but he knew it had only a
thirty-second time-fuse and he shouted out a warning to the
others. Without any more ado they all jumped out of the car
and ran away from it as fast as they could. A few seconds later
it blew up with a roar, and looking up from the ground they saw
the tangled burning wreckage that remained, and realised how
narrow had been their escape. After that little episode they were
obliged to walk the remaining distance to the rendezvous. But

in this respect they were fortunate, for it was only a matter of four miles or so, and they were able to spend two lazy days with the Arabs before the L.R.D.G. patrol picked them up and took them back to Siwa.

So that was Paddy's story, and taken by and large I believe he really did enjoy these quick raids which were crowded with action. For there had not been any hiding up in a house in Benghazi for a day, which must have made the previous raid such a trying experience. Then, too, Paddy was a bit different from the others—this sort of fighting was in his blood ; he thrived on it. There was no give or take about his method of warfare, and he was out to kill when the opportunity presented itself. There was no question of sparing an enemy—this was war, and war meant killing. No quarter was asked and none was given. Nor can I remember having heard him complain about the enemy's methods of warfare in the desert, for to him there were no rules. Once or twice I heard him question the value of the red cross, remarking that a soldier who was going to be built up to fight again should, in his opinion, be a perfectly legitimate target. He observed the rules and the red cross, mind you, but *his* theory was that the days of *noblesse oblige* and the Knights of King Arthur stuff had drawn to a close, and that now it was all or nothing. (Women and children, bombing of towns, etc. did not enter into this argument which concerned only the desert war.) Neither did you hear him complain when his friends were killed ; but I always felt, although he would say nothing other than giving an expression of sorrow, that a friend's death meant so many enemy lives in a form of personal revenge, a wiping off of the debt as it were.

On this particular evening, however, I did not know him so well. One only sensed that here was a quietly forceful and rugged leader who could be relied upon in any emergency ; a man who was as ruthless as he was quick-witted in action. Later on I used to think that you were as safe as you possibly could be when you were with Paddy, because he took such great care of the people who were under him. But there was one thing that it did not take long you to find out, and that was his shrewd judgment of character. " Shooting a line " cut absolutely no ice at all with him and he could detect it straightaway. Some people, anxious to create a favourable impression, thought that because he was so quiet then they had better do most of the talking, but he could ask the most discomforting questions in the blandest of manners, and he could cut a person short with hardly a word spoken. No, it did not pay to pretend when you were with him, and this evening you could almost see him sizing people up from the very questions they were asking.

What of David Stirling? At the moment, Paddy said, he was up at G.H.Q. in Cairo. Was he reporting on the results of these raids, we wondered, or was he making plans for a fresh attack? Probably both for when, a few days later, we went up to Cairo for the wedding of our engineer, Bill Cumper, there was David looking as languid and as well turned out as only a Guards officer can look and talking of bigger operations to come.

Jellicoe, too, was at the wedding reception and seemingly little the worse for his savage experiences in Crete. He had only just returned and thought that his party destroyed about twenty aircraft on Heraklion aerodrome. Three of the French officers with him had been captured, the fourth had been killed. He, himself, owed his escape to having left the others to make contact with the guide who was going to help them get away over the mountains. When he returned to the place where he had left the French, he found that one had been killed in a brief shooting fray while the others had been rounded up and marched off. In addition, sixty Cretans were shot for the part they were supposed to have played in this affair.

From him I enquired about our future activities, and he seemed to think that the next operation would be quite a big affair. Any chance of a doctor being wanted? Yes, he thought so quite definitely as it was more than possible that a little blood would be spilt. No, he did not think it would be a case of parachuting or using submarines, but he gathered we were having some jeeps specially fitted up with mountings to take two twin sets of machine-guns, one fore and one aft. In this way we should be able to concentrate a pretty strong fire power!

As I looked round the reception room I wondered just what headaches were in store for the Germans. For here were the people who were going to cause them, difficult though it was to realise, and one bomb in this room now would save the enemy

B.D.   F a great deal of worry and foreboding in the days to come. Yes, it was all such an individual affair. There was David looking so cool and imperturbable ; and Paddy dwarfing the very chair on which he sat as he argued with Jim Chambers over past rugger players and match results ; and Jellicoe, full of energy and being bombarded with questions about his raid on Crete. If these three were to be killed to-night, I asked myself, would the S.A.S. continue, would it survive ? For at this time these three were the real hub of the thing, and on them was to depend very largely the results of future raids and the part the unit was to play in relation to the war as a whole.

We got to bed late that night, I remember, and Bobby Dodds, Eric Parten and myself almost fell asleep as we returned in an erratic Egyptian taxi through darkened Cairo streets to our pension at Heliopolis. I record this because, although I was very nearly asleep before I got into bed, after three hours of being bitten alive by bed bugs, I eventually decamped to the sofa where I dropped off immediately. The sole comment that the landlady had to make the next morning about the livestock in the bed was that, if bugs indeed were there, then I must have brought them with me. Nothing, it appeared, could have been more logical. Fancy me daring to tell *her* that there were bugs in my bed ! Why, I condemned myself with my very own words ! I retreated and gave it up. Oriental logic could afford to be inscrutable in these times when it was so difficult to obtain any accommodation in Cairo. Nor was it any threat to suggest that you would leave the place in indignant wrath, for you knew that your apartment would be filled by someone else before your back was even turned. In short, there was not enough room for men coming back on leave ; for, after all, the staff officers had to be housed in quiet luxury and they, in themselves, formed *such* a superior army. At this time there was a story current to the effect that there was absolutely no need for any one to worry about the situation in the Western Desert, for even if the Germans did advance on Cairo they would only find themselves confronted by the vastly superior numbers of the G.H.Q. staff.

But to put that matter on one side and to return to the subject of livestock, I might as well add that I was extremely surprised to find that there were no bed bugs to bear me company on the following night, and accordingly I fell asleep with the firm conviction in my mind that I must, therefore, have taken them somewhere else.

We enjoyed our short stay in Cairo very much, and what a difference, I thought, it made to be in such good company when you were on leave. I remember one morning that we spent at the Heliopolis open-air swimming pool. Eric Parten, an Air Force officer, and I were sitting beneath a sunshade sipping " lamoons " and watching a very expert Egyptian diver giving a free perform- ance for the benefit of the onlookers. As he surfaced after each dive, there was a little burst of clapping from the people sitting around the pool, and he would strut back very proudly, puffing out his chest and showing off his physique preparatory to the next dive. All of which was very pleasing until Bobby Dodds decided to take a hand in affairs. Lumbering over to the diving board in his usual unconcerned sort of way he watched the Egyptian execute a neat somersault and then proceeded to do one of his gorilla imitations. This consisted of his ambling sideways down the board on all fours, pausing at the end to scratch one armpit in meditative manner and then, with a most animal cry, jumping into the water like a frog and landing with a huge splash—flat on his belly.

The Egyptian, strutting back for his next dive, could not quite understand the titters and the laughter. He looked rather angrily round the pool for a moment but could only see Bobby swimming in meekly to the side. With a final survey of the audience he embarked upon a superb back flip and turn, but hardly had he come to the surface before Bobby had followed him with a very good ' pansy boy " dive, falling down sideways through the air with one hand behind his neck and the other resting grace- fully on the opposite hip. There was no doubt about the laughter this time. The Egyptian champion clambered out and looked round with an expression of baffled fury. What the devil *was* the joke ? Had he made a mistake and fallen in with a splash ? Or was it just that silly clown of a fellow lying in the water there and blowing up little fountains out of his mouth ? Anyway, no longer would he continue to dive while these people obviously were not in the mood to appreciate his art—and that, I fear, was the end of his exhibition.

But we splashed around merrily throughout the afternoon with cock-fights and pick-a-back races up the shallow end. The latter event provided some amusement if only because I was carrying Bobby on my shoulders and, urged on by his voice in my ear, fairly excelled myself in jumping across the bath. It was only after we had reached the other side that I was given to understand, beyond any possible shadow of doubt, that his cries had not been of exhortation or encouragement but rather of exquisite agony, since his hind quarters were still very sore from his last parachute jump !

Yes, these days were most enjoyable and passed like the wind ; and it seemed as if we had hardly arrived in Cairo before we found ourselves tearing back fast in the Bedford fifteen-hundredweight, with Bobby at the wheel, trying to pretend that he was an ace-king on the Brooklands' track.

CHAPTER FIVE

" Wherein of antres vast and deserts idle,
  Rough quarries, rocks and hills whose heads touch heaven,
  It was my hint to speak."

Othello. SHAKESPEARE.

A FEW DAYS later David Stirling. came down to our camp at Kabrit. At the end of the week, he said, we would be setting out on the next operation. Most of us would be wanted. Yes, Bill Cumper ought to come ; and I would be needed since it would be quite a big party in all. He went round talking to each one of us, encouraging, persuasive, listening to what we had to say, and making every man feel that he was absolutely indispensable. Never forceful, there was almost a magnetic quality about his quiet charm : within five minutes he could persuade you that black was white, within a minute he could convert the cynic to the enthusiast.

From us to the French. (Yes, of course they had to come ! Why, the party would not be a success without them !) and from them to the sergeants' mess. It was just the same there. They all grouped round, hanging on his words, eager in their listening ; and when he had left they were just waiting for him to say the word " go." Then finally to the men's canteen to give them news and encouragement.

Later on I heard of one occasion how he had said to a man who was just going out on a job : " You know, to-morrow night you will be doing something far more important than any major in the army has ever done."

It was not surprising then that these chaps were ready to go out on a raid, neither knowing nor caring where or how they went, but certain only of the one thing—that their job was going to be very well worth doing.

He set off again for Cairo that same night, quite tireless in his impulsive energy and driving back the ninety odd miles in as

many minutes. On the next day he was going to army headquarters, some distance outside Alexandria on the main Cairo-
Alexandria road, and it was here that we must pick him up before
we set off on the operation.

From that moment on, there was an air of activity about the
camp, a restless activity combined with a sense of expectancy and
a prevailing eagerness. Throughout the day men were filing in
and out of the quartermaster's tent from which they drew their
compasses, binoculars, water-bottles, emergency rations, rubber
tubing, head-dresses and so on—they reappeared at the far end
of the tent heavily laden, and staggered off to their quarters to
sort out the kit they had obtained. In the armourer's store there
was always a group of men clustered together examining the
automatics and revolvers, fingering the tommy-guns, and making
their choice from the weight, the balance, or the sights of the
weapon. Every now and then there came the crackle of rapid fire
from the rifle range, and the sand would spurt up in vicious little
kicking clouds from the protecting bank behind. Over at the
M.T. section, too, they were doing overtime, stripped to the waist,
sweating and cursing as they worked at the welding and oiling of
the special fittings. You could see them lying on the sand under
the belly of a lorry, leaning over the bonnet and checking on the
engine, while the whole day long there came from that quarter the
confused sound of banging and hammering. And even we, in the
medical tent, were kept busy enough making first-aid packets for
each man, wrapping them up and issuing them out. The men
would hold them in their hands, weighing them up and down
and trying to gauge the potency of the contents. " This ought to
fix us, Doc ! " they would say, with a grin and a shake of the
head, as they marched out.

The work went on until late at night, and as it grew dark the
doorway of each hut threw out a warm pool of light from the
hurricane lamp within. At the vehicle pits the naked whiteness
of the arc-lamps shone down on the fitters as they clambered over
and under the three-tonners which they were inspecting, one after
the other. Then, when the mechanics had finished with the
vehicles, they were driven back to the M.T. park in an orderly
row, the jeeps side by side in front, with the massive lorries lined

up behind. Those who were not working would bring out beer to those who were; and every now and then you would see one of the men, outlined by the white brilliance of the light, throw back his head, drain a bottle in a few gulps, and then get down to it again.

From the direction of the sergeants' mess came the sound of singing, and we went over to them the evening before we set off. They were a grand crowd, these sergeants, and I can still see them quite clearly in the mind's eye, laughing, boisterous, and so full of vitality and rude health that you could feel the throb of life in the very atmosphere.

There was Sergeant Lilley with his black tousled hair, his serious voice, and his small dark eyes which wrinkled up when he laughed. I can hear him now singing " Ole Man River " in a deep trembling bass, with that way he had of modulating the volume until he came to the " Tow dat barge ! Lift dat bale ! " line, which he fairly spat out at you. There was a very sincere philosophy about Sgt. Lilley, and he reasoned and puzzled everything out for himself. Later on I can remember the long debates we used to have about this and that, for he dearly loved a good argument to help pass away the time. Sometimes, too, we used to play chess with a set that we had made for ourselves, although draughts was really more to his liking. Yes, there was something very kind and homely about him, you felt, as you stood talking with him—no acting, no showing off, but just very straightforward and honest. Funny to think that he was nearly forty, married and with children, and yet one of our oldest operatives in length of service with the S.A.S. Hard to advise him what to do after the war. When I started talking to him—perhaps trying to be a little clever and worldly wise—of the bright chances of a colonial life, he just pulled me up quietly and told me what were the real difficulties of obtaining a decent job, for he himself had tried. " It's not easy for a married man, you know, Doc," he said simply. " It looks so nice on paper, but it doesn't work out quite the same in real life."

He and Sergeant Bennett—pale, thin and with hair falling lank over his forehead—were great friends, drawn together by a mutual disapproval of class life in " civvy street " and a similar

sense of unjust treatment by the world' in general. " There's a
a law for the rich and a law for the poor " they would say with
an emphatic shake of the head as they talked of their earlier
experiences. Yet once Sergeant Bennett had thrown the cloak
of disapproval on to one side, there was absolutely no holding
him ; and when it came to ragging, he would be the capricious
schoolboy all over again. He always looked so worried and
baffled ! But, looking back on it now, I think it was only a way
of his and I do not believe that anything really upset him very
much. Except, possibly, when he was detailed as acting quarter-
master-sergeant later on at the rendezvous, and I had the
misfortune of being the quartermaster. " That's funny ! " he
would say when we came to check up on the stores together, " I
could 'ave sworn I put that tin of biscuits there with my very own
'ands." And there was all the wonderment of a mystery story
in the way he said it. Yes, I think that job had us both worried
a bit, for it was a responsible task trying to keep pace with the
dwindling food and water reserves.

Then there was Sergeant Hardy with his small, very powerful
frame, and a face that continually changed expression as he acted
to the words of his numerous songs and stories. Looking at him
I felt that people had missed a great deal in life if they had not
heard him sing " The green eye of the little yellow God," or recite
with forceful gestures, " My *friends* who stayed at home ! " These
were his preserves ; nobody else was a patch on him at that sort
of stuff. The way he would tap you on the shoulder or give you a
nudge as he remarked " the billiard cues " *their* gun, me lad—the
dance saloon's *their* home ! " I forget the exact words. But he
certainly was an actor and you could feel the deep bite of the
thing in the way he said it. He was very much the individual,
and I dare say that he will go on knocking round the world for
many a year to come, and never die in his bed.

Or Sergeant Bunfield with his extravagant knowledge about
everything, and his remarkable (not incredible, mind you !)
stories of life and hardship on the North-West frontier in the good
old days. You were seldom with Sergeant Bunfield for as long as
five minutes without him having been caught up in some argument or other. Being a knowledgeable person and not averse to
airing some of his views in a " contradict me if you dare " sort of

manner—whether on the subject of electricity or Drake's voyages
—he would soon get pulled up by somebody on some point or
other. For a short while the debate would flash backwards and
forwards in heated fray, becoming more and more personal and
emphatic over the contentious point at issue, until at last Sergeant
Bunfield, as if goaded beyond the point of human endurance,
would rap out with a " Right ! What d'yer bet ? " Then, for a
moment or two, the opposition would be silenced, considering
what, if anything, they were willing to lay on the subject over
which they were at variance. " There you are ! " Sergeant
Bunfield would say in triumph, " Now I'll bet you a pound ! I'll
bet you ten pounds ! Right, I'll make it a thousand pounds !
Drake sailed up the West coast of America ! " and he would look
round as if daring anybody to defy him. To listen to one of these
arguments was really most amusing, and you could eat your hat
if it remained on the same subject for more than a minute or two.
For all of a sudden, without a hint or a warning, the contestants
would be arguing about something completely different, and it
would be quite impossible to trace any connection between the
themes or any reason for the dramatic change. Mocking questions,
rude answers, and insults all helped in this respect, making it
extremely difficult for an onlooker, let alone those taking part, to
decide just exactly what it was they were arguing about. But it
always ended with a " Right ? What d'yer bet ? " and Sergeant
Bunfield jamming his pipe into his mouth and sucking at it in a
most determined and defiant manner. As a result of his social
debating activities his name became twisted up into " Bag-
tweazle " " Bagonwheels " and " Bilgethrostle " without very
much effort on anybody's part. But it was all given and taken
in very good humour, because every one was well aware, really,
that Sgt. Bunfield was right nine times out of ten in what he said.
And, of course, he was extremely efficient in whatever work he
did—it was just that you could not resist ragging him.

Or again Sergeant Rose with his happy nature and pleasing
manners. He made a very good sergeant-major to Paddy Mayne's
squadron later, and seemingly could turn his hand to any sort
of a job, without much effort on his part. But I shall never forget
the way the jumble of voices and the noisy laughter would die
down to an attentive hush when he started to sing, and I doubt

if a much higher or more sincere form of compliment could have been paid to him.

Or Sergeant Kershaw with his lean look, and eyes—bloodshot from desert strain—giving him a piratical sort of appearance. There was another fighter for you ! For he had fought in the Spanish civil war and this sort of thing seemed to suit him right down to the ground.

And Sergeants Cooper, Badger, Cantell, Almonds, White and Tate—the names come crowding back and the memories are very clear. And Pat Riley, the sergeant-major, huge and burly, who kept a rough law and order over all. Yes, I can still see him laughing boisterously and slapping his thigh with a great hand as he spoke of a past raid or discussed the merits of Italian sentries. Both he and Sergeant Cooper were later to become commissioned in the S.A.S., for this was one of the few units in which the men could become commissioned and yet remain with us.

I think that when I joined the S.A.S. there was a high proportion of sergeants relative to the men. Or was it that one did not come into contact with the men so much until you went out on the raids ? Certainly as the volunteers came in, the proportion dropped away ; for every man lost a stripe on joining the unit (and every officer a pip), and consequently no sergeants came fresh to us, which was a very good thing. I should put the total strength of the unit at round about one hundred and fifty men at this time, with a proportion of one officer to every ten men ; the high ratio of officers being due to the small numbers involved in a fighting patrol. Then there were, of course, the " non-operatives " who consisted of those attached to the administrative and parachute training branches—the latter really making up a separate unit in itself and working in liaison with the R.A.F.

So we were all set to go. Our packs and blankets were rolled up, the trucks were loaded, and this was the last night we should be drinking beer for some long while. Well, I thought, as we banged our glasses down on the bar and prepared to take our leave, going out on ops. could not fail to be enjoyable in such fine company as this.

We set out the next morning after a rather late start. For

there were all those little last minute things to be done, and final affairs to be tended to, so that the minutes lingered and crept into hours and seemed slow in their passing. I had been detailed to a three-ton lorry—we had half a dozen of these in all, together with a dozen jeeps—and in the back of it I had packed away my medical supplies which, I reckoned, should last out for about a couple of weeks. There were approximately fifty men going out on this raid which, I might add, was surrounded by an atmosphere of delightful vagueness. I, for one, was under the impression that we would only be out for about five days—ten days at the most— and little did I realise that it would be more than five long dusty weeks before some of us returned. I wondered whatever my aunt would have thought of all this, for she was so particular in being correct about the time ; and the thought of strolling to a railway station " to pick up a train " without knowing every exact detail— where it had started, at what stations it would stop and for how long, and when it would arrive—was absolute anathema to her. For here we were slinging the odd " buckshee " article into a lorry in case it might come in handy, not knowing where we were going, what we were going to do, or when or how we should return ; and I do not think that anybody cared two hoots. The men were going to see some action, or " have some fun " as they put it, and that was quite enough to render them light-hearted and care-free.

We made a strange little convoy wending our way along the monotonous road towards Cairo with " les petits jeeps " (as the French would say) driving in and out amongst " les grands trois tonneurs." And so by midday we found ourselves in the outskirts of Cairo, already feeling a little thirsty, and with the drivers swearing volubly as they tried to maintain formation amongst the rest of the traffic. Keeping position while driving through a city is never an easy business, but in Cairo it was doubly difficult with all the taxis and peculiar varieties of Egyptian family cars weaving in and out amongst our vehicles. The men were in great form, however, singing and shouting ; and you could not help laughing as you watched them remove certain attractive articles from the stalls of the street-vendors. For you would see the jeep in front of you proceeding along the Egyptian highway in a very dignified manner, when all of a sudden it would swing in to the side of the road near a fruit-barrow, a large brown hand would shoot out, and a succulent water-melon would disappear as the jeep accelerated away again. All of which was very bad form, of course, with nothing of the white-man touch about it, but nevertheless extremely amusing to watch. The Egyptian merchant, having realised that he had been shamefully robbed and deceived, proceeded to raise his arms to high heaven and call loudly upon Allah to punish the infidel. But since it required only the slightest of incidents to make a native behave in this fashion, none of the passers-by or onlookers took the slightest notice or was in the least bit concerned. For to the casual observer it was merely another Egyptian passing away the time of day with old acquaintances in light and airy banter ; and anyway, although one realised that this might be rather poor form, I doubt if it did much harm, since the Egyptian gentry sold their vegetables at such vast profits that a melon or two could not have affected their turnover much.

We halted on the other side of Cairo for a meal and then pushed on again, choosing the delta road to Alexandria in order to avoid the traffic on the desert by-pass. Probably we took up more time in going by this route, but certainly it was quite pleasant over those bits of road that were not so dusty, with the rich agricultural fields slanting away on either side of us and the ships, heavily laden with fertile produce, moving slowly down the networks of water-channels. Camels abounded everywhere, walking delicately along the " towpaths," munching with noisy regurgitation and vacant stare as they lay by the roadside ; while oxen, blinded like Samson, turned hopelessly at the water wheel. This, the romancer or tourist would have said, was the Egypt of two thousand years ago, the land of the waving palm-trees. But in the dirty squalid villages round the next corner were the children in their rags, chasing each lorry and hurling their filthy epithets after us—a touch which, I fear, tended to spoil the effect of the picture somewhat.

Soon after it had grown dark we halted for the night, and from the direction of the cooks' lorry came the welcome clinking and banging as they got the grub ready. We were dust-coated and feeling pretty hungry ; so, after we had unrolled our blankets, we squatted round the fire, watching the hissing flames and waiting impatiently for the water to come to the boil. It was a humid sort of atmosphere, for we had drawn up in the long grass beside the road, and from the slow moving stream that ran alongside came the clamour of hundreds of frogs as they woke up for the nights' activities. Mosquitoes, of course, were rife ; and, as soon as we had settled down to rest, they descended upon us, giving us brisk periods of wakefulness throughout the night and an uneasy slumber. And if there was one thing I could never learn to do, I thought as I took a blind swipe at one that hovered overhead, it was to go to sleep while there were mosquitoes in the offing. . . .

We were away again by sun-up, driving through the outskirts of Alexandria and along the main desert road to army head-quarters. Here we found ourselves amongst a mass of dug-in tents, in the midst of which was Auchinleck's private plane ; and after a little searching we came upon David Stirling and Robin Gurdon. Robin I had known from earlier days in the regiment, but now he had transferred to the Long Range Desert Group ; and here he was as immaculate as ever in his clean shirt and corduroy trousers ; for it did not matter whether he was back in a company mess or out with a patrol, he always managed to preserve that air of being very much the nobleman. Proud and headstrong, with a temper that chafed at any delay, there was something very human and lovable about him. In many ways he was the perfect officer with the men : always looking after their needs and attending to their comfort before he settled down himself, and yet with all this he still maintained his air of superiority. From him I gathered that he was going to navigate our party to the rendezvous of his L.R.D.G. patrol, which was situated somewhere south of Mersa Matruh. "But how do we get past the enemy lines ? " I inquired innocently. "Oh, just drive round," he replied with superb confidence. And that, I suppose, is what we did, for at this time the enemy's line at Alamein did not extend as far south as the Qattara depression.

After a brief lunch at Army H.Q. we moved back towards Alexandria with Robin in the lead, but before reaching the city we turned south into the open desert. Here we immediately found ourselves in difficulties, running into one long stretch of soft sand after another. It made very hard " going " for the overloaded lorries, and time after time they kept bogging down, getting stuck, and having to be dug out and run off on the sand trays. With these frequent delays it was obvious that something would have to be done, and that evening it was decided that a small party of men and one or two lorries would have to turn back after having removed whatever was not absolutely necessary in stores and kit from the other lorries. In other words our lorries were lightened at the expense of those which were going back to Kabrit, and our water supplies, for example, were reduced quite considerably. An officer would have to return with the party, and I thought that Jim Chambers took it awfully well when he was told that the lot had fallen on him. It was just typical of him that he never made any query or complaint although, God knows, he was probably twice as keen as any one to go on. Bill Cumper, too, had to turn back here, but he left his engineer sergeant to carry on with us.

So that night we camped down and sat talking round our trucks while the desert breeze blew fresh and cool from off the coast. How good it was to be alone again, just our little party, away from the stench and filth of agricultural Egypt and back to the clean sterility of the sand. Away to the north we could see Alexandria being raided and it was strange the sense of detachment and isolation that it gave you. For we were just spectators of this impersonal firework display, and it was difficult to appreciate the human element involved. We could see the momentary specks of the little shells pricking cleanly against the blackness of the sky, the occasional flash of bomb explosions ; and then would come the deep heavy rumble on the night air. I tried to realise how, up above, there were Germans peering down their bomb-sights, selecting their targets, and coming down to dive through the flak ; while far below were poor terrified people cowering in their shelters and homes, holding their breath in sudden fear, and praying confusedly that God might be kind to them this night. Yet from where we sat watching, dusty and sleepy, it might have been merely a spectacular performance, so detached and impersonal did it seem.

We awoke the following morning to find ourselves blanketed over by a thick white mist which crawled along the ground, enveloping us all in its damp clinging embrace. Our clothes were wet, the lorries were wet, the seats wet—in fact everything seemed to be soaking. Under these conditions driving became very

difficult ; and after we had said farewell to the small returning
party, we set off in slow time, being unable to see one another and
fearful of a collision. It was just as bad as a London fog, I thought,
as I peered out, trying to discover the outline of the truck ahead,
and not knowing whether we were going too fast or too slow.
Every now and then we would come into a clear patch, only to be
lost to each other's sight a moment later. After a while, feeling
certain that we had become separated from the rest, we stopped
and switched off our engines. All around was the woolly whiteness,
the dampness and, to my alarm, the utter silence. What a fine
old joke this would be if we were to become lost almost before
we had started ! We sat there for a moment, speaking only in
whispers, and trying to pick up the slightest sound that might tell
us where the others were. Then we heard a lorry go grinding
along somewhere to our left : suddenly the engine was switched
off and the voices of its occupants came to us quite distinctly from
not far away.

" Blime, where the 'Ell are we now ? 'Ere matey where the
blinkin' 'Ell are we ? "

And the rather surly response of the driver, " 'Ow the 'Eck
should I know where the blinking 'Ell we are ? "

Then the first voice again, " Owkay, matey, owkay ! I was
just wonderin' where the blinkin' 'Ell we was, see. Don't get all
worried ! "

" 'Oos worryin' ? "

" Wot yer say ? "

" I said 'oos worryin' ? " There was no mistaking the tone
of the voice this time.

" Nobody's worryin'."

" Oh, yes, they blinkin' is, see, 'cos you're worryin, 'see !
That's 'arf the blinkin' trouble ! You worry too much, see."

It certainly was a bit of a relief to hear the old voices we knew
so well, for one could not mistake that sort of argument. It was
a strange thing, I thought, how in the Middle East the phraseology
was such, that to suggest a person was worrying, or worried, in
the slightest degree was equivalent to the vilest form of abuse.
At least that was the reaction it appeared to provoke, and I could
not help smiling as I heard these two going at it hammer and
tongs. We took a compass bearing on the sound of their voices

and located them without much difficulty. That, at any rate, made two lorries. We switched our engine off again and listened hard in the damp silence while the mist eddied and swirled about us. After a short interval we heard the brisk crackle of machine-gun fire, and taking another bearing on the sound we eventually reached the main party. So we continued on our way, with halts every now and then to recall any truant trucks that had lost their direction. It was a slow business, but by ten o'clock the sun had begun to break through and soon afterwards it was perfectly clear. We found ourselves travelling across even undulating ground with scrub-hummocks dotted sparsely here and there, and as we came over the breast of one of these undulations we caught sight of some transport in the hollow below. We halted at once and surveyed them through our field-glasses, then the jeeps scattered to form a protective ring round the three-tonners, the guns were set ready and we drove on. This apprehensive be-haviour on our part made the people in the hollow very suspicious, and they sent out a car to watch us as we went past. Of course they were as British as we were, but it was wiser not to take any chances ; so accordingly we both behaved rather frigidly towards one another, like ladies who are not very well acquainted.

We were driving on a south-westerly bearing which should take us down to the northern border of the Qattara depression somewhere in the region of the Eighth Army positions. As the day wore on it became very hot, and we started the strip-tease act which was our usual custom on these desert drives. For by day we found it hard to believe that it could be so cold at night, and vice versa, the more especially so when we were sitting in an open truck. It could be bitterly cold at about five or six in the morning, and boiling hot by midday ; so we started off wrapped up heavily in battle-dress tops, greatcoats, and blankets, and by early afternoon we were semi-naked, with only a pair of shorts, sandals, and some form of head-dress to our credit. It was in this sort of attire that we passed through the Eighth Army positions ; and seeing their trucks and guns well dispersed and scattered one could not but help feeling how frail and thin the line looked to be holding Rommel in check before the very gates of Alexandria. But this was right down in the south, and I suppose most of our forces were concentrated further north and nearer the coast line.

Mike Sadler, M.M., with David Stirling, D.S.O., planning patrol route to join the First Army. Taken at Bir Zalten about eighty miles south of El Agheila.

Soldiers brewing up tea. The bitter desert cold was due to the North winds. One night when sleeping on the ground I found the rain water frozen to ice around me.

Digging a battle jeep out of the Sand Sea, after the raid on Benghazi. Note twin machine guns fore and aft.

Paddy Mayne, D.S.O.

Parachutist Sillitoe, after his lone march of 180 miles from Tobruk to the Sand Sea.

Caravan route to Kharga Oasis. The bleached skeletons of animals (bottom right) indicate that this caravan route had been used for centuries.

Two stalwarts, Cpl. Austin and Sgt. Hevans.

Cook-house scene in Kufra Oasis. First come, first served: Officers and NCOs had to queue up as they arrived.

Bill Fraser, the author, and Jim Chambers. Note bandages for desert sores on Bill Fraser's hands.

Paddy Mayne, with cap, sharing news from home with members of his squadron.

Mike Sadler, chief navigator to the SAS.

Sgt. Bunfield.

"Shooting the Sun". Sgt. Badger, M.M. and Sgt. Cooper, D.C.M.

Sgt. Lilley, M.M.

My Red Cross jeep approaching Wadi Sura

Parachute training: on the swings.

Desert Oasis. The water was beautifully cold, but could be brackish at times.

The author.

As we went through their line we waved and gave them a cheer, together with variations on the V for victory sign ; and they ceased from their digging and labours to wipe their brows, shield their eyes against the sun, and watch our noisy passing. Then we had left them behind and were alone, once more, just a handful of trucks and jeeps moving westward, very much on the look-out and wondering if the enemy was in the offing. According to information received, the enemy had not yet extended his positions as far south as the Qattara depression, but one never knew what might happen from day to day. Nothing occurred, however, apart from infrequent halts when aircraft were sighted flying high and to the north of us. The sun grew low in the west, our shadows lengthened behind us, and slowly the evening coolness brought a welcome relief and a more yielding harmony of colour to the surrounding desert.

That evening we camped near soft sand and bedded down in the luxury of comfort ; but we were away again the next morning, still on the same bearing, until we had reached the rough jagged country, with sheer falling cliffs, that surrounds the Qattara depression. Driving in and out amongst these satellite depressions, we came at last to the old Arab track that runs along the rim of the main depression, and here we turned west. Looking down to the south we could see the vast arid plain, nearly a thousand feet below, as it stretched out flat and utterly dead to the shimmering horizon beyond. The rocky cliffs fell away in pre-cipitous confusion ; and somehow, as we crawled along the top in single file, it made one feel extremely minute and unimportant, venturing in this solitary way amongst such a stricken landscape. For it was so silent and broken that it seemed as if God had passed by and forgotten this land in its lifeless eternity. Only the old Arab track to show that man had travelled this way before, with here and there the smooth bleached skeleton of a camel, so old that the bone crumbled in the hand. . . .

From time to time we came to hollows where the white sand had drifted, and lay deep and treacherous to the vehicles. We would change our gears into four-wheel drive and charge furiously into the sand, churning it up behind the spinning wheels in great white plumes ; while the engines raced and groaned as we tried to get across to the firmer ground on the other side. It was a very good test of driving ability, and when our driver had got us across safely, he would turn our lorry into such breeze as there was in order to cool off a bit, and then watch the others in their attempts. He was extremely good at his job and during these intervals he would tell us of some of his experiences when he was a test-driver for tanks in desert warfare, and of some of the tricks he had learned in getting across soft sand.

As the day went on we left the Qattara depression ; and the cliffs gave way to small flat-topped hills with conical slopes, coal-black in colour and scarred by little dry river beds where the sand had settled in colourful contrast. The track weaved in and out amongst the hills, this way and that, until at length we came to the main Qara Matruh track as it crossed our own course and ran up towards the coast.

After a brief halt to check our position we turned north and followed its direction. Already the hill shadows were beginning to fall slantwise across the hollows, and already the aching white glare of the day had begun to soften into the kinder shades of evening, for by now the blues and delicate mauves had lent their perspective to the receding landscape.

After about five miles we halted suddenly, as if in doubt.

" Look ! " said our driver.

We followed his pointing arm and there, about half a mile away on a hill crest, was the tiny figure of a man. His outline stood out in such stark contrast to the setting sun behind, that it might have been cut out of a little piece of black paper. I think I shall never forget that moment, and the quick catch of the breath that it gave me to see just one solitary human being in this desolate wilderness, standing up there like an Indian scout and watching our movements below. How long had he been observing us, I wondered, and even as the question crossed my mind he began to signal to us in semaphore with his arms.

" Guess it must be the L.R.D.G.," our driver remarked in an unimpressed sort of way, and picking up his waterbottle from the floor-board he rinsed a little round his mouth and swallowed noisily.

So this was my introduction to the Long Range Desert Group. Perhaps I am too romantic ; but the memory of that lone figure, and the uncanny sensation of the realisation of having been watched in that bleak wilderness, remain as vivid now as they were real then—and somehow such a fitting symbol of this fine unit.

After a brief interval we altered our course slightly and drove over towards him, and just as we were rounding a nearby hill we came on their patrol. They were sitting round having their evening meal as we arrived, and at our approach they put down their mess-tins and mugs to come and welcome us. I looked down at them from my perch on the lorry as they clustered round our trucks. Lean, deep brown, and heavily bearded, they greeted us with broad grins and queries about the local news.

" Any letters ? "

" Brought up fags with you ? "

" What does beer taste like, chum ? "

And Robin Gurdon had his work cut out to keep up with their questions, to give them unit information, and to hand out their mail. Then, too, there were many friendships to be renewed and stores to be exchanged, for not a few of these men were old friends with some of ours, and you would see them wander off in little pairs and groups as they swapped yarns and recaptured their intimacy. For my part, a newcomer and a stranger, I was content to watch and note the way they had hidden their trucks in the little rocky hollows, and cleverly concealed them with netting and scrub ; the way the wireless operator sat there with headphones on, ready to pick up any signal from another patrol ; the alertness and the general sense of happiness that seemed to radiate from these men. And all the time the sentry was standing up on top of the flat hill nearby, watching for any sign of life or movement, and searching the further distances with his glasses.

Slowly the sun moved down over the skyline leaving a deep orange glow in its train ; and now, before it was yet dark, we moved away a little and dispersed our trucks amongst the rocks and hills. Each truck cooked for itself that night, and we unrolled our blankets early for David Stirling had told us that we were going to start raiding to-morrow. Better, then, to get a good night's sleep while we could ; and looking up at the brilliant stars overhead I wondered just where we should all be this time to-morrow. It must be about ten o'clock, I said to myself, and at home my mother and father would be preparing for bed after listening to the evening news, while my aunt would be busy calling in the cats and reproaching them fondly for being such naughty tipsters and staying out so late. . . .

There was a little breeze playing up and down the wadi, and it was nice to lie still and think a bit before I dozed off. Yes, life was very good, my belly was full, and I was content. At this particular moment it seemed as if there was nothing lacking, and I fell asleep wondering if I should ever be able to grow a really decent beard like some of the other chaps.

CHAPTER SIX

" Deep into that darkness peering, long I stood there wondering, fearing."

The Raven. EDGAR ALLAN POE.

THERE was a certain amount of adjustment and final rearrangement necessary the next morning before we were ready to move away. Firstly there were the plans of the raids which we had to get quite clear in our minds, in case anything should go wrong and we should be obliged to act on our own initiative. Our position at this time was, as I remember, situated about seventy miles to the south of Mersa Matruh, and from here we were going to set off in three separate raiding parties. Jellicoe would be proceeding with a few jeeps in a north-easterly direction towards El Daba where he was going to strafe the coast road and do what damage he could to vehicle parks, etc. ; in addition, we thought that Rommel's headquarters were situated in this vicinity and by sheer luck (for it was always on the cards) it was just possible that this little party might catch him.

Secondly there would be a larger party, incorporating a small group of the Long Range Desert Group under Robin Gurdon, and this was the one to which I was detailed. David Stirling and Paddy Mayne were coming with us as far as the escarpment, and at this point they would turn westwards in their two jeeps and carry on until they reached the Bagoush airfields, which were their objectives. We, on the other hand, would go down the escarpment and raid the Fuka airfields on the coastal plain below. Our transport consisted of one jeep and two three-ton lorries, together with such trucks as Robin would bring along ; and our party was made up of a small British patrol under Bill Fraser, another under Arthur Sharpe, an Air Force liaison officer, and a third consisting of Fighting Frenchmen. Bill Fraser and the French would raid the main airfield at Fuka ; while Sharpe was going to raid the satellite airfield a little later on, after the enemy's attention had been drawn to the main airfield.

Thirdly another small combined patrol of S.A.S. and L.R.D.G. would proceed north-west towards a landing ground in the area south of Sidi Barrani, and their instructions were to keep a close watch on the whole of this coastal area and to destroy any aircraft that might be using the field. Since, however, we had been informed that the field was used only for refuelling, it was more than likely that the latter objective would not materialise. Reconnaisance, then, was the main feature of this patrol which would report its findings by wireless communication and which would remain observant until such time as food or water supplies ran low, or until it was recalled to the rendezvous.

So those were our plans. With regard to getting back, we, in the fighting patrols, had to use our own intelligence. Our rendezvous would be at a Bir about thirty miles north of our present position : we had to try and reach this before nightfall of the day following the raid, but if air activity made movement impossible then we were to lie up during the day and get back under cover of darkness.

It took us a few hours to clean the guns, wipe the dust off the springs and feeding clips, load the pans, see that the vehicles were in good running order and correctly rationed with food, water and petrol. Stocking was always an important feature of these raids ; and once it had been completed Jellicoe's patrol, piloted by the L.R.D.G., set off, leaving a little cloud of white dust hanging like a curtain in the wake of their departure. Shortly afterwards we followed them, heading towards the Qara Matruh track once more ; but scarcely had we started before the sudden shout of "Aircraft !" brought us to an abrupt halt and sent us scuttling out of our lorries. Not quite understanding what was going on, I followed the example of the others and hid behind a boulder : there was no time to consider camouflaging the vehicles. Looking down the wadi I could see every one crouching down, absolutely still. Like animals, we had frozen at the first sign of danger. Then I heard the steady zoom, zoom, zoom of approaching aircraft and, a moment later I caught sight of them—two M.E. 110's to the north of us at about five thousand feet. They were flying westwards, looking pale as moths against the flower-blue

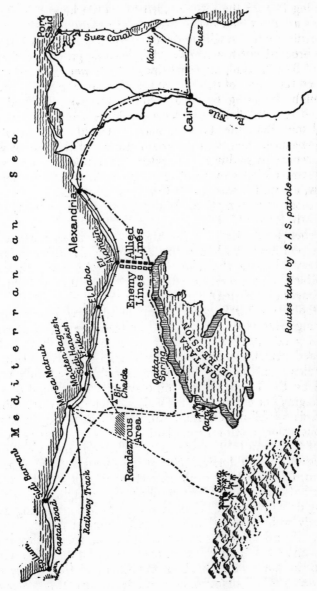

AREA OF OPERATIONS AND RAIDS ON AIRFIELDS.   JULY, AUGUST, 1942.

of the cloudless sky, and every now and then the sun would catch them and turn them to a bright silver as they passed slowly overhead. We watched them silently and furtively until the drone of their engines had died away. Then the wadi came to life again.

I felt rather puzzled by all the caution since, in my previous experience, aircraft had never necessitated any action other than jumping into a convenient slit trench when the occasion demanded. I walked over to Paddy as he sat in the shade of his jeep.

" Do you reckon they saw us ? " I asked.

He looked at me straightly for a moment and then shook his head, " Och, no," he said, " I doubt it."

And then he went on to tell me quite briefly but very decidedly that you had to remain absolutely still as soon as you saw or heard aircraft. Get behind a boulder or truck, get ready to use the guns if need be ; but you must remain still at all costs. Movement was the first thing that betrayed existence. Moreover, the danger did not lie so much in the immediate offensive action which these two aircraft could take, as in the fact that they would report our presence and locality, and then the fat would be in the fire with a vengeance. It was very necessary to be cautious in approaching or leaving an objective, but of course you could be as reckless as you liked once you were attacking the target itself ; for although we were fighting patrols, our intention, strangely enough, was not to fight but to remain undetected for as long as we possibly could. Our numbers were far too small to risk an open engagement ; therefore when we did fight it was with surprise and darkness to help us. All this Paddy explained to me in a very matter-of-fact manner and then, feeling a trifle chastened, I returned to my lorry.

Having reached the Qara Matruh track, we followed it northwards, bumping and jolting along at a fair speed until we came to the Bir Chalder. At this point we branched off on a north-easterly bearing, heading direct for Fuka, and after an hour's run we chose a piece of thick scrub in which to halt and have lunch. We were well up to our time schedule, the only drawback being that one of the L.R.D.G. trucks had developed engine trouble and another had remained behind with it in case help should be needed. Not only in order to help, I should add, but also to observe the rule that one should never travel singly in the desert in case of just such an eventuality taking place. However, they did not turn up, and after waiting for a while we continued on the same bearing. Throughout the afternoon we were passing derelict trucks, burnt-out vehicles, trackless Bren-gun carriers, and all the sad forlorn things that remain in the path of a retreating army. Here we could see the charred ground where men had brewed up during a halt, and the half-dug slit trenches nearby ; here we could see blankets and bits of clothing lying scattered about ; while over there was a lorry, leaning over in drunken abandon, with creaking rusted framework, and canvas hood flapping desolately in the hot breeze. " It made yer think," as our driver remarked meditatively, scratching the bristle on his chin with oily fingers. " Where all the money came from fair beat yer ! " Shocking waste, he reckoned. Actually it did more than make one think, since every time we sighted one of these vehicles we had to stop and watch it closely, to make quite sure it was not an enemy truck or armoured car ; consequently our afternoon was made up of a series of halts and short advances. It was not until about five o'clock that we saw any sign of movement and then, coming over a shallow rise in the stony ground, we suddenly caught sight of a column travelling across our front at a fair speed.

" Jerries ! " said our driver tersely, as we halted once more. Looking at them through our glasses we could see that they were bunched closely together—that, at any rate, was a typically German habit, since they seemed to hate dispersing or travelling in small numbers. But the strange thing was that we could pick out what looked like our own army trucks, guns and armoured cars in the column. We watched them move past in front of us, with the sun flashing off the windscreens of their vehicles, until they had become small moving dots on the western skyline. Then we felt it was safe to move. David and Robin were frankly puzzled and did not know what to make of it. The final conclusion we reached was that this column could only be one of two things : either it was captured material being taken back by the Germans for refitting, or else it might be one of our own columns—though Heaven alone knew what it was doing up here.

Our uneasiness was increased when David turned round to speak to Robin and suddenly caught sight of something behind us.

" Who the devil are they ? " he asked abruptly.

With a nasty sinking feeling we turned round to look in the direction in which he was pointing, and there were three more trucks, scattered well apart, and approaching us from the south. When they were within half a mile of us they halted, and remained watching us.

" I'll soon find out who they are," said Robin, sounding rather as if he was about to chase some poachers off his land ; and jumping into his truck he set off in their direction. But no sooner had he started than the three trucks turned round and began to move away like scolded dogs. He returned to us looking a bit nonplussed while the trucks halted and watched us once more.

" I just can't make it out," he said. " If they are my L.R.D.G. trucks, why don't they come up to us ? They must be able to recognise our jeeps. But even so I don't understand where the third truck has come from ! "

It certainly was a bit of a mystery, but since we had no time to spare we decided to ignore them and carry straight on. David called us all together.

" From now on," he said, " you must keep your eyes skinned for enemy aircraft and armoured cars. Remember that we are targets for British as well as enemy planes, and if we are attacked and get separated you must all drive on towards the airfields. Remember that ! Nobody turns back. If we have to take evasive action we must still head northwards for our objectives."

He tapped out his pipe on the sole of his boot and then gave his quick, shy smile. " It will be all right," he added. " But keep wide awake. Now let's get going ! "

We continued once more, bumping along unevenly until we sighted an enemy camp, which looked very peaceful and serene with its clean white tents catching the glancing rays of the evening sun. We made an easterly detour round it, just keeping it in sight the while, and looking back I could see the three trucks following in our tracks. Whenever we halted, they halted. When we changed direction, then they followed suit. Who they were I shall never know, for after the sun had gone down and dusk had closed in around us, they disappeared quietly from our ken. I should think that probably they were our own trucks, but that they were very uncertain of us. For in the heat haze which, throughout summer, persists almost until sundown, it is more or less impossible to recognise a vehicle at a distance, even through glasses. What appears to be an armoured car turns out to be a three-ton lorry, and an apparent piece of scrub might materialise into a tank. You could never be certain.

Soon after sundown we came to the escarpment edge, with a minefield blocking the entrance to the track leading down to Fuka. This was where David Stirling and Paddy took their leave and, after wishing us good luck and exchanging a brief farewell, they went jogging off into the gathering darkness and the noise of their jeeps faded away into silence. We turned and took a closer look at the fenced-in minefield. Then, following its perimeter, we proceeded in single file along the narrow ledge between its border and the brink of the escarpment until we had reached the track as it emerged from the northern side. What an appalling noise we made as we drove down that escarpment track ! It was not an easy piece of driving in daylight, but it was far more difficult now ; and with racing engines and protesting gears we lurched and skidded down, with boulders tumbling away from our wheels and over the steep slopes on either side. Now, I thought, if the whole enemy force cannot hear us coming then it certainly is not our fault and, as if in answer to my considerations, the guns on the airfield below suddenly opened up. " All right ! " they seemed to say, " All right, we are ready for you. Don't worry, we know you are coming ! "

Eventually we reached the bottom, and halted to try and make what we could of this fresh mystery. They were firing low, with the tracer criss-crossing in slow, colourful parabolæ over what we assumed to be the airfield. Then, for no apparent reason, the firing ceased as suddenly as it had begun. On thinking it over, we decided once more that it could be one of two things : either they were clearing their guns or else they were firing at a low-flying aircraft. But we could hear no sound of a plane, and anyhow we had requested our Air Force to keep away from these airfields on this particular night. So that explanation did not seem to suit the book very well.

Feeling a little dissatisfied we got going once more and drove along the narrow track as it led straight towards the airfields, drawing up to a final halt when we had come to within a few miles of them. Between our present position and the airfields was the railway line running from Alexandria to Matruh and beyond (which, incidentally, the S. A. S. had already blown up on previous raids), while on the far side of the airfields was the main coastal road.

I think that by now it was about ten o'clock and I remember Robin Gurdon coming up to me in great glee.

" What do you think of that Doc, eh ? " he asked. " Perfect navigation ! Dead on the spot and right on time ! "

I can see him now as I did then in the milky starlight, wrapping his Hebron coat about him, his Guards cap pushed well back off his forehead, tugging at his bristling moustache, and as confident as ever. He was a great man, Robin, there was no getting away from that. Proud as Lucifer and as brave as a lion ! Sometimes I wondered if he knew what fear was, for it was something so completely alien to his make-up. You would never see *him* running away or doing anything undignified—not Robin.

Why, I can remember an occasion when a convoy was being strafed by low-flying aircraft, how everybody but he had run for cover. But not Robin. Oh no ! He had just stood there in his Hebron coat and fired at the planes with his revolver. Of course it was a foolhardy piece of courage, and the chances of him hitting anything of value were more or less nil ; but it does just serve to show the spirit of the man and his great pride in himself. . . .

We sat round the trucks eating some cold sausage and feeling the breeze on our faces, fresh and cool from off the sea. Every now and then we would pause to listen for any sound of movement, but it was all very quiet and it was hard to realise that we were so close to the enemy. Nor did there appear to be any traffic on the road, a fact which perturbed Robin a little for he was hoping to drive along it towards Bagoush and do some strafing on the way.

" Now, what do you think, Doc ? " he looked up from his tin plate. " Shall I drive down the road with my lights on or off ? "

I thought for a moment. It seemed to me that the wisest thing he could do was to take his cue from any enemy transport he might see.

He nodded. " Do you know this place, and which would be the best place to cross the railway line ? "

Yes, I did know it slightly ; for I had driven over here one day last summer to see a doctor in the Air Force, and it seemed so strange to think that now the enemy were bathing from the sandy beach where once we had lazed and swam. To the best of my knowledge the railway line was running along a slight sandy embankment, which might be difficult to cross in one of his trucks. About five miles to the west there was quite a steep rise in the ground with the road winding sharply as it surmounted it ; and at one of these hairpin bends the road crossed the railway line. Straight in front of us was a level crossing where our track and the railway line met, and just to the east of this was the little platform that served as a railway station.

"So you think I had better go over at the level crossing ? " he asked.

"Yes," I said, " but what are you going to do if they challenge you ? "

He looked at me in blank astonishment. "Why, I shall shoot them of course ! " he answered, and then he threw back his head and laughed as if it was the best joke in the world.

By now it was about fifty minutes to zero hour and our patrols began to get ready, slinging the bombs on to their belts, or carrying them over the shoulder in a small pack. Bill Fraser gave his men a few words of advice, and then away they went, their figures bobbing up and down until they were lost in the darkness. Five minutes later the French followed them ; and soon afterwards the third patrol, under Arthur Sharpe, walked off in a north-westerly direction towards the satellite airfield.

For a little while longer Robin and I stood talking of the old days in the regiment, and then he yawned, stretched himself, and said that it was time for him to be getting along.

"Let us hope I shall not need to consult you professionally, Doc.," he remarked sagely, as he wrapped his white fleecy Hebron coat once more around him and fastened it in position with a piece of cord. He stood for a minute breathing in the sea breeze and then stepped up into his truck.

"All set, Wilson ? Right ! Good-bye, Doc," he called out over his shoulder as the two trucks moved off slowly down the track. A few moments later and it had become perfectly silent once more.

That left the three of us—Macpherson and Holmes, the two

lorry drivers, and myself with the jeep. Our orders were to go
back a short way along the track to the point where it was crossed
by the telegraph line, and there we should turn left and wait at
the fifth telegraph pole from the track. We were to shine a torch
at ten-minute intervals between the hours of two and three o'clock
to guide the operatives back to the trucks. If any of the men were
unaccounted for by three o'clock, we were to move off and leave
them ; hiding up during the following day and returning the next
night to pick them up. Those were the orders.

We got back into our vehicles, wheeled them round and drove
back a few hundred yards to the telegraph poles. Before we
reached them, however, we suddenly saw a light ahead. It
appeared to be on the track and about a mile away ; but it would
be a bold man who would try to estimate the distance of a light
at night time with any accuracy. We turned left and as I drove
along slowly in front with one wary eye on the light, there was
a sudden bang, and I was thrown against the steering wheel as
the jeep stopped dead in its tracks. Then there was a hideous
noise as the drivers behind jammed on their brakes and swerved
away in order to avoid hitting me. For a moment I thought the
jeep had been hit by a shell ! Which just shows how one's nerves
can become keyed up without one being aware of it. But, peering
ahead, I saw that I had run straight into one of the wire supports
of the second telegraph pole. With a mental curse I backed away
and we carried on to the fifth pole where we hid the vehicles
amongst the surrounding scrub. Then we cut off the engines and
a welcome silence descended over our activities.

We turned our attention to the light ; it worried me more
than I cared to confess. Looking at it through the glasses it
appeared to be a fire flickering up and down, and yet it was too
white a light for a flame. Macpherson thought he saw the
opportunity for a little action ; this job of sticking around with
the trucks was not much to his liking.

" Wud ye no like me tae tak' a wee shufti roon' there ? " he
asked in his very broad Scots. " It wud hardly tak' a minute,
and if there's only a few o' them I cud sune fix it."

But I was all for caution and thought it much wiser to remain
with the transport, which was really our most valuable possession.
Obviously Macpherson was disappointed in me, " But I wud only

tak' a wee shufti," he said, " I wouldna make any noise." And
then, seeing my lack of enthusiasm, he hunched up his shoulders
in Celtic resignation.

We continued to watch the light, arguing amongst ourselves
as to whether it was on the track or not. It would be strange for
people to camp on the track when they were so close to Fuka ;
but if this was the case it would make our return journey more
tedious, for the ground was very hummocky and it would mean
a wide detour. And as we debated the point a plane passed over,
droning monotonously against the stars ; and all at once we
realised it was a ground flare that had been dropped to mark out
the course for later planes. That, at any rate, was a welcome relief,
and without giving it a further thought we turned our backs on
the light.

It was quite chilly standing there, with the breeze coming
fresh from the north and giving a little tugging movement to the
thick scrub around. It did not do to peer into the darkness too
long, I decided, or else you began to think you really did see
things moving. First it was on one side and then on the other,
and as you looked away you could swear that this or that shadow
had moved and you would rivet your attention back on to it. It
was a most eerie sensation. Bits of scrub, light patches of sand,
dark shadows and hummocks, all seemed to be on the move,
approaching and receding with stealthy silence. I recalled what
my batman had told me of a night patrol when he had been
detailed to guard the transport.

" It don't do," he had said with solemn emphasis, " it don't
do to stay behind when the other blokes 'ave gone on a raid, cos
all of a sudden things starts to move. First they moves towards
yer, then they goes to one side ; one minute they does a slow
step and the next it's a quick march. Blime ! 'Fore yer knows
where yer are, they've started to form fours and do every blinkin'
sort of thing."

I had been a little amused at his words when I had heard
them, but now I realised how true they were, and it needed very
little imagination for you to feel that you were encompassed about
by silent moving hosts.

I looked over at Macpherson and Holmes as they stood with
shoulders hunched, chewing away at some gum to make up for

the lack of cigarettes. What were they thinking about ? I
wondered ; and realising that I scarcely knew them, that we were
as good as strangers, I walked over and joined them. We started
talking in hushed voices, as if afraid that someone might overhear
us ; waiting, yes waiting all the time for something to happen and
break the suspense. Macpherson, I remember, started to tell us
of his home in Glasgow and of all the haunts that he knew so well,
and of some of the better known characters, too ; and of how he
and his friends would go sailing down the Clyde in the summer,
exploring each loch and inlet ; and how they would take down
the sails and row ashore and walk far over the rough hillsides
amongst the gorse and bracken. And Holmes, who came from
Brighton, told us of his little house, exactly like all the other
houses in the street ; and of the canoe he had shared with the
chap over the road ; of how he used to take out some bread and
sardines to last him for the day, and paddle over towards Rotting-
dean. There he would come close in to the cliffs and, lying face
down, he would lean over and feel the sun warm on his back as
he watched the fish swim in and out of the waving seaweed below.
It would be very quiet and peaceful ; and you could almost drop
asleep as you listened to the lisp and swish of an occasional wave
against the side of the canoe.

Then they asked me about medical work, and what it was
like to carve up dead bodies and do operations on live ones. So I
told them : it wasn't much really—only a question of getting to
know your job thoroughly. And as I was talking the memory of
those student days came back in a flood. Of the fountain in the
square, and how we used to sit round it, waiting for the chief to
drive up in his luxurious car and do a ward round. Of how the
patients would be wheeled out to get a little of London's dusty
sunshine ; of the way the nurses would tuck a blanket round
them and leave them to read and talk with the students. Of the
wards rounds themselves when we, who were mere dressers, put
on little white jackets ; whereas the newly appointed house-
surgeons, full of their dignity and conscious of their importance,
would be wearing long white coats. Of how some chiefs would
enjoy asking you absurd questions, and making you look foolish
and stupid in front of the patients. Of the lectures in the old
anatomy room with the students running and making a noise on

the wooden floor as they came in late, and of the sudden hush as
.the lecturer made his appearance. Of the stillness in the dignified
library where we read and read for the examinations ; and how
in the winter we would group round the open fire and get out
our notes to study. Of the hard and heavy reading at nights, when
it seemed at times as if our learning would never come to an end,
and as if any sort of break or variation would be such a relief. . . .

And then, all at once, the Breda started and we looked up,
suddenly startled back into reality. Slow red tracer was arching
across the ground, this way and that—long strings of red beads
which stopped sharp, every now and then, as if smothered by an
invisible hand, while the throaty cough of the staccato fire echoed
in their wake.

" Poor Bill ! " I thought. " God, I hope they don't get him,"
for he seemed almost too young and boyish for this sort of thing.
On these occasions you always feared the worst, and suffered in
consequence when you saw the fire criss-crossing and sweeping
low over the ground.

Then there was a white flash followed quickly by the blast of
an explosion.

" Bet that's Nobby," cried Holmes. " I *bet* that's Nobby."

Then three more flashes, quick and white and sharp ; stabbing
into the blackness of the night—and all the time the guns kept
stuttering and ranging blindly round the field.

" Cor—look at *that* one, sir, that's a beauty all right ! "

Over to the west of us there was a terrific flash which lit up
the skyline like summer lightning. We waited, listening for the
explosion, and then it came, a slow heavy rumble which gave the
earth a little shudder as it passed. Now there was a dull red glow
over the western sky, and through our glasses we could pick out
the small pinpoints of the fires.

" That's Major Stirling and Captain Mayne," they cried
excitedly. " You bet there's some fun over there ! "

In truth, the war had suddenly come to life on this dark night,
and explosions in the direction of Bagoush interrupted our concentration on the airfields close by. Things had become quieter
here during the last few minutes. Then there would come another
explosion ; then two, one after the other, in quick succession ;
and after each explosion the Breda would rap out angrily as if in

reply. But the intervals of silence grew longer and longer; and just as I was thinking we had finished for the night, some more banging started up from the direction of the satellite airfield. It did not last long, however, and within twenty minutes there was a deep brooding quietness over the night, with only the fires flickering up and down to show that anything had happened at all.

I looked at my watch. It was getting on for two o'clock so I got the torch out of the jeep. How strange and unreal it seemed to be shining that torch round in a slow arc, from the direction of the satellite to the main airfield, and then back again. Have thirty seconds ever passed so slowly before? I wondered, as I held it up high, feeling that I was the most conspicuous person in Africa. For it seemed as if every one must see that torch wave steadily from one side to the other, and I felt that guns were being lined up on me from everywhere around. Thirty seconds every ten minutes! In the intervals we listened hard for any sound of movement.

It must have been about half an hour later that we heard the sound of voices coming closer, and jumping up on the lorries Holmes and Macpherson trained the guns in that direction. Feeling very foolish I got out my revolver and flicked back the safety catch. At any rate, I thought, we were ready for trouble; but as the voices grew more clear, we heard the same old repetitive swearing that one knew could be nothing other than true British. What an infinite relief and homeliness there was in those old swear words! Nevertheless we challenged them and then they stumbled over to the trucks and lay down, very tired, and angry in their disappointment—for they had had no success with the planes. Bill Fraser was very fed up about it; the more so as it was due chiefly to a misunderstanding with the French, and not to an error in his own plans.

The French themselves came in soon afterwards, and as soon as they had caught sight of the dark shadows of the trucks, they came running towards us and threw themselves face downwards on the ground nearby, as if they had just completed a marathon. It lent a theatrical touch to our affairs, and one could not but help comparing it with the return of our own men. When they had regained their breath they started talking in fast excitable voices.

One of their sergeants had been hit ; a trivial affair with the bullet slicing across his little finger. I took him behind one of the lorries and bandaged him up, clumsily enough, and while I did so he told me that they had blown up nine planes for certain. As we were talking together the third party came trudging in from the satellite airfield ; they had destroyed at least six planes and thought they must have got more. Well, that made fifteen for a minimum which was not too bad ; but it was a great pity that Bill Fraser's party had been out of luck. From their angry remarks I gathered that they had expected the French to sneak their way between the sentries and on to the airfield in the usual manner. The French, however, had decided that the best plan was to walk straight on to the field, pretending that they were Germans. Unfortunately it had not worked out as they had anticipated. They were challenged, and their reply and subsequent evasive action had given the warning. That explained why the Breda fire had come before the explosions. Once the French had got into the field they had done well in locating the planes ; but their discovery had raised the alarm just at the very time when Bill Fraser's patrol was crawling between two sentry posts. This put the British in a most unenviable position and their only line of action was to get away, if possible, without being detected. This they had managed to do ; and the only relieving episode of the whole business had been the querulous voices of the Italian sentries as they called out to one another in the darkness for reassurance, and prayed loudly to the saints to intervene in their protection.

As Bill Fraser was crawling away behind the cover of a little rise in the ground, he passed within about ten yards of one of these little groups of Italians. He stopped for a moment to draw a hand-grenade from out of his pack and was just fingering the pin, when he thought better of it and put it back again. Perhaps he thought that they were too childlike to be killed in cold blood. I do not know ; but I dare say there have been many similar cases, and probably quite a number of Italians are walking about, wholly unconscious of their narrow escapes. It was a minor incident, yet it does serve to illustrate the chancy way in which our lives are governed. But for a kind thought, which many an armchair critic would condemn, three or four Italians would now

be buried under the sand at Fuka, three or four families would
be bereaved, and the whole lives of the offspring of these men
would be altered. These were the things that were dependent
upon the mere whim or impulse of an unseen enemy. During
that split fraction of a second while Fraser had fingered the pin
on his hand-grenade, the future of quite a small number of people
had trembled and hung in the balance.

By now it was nearly three o'clock ; and as it would be
getting light soon after four, we decided to get away as far and
as fast as possible. All our men had returned, and we knew that
Robin Gurdon would be coming back independently. We were
just about to climb aboard the trucks when we heard a plane
approaching from the east. Immediately the searchlights snapped
on, clear-white and penetrating as they probed up straightly into
the night's blackness. It was only a matter of seconds before they
had caught and held the plane—a Wellington, flying at about
five thousand feet. With a horrible fascination we watched the
coloured tracer tearing up so accurately that we thought the plane
must be hit at any moment. We saw it twist and turn, looking like
some wild thing trying to shake off its pursuers and avoid capture ;
and although we hated the very spectacle, we could not drag our
eyes away. We gazed as if hypnotised. Suddenly the plane banked
and dived—right through the tracer it seemed—and the next
moment it was lost to sight and had gained the cover of darkness.
It was all we could do to suppress a muffled cheer. Then it roared
over our heads, outlined against the stars by the exhaust flames,
and still heading due west. A few minutes later there were some
heavy explosions further along the coast ; and the next day David
Stirling was extremely angry when he spoke of how he had been
bombed while he had been operating on Bagoush airfield. " I
told them especially to stay clear of the airfields ! " he remarked
with a frown. But we, who had seen the plane's escape, could
hardly share his annoyance.

By now it had become quiet again so we started up the
engines and drove back on to the track, turning south as it led
towards the escarpment. Here we must have missed our way, and
how we ever got up is still a bit of a puzzle, but when eventually
we did reach the top, we found ourselves inside the wire that
surrounded the minefield. This was an unhappy discovery and

gave rise to some anxiety, since there was hardly sufficient space between the wire and the escarpment edge for us to back out the way we had come in. Consequently we made for the nearest piece of wire and ran that down, only to find another wire fence ahead of it. In this way the darkness gave us some relief for frequently we thought we were clear of the field, only to realise our mistake when we reached the next wire barrier. I would hesitate to say how many fences we knocked down that night, but time seemed to pass very slowly as we blundered around like so many bulls in a china shop. Sitting in the back of the lorry we waited expectantly for the moment when we should be blown from off our insecure perches. It was our good fortune that the mines could not have been fused.

But at last we ran over what turned out to be the final wire fence, and as we bumped away at good speed we pulled the blankets closer round ourselves to shield off the bitter night air, and settled ourselves down to try and snatch some sleep. There were no more alarms. Slowly the stars began to pale and disappear, one by one ; the sky lost its blackness and the first pale touch of colour crept into the east. In the luminous half-light of dawn we could just make each other out : the little jeep appearing to scamper along in front while the two lorries lumbered heavily behind like faithful watchdogs. Then, as the light spread softly like a painter's wash over and around us, we began to disperse ; for the sun was our enemy, and in the solitude of darkness lay our safety.

The first morning rays lit up and threw our lines into staring relief, whilst our shadows, exaggerating and distorting, raced lengthily beside us. The cold was piercing, and we had huddled ourselves together for warmth when, quite unexpectedly, we halted. Looking round we saw the rest had done likewise. Apparently the other lorry had developed engine trouble and, jumping down, I started to walk over towards it, stamping my feet hard and blowing on my numb hands to try and restore a little warmth into them.

" Aircraft ! "

It was a sudden cry that seemed to cut through the morning air with the keenness of a knife. Turning round, I just had time to see two planes skimming over the ground towards us before I fell flat on my face. Looking from beneath the crook of my elbow I watched them come racing along until the roar of their engines was almost deafening. They were two M.E. 109 F's, about fifty feet from the ground and a little to the north of us. As they swept past we could see the heads of the pilots outlined all too clearly in the semi-circles of the cockpits. I felt sure that they would turn round into the sun and come back to machine-gun us. Such moments are engraved with remarkable definition on the memory, and even now I can see the French playing their sort of cat-and-mouse, hide-and-seek game. For they were crouched down behind the radiator of the lorry—about four of them all jostled together—and as the planes approached and flew past, they crept stealthily round the front and so to the other side. It seems amusing, now, the way they prowled round, always keeping the lorry between themselves and the planes ; but at the time of its occurrence I was only acutely aware of what was happening and the painful way in which my heart seemed to be thudding against the hard, rocky ground on which I was lying. We watched the planes grow smaller, become black specks against the rising sun, and vanish over the skyline leaving only a thin menacing whine in the air behind them. Once again our luck had held, for, in our immobility, they had mistaken us for derelicts of Auchinleck's retreat ; and if our lorry had not broken down at that particular moment, things might have been very different.

But it was high time for us to hide—we all realised that !— and within a few minutes the engine trouble had been remedied and we drove on towards a nearby ghôt.[1] There was insufficient cover here for the lorries, so it was decided to gamble on the chance of their being mistaken for derelicts again. Accordingly we left them out in the open, facing in different directions ; and by throwing back the engine-hoods and the tailboards, we managed to make them look fairly forlorn and deserted. The jeep we camouflaged closely, in amongst the scrub, until it resembled a little bush. Then we lay down and fell asleep.

It must have been an hour or two later when I was wakened by the sound of approaching planes ; and looking up through the bare patchwork of scrub over my head, I could make out two CR. 42's flying directly above us. They looked so harm-

[1] The word " ghôt " is used to denote an area of scrub-covered desert.

less and toylike with the sun glinting off their airscrews, that it
was hard to realise they were out after us and us alone, to kill
and destroy us. I was filled with the unreality of it. To think
that up there were men searching the face of the desert in order
to find some sign of our tracks and put an end to us. It was
all so personal, and so unlike the war of an army where the
very word enemy just meant a multitudinous plural. Here it
was the first person singular with a vengeance ; and, as the hum
of their engines died away into silence, I found my thoughts
wandering.

It was pleasantly warm in the early morning sun and I felt
very peaceful and drowsy lying there. I watched a bluebottle,
all resplendent in his bright varnished colours, approach my out-
stretched hand with quick lateral advances. He stopped to wipe
his head with a little jerky movement and give his tail a brisk
rub. Then he paused for a moment wondering what to do
next, and as I moved he flew away with a quick warning
buzz.

I saw a large spiky beetle crawl past, ungainly and slow, his
heavy body drawing a smudge in the sand behind him, while his
legs left fine tracing patterns. I stopped him with my finger and
he halted then, his head drawn down and his antennæ waving
cautiously in front of him. This was something quite new and
alien to him, but evidently he decided that there was no danger
here, and crawling over my finger he plodded round a white stone
and out of sight. Later a lizard came to investigate my body and
paused, still as an image, with grace in every line as he inspected
me closely with bright beady eyes. When his curiosity had been
satisfied he jerked his head away and, with a delicate scratching
movement of his forefoot, darted off in search of food.

Yes, in the coastal desert there was life abounding ; not very
beautiful perhaps, sometimes almost weird, but there it was. In
my regimental aid post, I remembered, I had kept five chameleons, named, with an imposing solemnity of which they seemed
to be well aware, after the Churchill family. With lower jaw
thrust forward and with slow and pompous determination they
pursued their prey, and nothing, it seemed, could alter their
purpose or deflect their course. Their characters remained true
to type and the two baby chameleons, less than an inch long,

would imitate their elders in the most amusing fashion ; and if you approached them unexpectedly, they would try to swell up and look threateningly and diabolically ferocious, despite their minute size. A fly, for them, took a great deal of digesting, and incurred much swivelling of their periscopic eyes and a very deep concentration.

There were many insects, too, strange and curious, which must have led a very dull, sandy sort of existence. Once I had kept one in an old cigarette tin. I believe he was a larva of some moth related to the clothes moth at home, and he weaved around himself a little protective pyramidal shaped box with a trap-door at one end. This he would drag around behind him in a hermit-crab manner as he nibbled away at the tender green pieces of scrub. But if any one intruded upon his privacy he would shoot back into his little home and slam the front door fast shut behind him. He was an amusing little fellow to watch, always busy eating and reinforcing the framework of his house.

To my very amateur way of thinking there seemed to be several species of praying mantis, or at any rate a large number of insects that adopted their characteristic attitude. But a thing I had never realised previously was that they could turn their heads round and thus assume the most intelligent and interested expressions. The way they watched you when you were shaving or holding a sick parade, for instance, with head cocked on one side like a dog—the very embodiment of natural curiosity.

I suppose it was these insects that attracted so many birds ; and in late May and early June you could see the swallows hovering near your dusty footsteps, ready to snap up anything that you might disturb. These swallows seemed far more tame than they did at home, and they would flutter very close to your hand. Then there was the common desert lark who seemed to be the only real native of the place, a bird reminiscent chiefly for its mournful metallic note and its reputation for battlefield gluttony. Duck would come swinging along the coast, alighting in their hundreds on the salt lakes and lagoons. Once I saw a heron and twice I saw kingfishers. The first was of brilliant plumage flying round the rocks near El Daba, while the other was a black and white kingfisher diving for fish in the Bitter Lake. Wagtails, hoopoes, hawks, owls, doves and pigeons were other

birds that helped to remind one that this part of the desert was
not what it was made out to be, and often, with a flutter of wing
and a musical cry, brought back memories of green meadows
and leafy woods.

Then there was Mrs. Hazledene who came to live with us
for a while, and whose stay was so unhappily cut short by her
untimely end. She was a beautiful tern, about the size of an
ordinary gull, with bright beady eyes and a long sharp red beak
that looked much more formidable than it really was. The men
brought her to my regimental aid post one day, for she had been
discovered on the sea shore with a broken wing. " What shall
we call her ? " I asked. " Why, Mrs. X," replied an officer,
naming a well-known London hostess ; but here, for purposes
of anonymity, she shall be known as Mrs. Hazledene.

Well, there was nothing shy or backward about *her*. She was
as bold as brass, and she made it quite clear to all of us right
from the very beginning that if she condescended to receive
medical treatment as an " in patient," then she would see that
the department was run according to her liking. Her left wing-
bone was snapped right across in the part corresponding to the
human elbow, and I suppose really that we were highly optimistic
in thinking that we could set it. I do not know how old the
fracture was, but it seemed to be quite painless, and she would
let me do what I wished with it, only giving me an occasional
nudge with her beak to show that she was still alive and kicking
so to speak. For a splint we chose a flat piece of wood, kept in
position with adhesive tape ; but the pity was that it weighed
that wing down so that it drooped on the ground. Every now and
then Mrs. Hazledene would pull it up in the business-like way in
which a woman will tuck an umbrella under her arm, but
obviously the splint was too heavy. We tried to keep it up by
strapping the wing to the body ; but this she would not allow,
and within a short while she had pecked it off. Eventually we
splinted the wing with the lightest and thinnest piece of wood
that we could obtain, and with it in position Mrs. Hazledene
would stamp up and down the medical tent making quite sure
that everything was being done to her satisfaction. The sandy
floor of the tent had been trodden quite firm, so that you could
hear her determined step quite easily as she poked her way in and

out of the boxes and stores, while every now and then would come a metallic clink as she thought she had found something in a tin which appealed to her fancy.

The men, too, became quite fond of her during the short while she was with us ; and on the sick-parade queue they would stand respectfully to one side in order to allow her to plod past, knowing full well that, if they did not do so, they would receive a sharp tap on the legs from her beak, just to remind them that it was a case of ladies first. Yes, she was a real martinet, and was becoming accustomed to drinking her water out of a bowl and taking an occasional scrap of food when, foolishly enough, we conceived the idea of letting her go for a swim on the little salt lake near by. So we carried her over to the water's edge—for she was by no means averse to being picked up and petted—and away she swam, enjoying herself hugely and making a proper bath of it. After about ten minutes she returned, stamping out of the water in a way that made it perfectly clear that that was enough for one day, thank you. On the following morning she was ill and stayed in her box, shivering hard despite our efforts to keep her warm, and she died during the night.

Poor Mrs. Hazledene. We all missed the tap, tap, tap of her feet as she walked up and down the tent, and the way she had taken such an interest in whatever we had done. Why had she died ? One suggestion which probably came near to the truth was that, in her hunger, she had eaten the oil and fat from her body and wing feathers, and consequently had little resistance to the cold water. That would explain why she had looked rather bedraggled after her bath, and presumably pneumonia had followed and had been the cause of her death.

When you came to think of it there were a surprising number of animals in the desert ; and, quite apart from the chameleons, there were several varieties of lizards.

I remember how, at one time, we had pitched our battery mess tent against the rock face of a shallow wadi ; this did duty as one wall, and in its nooks and crannies lived a couple of lizards. Frequently we would see them dart up the rock during a meal, or pause, motionless, to watch us eating our supper by candlelight. They had a peculiar little cry all of their own which, for want of a more polite form of comparison, one might liken to a miniature belch : and sometimes they would utter this sound during the most appropriate silences. On these occasions the colonel, a most worthy gentleman, would apologise with a little bow of the head and an " I *beg* your pardon " or an " Excuse me," taking great pains that, if a visitor was present, he should not overlook the incident. It was his own little joke ; nobody else intruded or tried to apologise ; every one waited until the deferential apology had been made by the colonel, the lizards pointed out to the surprised guest who thereupon gave a satisfactory expression of his astonishment, after which the normal run of the mess conversation would start up once more.

Then there was the dreaded " asp." Now I had always understood that an asp was some sort of poisonous snake. But no, the troops informed me, I was mistaken. An " asp " was a lizard characterised, apparently, by its lack of hind legs, and it was as deadly as the devil. In actual fact these lizards appeared to have various sizes of diminutive hind legs, and presumably were merely different types of the same evolutionary process which gives rudimentary skeletal legs to certain snakes. As to being deadly, anything with a forked tongue was deadly to the troops and filled them with awe. I shall never forget a large monitor lizard we caught once—it was about three feet in length from nose to tail and possessed a beautifully forked tongue. The way the men scattered when they saw it ! They would launch an attack against the enemy—Oh yes !—but this old lizard had them all at sixes and sevens, and it was a long time before they would accept it as a pet.

As for snakes, of course, the men held them in deep and superstitious dread, believing implicitly that the soul of a snake never left its body until the sun had dipped down below the sky-line. They were not convinced even when I dissected one out ! Being uncertain myself just how many of these snakes were poisonous or semi-poisonous, I too gave them a wide berth. There was the horned viper, not often seen, and repulsive in its ugly squatness. He was a nasty customer and no mistake. But the others may have been quite innocent for all I knew, although each one suffered from a generalised evil reputation. I well remember a snake entering the medical tent one morning when we had detained a patient with a sprained knee ; a knee, by all accounts, so severely twisted that the slightest of movements produced the most exquisite agony. To put his foot to the ground? Ah, that was torture indeed! Nevertheless, hardly had that snake started to slither down the steps into the tent than he had sprinted out of the other end in a way that would have done credit to any aspiring athlete. Nor, oddly enough, did he report sick again.

Scorpions, too, were plentiful enough, the yellow variety being more common than the black. I shall not forget hearing a scratching noise under my pillow one night, and lifting it back to find a scorpion below. My subsequent movements were extremely brisk. Nor shall I forget an unfortunate officer who sprained his ankle, and, in sitting down with a yelp of pain to nurse it, was unfortunate enough to lower his posterior on to a sleeping scorpion, which awoke and reacted in the most natural manner possible.

Amongst the larger forms of animal life you might sometimes see a fox—we disturbed several once on Auchinleck's retreat from Agheila, and they joined in along the general line of evacuation. Or jackals occasionally would wake you at night with their banshee, bloodcurdling howls, which could strike sheer terror into the heart. And what of that shy little beauty, the jereboa— a regular peeping Tom as he watched you with his large round eyes from behind a piece of scrub? Why, even a hyena had been seen in Jebel country; while the L.R.D.G. had, for a time, made pets of two little cheetah cubs, with their vacant expressionless eyes which gave the impression of sightlessness.

We used to wonder where these animals and birds found their drinking water. From the scrub that sometimes was dew-sodden in early morning? From wells, by some clever animal means? Had they grown acclimatised to salt water? For we had seen duck settle and gabble at the floating weed of a salt lagoon, and mosquitoes had become accustomed to breed in water more saline than the sea. Or was it that desert life had adapted itself to its surroundings, and, like the camel, could manage with very low water supplies over a long period of time? We would propound and argue over each theory in turn.

In truth their life was one continual search for food and an everlasting battle for existence and procreation; the manifestation of the old law of the survival of the fittest. And now we human beings had come back to it again, living by our wits and good fortune, in constant fear of danger and always ready to kill or be killed. Why then, I asked myself, did we long so much for peace when this sort of life was our evolutionary heritage ? Why did we fear, and of what were we afraid ? Not of death, certainly, nor of the unknown. Rather, I supposed, it was the continual uneasy anticipation and the mental torture of anxiety. For death itself was not fearful, but almost a quiet absolution of fear. And if we died, what then ? Why surely the God that had made us without our asking—without giving us even the ability to query our own creation—why surely He could not then expect us to devote our lives implicitly to this dogma or that creed, and wait in dreadful questioning for the day of reckoning. Had we no right to decide for ourselves without being convicted for our decision ? And were we not given minds to judge for ourselves, rather than to follow blindly in the footsteps of such and such a teaching or such and such a theory ?

Yes, my thoughts were drifting along channels which by now had grown familiar. For it was very nice and warm lying there, and you could not concentrate on one subject for long. Soon it would be getting too hot for comfort and the very stones would become burning to the touch. But now it was just right ; and lying there in dreamy contemplation with the sun on my cheek, I found I had quickly dozed off to sleep.

We moved off again before midday, when we judged that the heat haze was sufficient to hide us, or at any rate to render us difficult to perceive. Continuing on our south-westerly bearing we reached the Matruh Siwa track, and after bumping along it for several miles, we branched off towards some rocks nearby. Here we stopped for a meal. Then on again down the track, until we saw the conical mound of the Bir Chalder reflected in the surrounding mirage and, in driving towards it slowly, we came upon some of our men. David Stirling was there, welcoming us as if we had just come back from a game of golf. Paddy was there, too ; giving us a sleepy grin as he lay in the shadow of his jeep reading a Penguin and flicking away an occasional fly. Somehow, I thought, even when he was resting, Paddy managed to give the impression of massive latent force and power.

" Hallo, doctor," he said in his Irish voice when I had sat down beside him, " and how did you get on ? "

" Well, we probably got about twenty planes," I replied enthusiastically, " but we only counted fifteen for certain—that's not bad, is it ? " I added eagerly, expecting a few words of praise at the very least.

" Och, no," he yawned prodigously and rolled over lazily on to his back. " How many did Bill get ? "

I told him of their disappointment and he remained silent, until, all of a sudden and quite irrelevantly, he remarked, " This is a very good book I'm reading now—have you read it ? "

Feeling a little surprised by the sudden turn of conversation I turned over the fly-leaf. It was Mottram's *The Spanish Farm*. No, I hadn't read it. In that case, he replied, I could read it after him if I wished. I thanked him and inquired what sort of a raid *he* had had, adding that I had seen some explosions from over in his direction. Yes, he said, stretching himself, there had been some good shooting. " Did you get many planes ? " Och, quite a few—couldn't say how many for certain—round about thirty he reckoned. Thirty ! That was pretty good going, even for Paddy and David. I did not know quite what to say, for it seemed foolish to try and congratulate someone with his record ; and with the stock expression of " Jolly good show " I felt I had done the best I could.

" So you only had one casualty ? " He nodded over towards the lorry round which the French were grouped. " Yes," I replied, " just a small affair," and suddenly I realised that Paddy observed far more than I gave him credit for, lying there as he did and seemingly taking little interest in what was going on around him.

" Aircraft ! "

The shout interrupted our conversation and we all crouched down beside the trucks and bushes and stayed motionless. Our vehicles were camouflaged amongst the patch of scrub which had been chosen as our rendezvous. But this ghôt was too small, really, to serve its purpose and consequently we were not sufficiently dispersed. However, there was no better cover in sight ; all around was the blank open stony desert, with not a hint of a hiding-place anywhere. Nearby was the bir—the sole relieving feature—and in a little ghôt on the far side of it was hidden a patrol of the L.R.D.G. David had just driven over to them to check up on one or two points.

The drone of the plane intruded on the desert silence ; it broke into it with an almost tangible and alien harshness, forcing itself in beating throbbing waves on our consciousness as we hid below. I peeped up and saw it was a CR 42, about four thousand feet up, flying directly overhead. The hostile sound of the engines began to recede. I took another look, praying quietly that we had not been detected. No, it has passed over all right ; and then I saw one wing tip over ever so slightly and the plane came round in a wide circle, losing height as it did so. It was at about a thousand feet, now, and the drone had become a menacing roar. Once more it circled over us and, just as I was wondering what was going to happen next, the L.R.D.G. opened up on it from the little ghôt in which they were hidden. That, of course, settled the issue ; and for the next five or ten minutes there was a lively interchange of fire over in that direction, with the plane coming down in low shallow dives, strafing furiously the while. This lasted until the plane, presumably, had exhausted its ammunition and had headed off northwards, becoming a small speck and quickly vanishing into the blue of the sky. Soon afterwards David turned up, very annoyed, for his blitz buggy had been shot up ; and now that our position had been located it meant a night drive in search of a fresh hiding-place. However, we should have been obliged to move anyhow, for the cover here was poor and there were more people yet to return.

We assessed the result of our night's activities. The Fuka patrol, David said, had destroyed fifteen aircraft for certain, so we could report that we had destroyed ten. By claiming two-thirds of the planes definitely destroyed in his reports to H.Q., he crushed any possible criticism of exaggeration before it was ever made.

Thus he claimed twenty aircraft in his raid and that, with our ten, made a total of thirty. H.Q. would be able to compare our claim with the reports and photographs sent in by a recon-naissance aircraft which flew over the morning after the attack. I always thought this rule of sending in under-estimates of results was extremely good, since stories were so liable to become exaggerated in this sort of work. And when exaggeration has been detected and realised, then people begin to lose faith and become sceptical. We, on the other hand, by under-estimating our results in official reports tended, I think, to reverse the process.

Shortly before sundown, George Jellicoe returned, and soon afterwards Robin Gurdon drove in with his two trucks. The former had not had much luck, but the latter had managed to destroy twenty to thirty vehicles. Jellicoe's party had brought back three prisoners, which meant more mouths to feed and bellies to water. They looked very disconsolate, I thought, as they sat grouped together under the custody of a sturdy guard and, judging by the expressions on their faces and the bleak way in which they viewed the surrounding desert, I doubt if they would have left us had we paid them.

So we had all returned safe and sound, except for the one Frenchman, whose finger I splinted after sundown with the aid of a little pentothal anæsthesia. His rambling talk as he " came round " caused no little merriment amongst his companions, and after that had all settled down quietly we had some supper and " went to bed." It was still early, I remember, when we tucked ourselves under the blankets ; for most of us were pretty tired, and we were due to move off at three o'clock the next morning in search of a fresh rendezvous.

CHAPTER SEVEN

GERMAN PRISONERS AND A RUM PARTY

" There is delight in singing, tho' none hear
  Beside the singer."
                                        W. S. LANDOR.

" Yo-ho-ho, and a bottle of rum ! "
                            Treasure Island. R. L. STEVENSON.

WE WERE WAKENED UP effectively enough the next morning by the guards whipping away our covering blankets and bidding us loudly to " Rise and shine, matey, rise and shine-o ! " It always took me a few minutes to realise exactly where I was on these occasions, especially if I had been sleeping heavily. Rather like the old midwifery days at hospital, I thought as I fumbled with my sandals, when the sudden glare of the electric light, a shaking of the shoulder and the rough voice of the night porter : " Mrs. 'Arris, 121 Clarence Road—I'll get a taxi " were the first things that penetrated the fog of sleep. And here we were now with the night still dark around us and the stars not yet pale ; with figures, crouching low as they rolled up their blankets, or sitting up as they stretched themselves with exaggerated contortions. Voices cursing—the old repetitive expressions ; shadows of figures dimly outlined as they clambered over the lorries ; the sudden throaty cough of the engines as they faltered and sprang to life, one after the other ; the quick flare of a match ; the deep red glow of a cigarette ; men urinating noisily against the wheels of the lorries. The laager as it came to life and got ready to move off. No clothes to take off or put on—we slept in our shirts and shorts—only a coat if you had remembered to bring one, blankets, or whatever you had added to the wardrobe to keep off the cold.

When everything was ready we set off on a north-easterly bearing, determined to cross the Matruh Qara track in darkness and to cover a good distance before it grew light. Probably the enemy would soon be coming down the track in search of us. For we were fugitives, I told myself as I watched the blurred shadows of our trucks and jeeps slowly move away, fugitives from the light, and children of the darkness. What a strange animal sort of life it was ! Hiding, always hiding during the day, and emerging from our lairs by night.

Slowly the dawn lifted behind us with a delicate rosy flush which touched and lighted the desert around, making it look clean and inviting as it stretched away in this morning coat of colours. We went rumbling along the flat stony ground as fast as we could, pursued by an intangible foe and our peril increasing with every moment that passed. For by now the enemy would be warming up their aircraft engines on the coastal airfields ; in a few minutes they would be taking off, and then the search would begin, with planes circling out in widening spirals from the position we had recently left. But our luck held, and, just before the sun had suddenly flooded the desert with brilliance, we came upon a small shelving escarpment, about fifteen feet in height ; and, running our trucks down the steep slopes, we quickly had them tucked away in the little inlets and wadis that scarred its regularity. Then, over with the camouflage nets, and soon we had torn large tufts of camel thorn and scrub from the nearby ghôt to sprinkle over them in order to break up the outline of the trucks beneath. Within half an hour we were hidden away from unfriendly, prying eyes ; and, clinking our mess tins, we made our way over to the cook's lorry where we waited hungrily for our breakfast.

For a few days we rested here while aircraft circled round in fruitless search ; and then more patrols went out, usually one or two at a time : small patrols, with jeeps heavily overloaded in order to be self-sufficient in supplies. As a rule they left after supper, the men singing and shouting, boasting of what they were going to do and hilariously happy in their expectations. And as the little jeeps clambered up the escarpment edge and then, setting off northwards towards the coast, grew smaller and smaller in their black silhouettes against the vivid hues of the evening sky, I could not but help wishing that I was going with them. But I had decided that it was wiser for me to remain at the rendezvous —a fixed place where every one would know where they could find me—rather than to go chasing out with a patrol of a few men, on the off-chance that one of them might become a casualty. As it happened we had only one man wounded in the following week ; a French officer who had been drilled neatly through the arm with a resultant ulna nerve palsy, and for such an injury it made no difference whether or not I was present at the time of its occurrence.

There was great excitement when the patrols returned a few days later, usually just after sundown or before sun-up in order that our rendezvous should not be compromised by aircraft. The men would come crowding down from their ridges and crannies in the rocks, persistent in their questioning and eager for all the details. I can picture the scene now, with one man the centre of interest, telling his story in his own strange slang, emphasising and describing certain points with forceful expressions and gestures. I can see the others, squatting round, sitting on their haunches, hugging their knees, interrupting here and there and all the while enjoying themselves hugely. They would be tanned a dark brown, a bit dirty without a doubt for there was no water for washing, and with the beginnings of whiskers and beards smudging over their faces. Almost I can hear their voices and the strange language they used, for in the desert such a group of men quickly coined its own phrases, and a stranger might well have found some of the conversations unintelligible. Were any men as happy as these ? I wondered, as I looked round at them. Was there another unit such as this, where each man had his own individual job to do, and where his success, failure and very life depended largely on his own skill and quick· thinking ? Where the war had become such a personal affair that you would see some of the men treasuring their notched sticks, with each notch representing the number of planes that they, individually, had blown up ? I doubt it. For you seldom heard a grumble here ; only when a man was left out of a patrol he might " tick " a bit.

Every morning after breakfast I held my little sick-parade, a strange affair and not as monotonous as one might suppose, although most of the cases consisted of desert sores. At this time I was not aware (although Sergeant Bunfield was !) that the best treatment for a desert sore was simply to stick a piece of adhesive strapping over it and leave it there until it fell off, when it could be replaced with a fresh piece. No, I was still trying this ointment and that ; and once I was foolish enough to try the method recommended officially which, if I remember correctly, started off by scrubbing the sore with a brush ! Under this treatment the number of personnel attending sick parades decreased in a most remarkable manner as far as the weekly returns went ; and hence, presumably, the recommendation of the high and mighty !

My few stores were tucked away in a little cave at the top of the escarpment, and solemnly we would clamber up to it over the rocks and loose stones. Having arrived, the men sat themselves down while I opened my monkey-box and endeavoured to look as medical as the circumstances allowed. Not very imposing perhaps, in dirty shorts and sandals, with nothing of the bedside manner or the "would you mind coughing just once more, please ? " attitude, and yet not ineffectual in its crude way.

To such a parade came one of the German prisoners. He was a sandy-haired chap, aged about thirty, I suppose, pale and obviously not very strong. In this respect he contrasted strangely with the other two prisoners, who were comrades and of the blond Nazi youth variety. For they were both from the Luftwaffe, whereas this poor fellow was only a humble postman in the postal service ; they were mere boys and looked it, whereas it was plain that he had lost his early convictions ; they were enthusiastic but he was doubtful.

Now he sat down on a rock and shaded his eyes with his hand, waiting patiently until the others had been treated. Then, when I had beckoned him over, he pointed to his ear.

" Batt ! " he said, " Eer batt ! "

" How long," I inquired, " wieviel Monaten ? "

" Ah ! Ein, zwei, drei Monaten." He held up three fingers. What could I do ? Precious little ; of that I was aware ; it was just a question of keeping it as dry as possible, and we started off by giving him poultices to relieve the pain. So he had had it for three months. Somehow I thought he must have had trouble with that ear for much longer, since already there had crept into his eyes that expression of suffering which is so characteristic of ear disease. I was reminded of the out-patients in the ear, nose and throat department at hospital. Walking past the long lines as they waited their turn to see the surgeon one would note just that expression of resignation to pain ; a tolerant acceptance of suffering as if it were, indeed, as much a feature of their lives as eating and breathing. So I found it hard not to feel sorry for this little German, who seemed so unlike a man of war, and all the more pathetic in his captive loneliness and unhappiness.

" Desert—no goot ! " he remarked one morning as he screwed up his eyes and surveyed the shuddering expanse of the wilderness around, " and war—no goot ! Englische and Deutsch, one race. Ja ! Why war ? "

But neither my German nor his English were sufficiently adequate for me to explain why there had been a war, although it seemed a foolish question, I thought, when the facts were so clear and positive. This remark, that English and Germans were of the same stock, was heard frequently enough amongst captured Germans and came, presumably, as a routine phrase of propaganda. Nevertheless it was interesting if only because it was largely true, and one had only to see the way in which the Germans and Italians mixed to become acutely aware of the difference between Saxon and Latin.

This little prisoner, I felt, was rather apart from the usual run of Germans. Had he shouted his " Heils " and waved his swastika with the best of them ? Had he goose-stepped down the bedecked streets in the military parades of 1939 ? I rather doubted it : for he was a simple countryman, and in relieving his pain I found a certain personal satisfaction.

It was our custom to linger over our evening meal ; waiting until the red sun had dipped behind the flat rim of the desert ; watching the transparent colours as they throbbed and pulsed and died away ; watching the filmy light as it caught the occasional flimsy cloud surfaces and was thrown back in soft reflection on to the ground below. Waiting and watching, watching and waiting, until we felt that first touch of coolness in the air ; the balm and solace of the wilderness. Then we would fill up our water bottles for the next twenty-four hours and, by leaving the bottle buried in cool sand, manage to keep the water beautifully fresh. And having filled our bottles, we would sit down and wait for the next event of the day ; the issue of rum and lime. For our time passed by in slow stages and repeated affairs, and this was the occasion to which we had been looking forward with silent longing throughout the heat of the day. How pleasant to sit round the cook's lorry, or perched up on the escarpment slopes nearby ; breathing in the coolness, conscious that you were alive once more, rejoicing in the relief from the blistering white light, feeling your temper mend, and watching the little stars prick out, one after another, as night drew over with a soft gradation of tone.

As a rule we sat talking and telling stories until somewhere round nine or ten o'clock, and then we moved off to the little patches of sand which we had staked out as our sleeping quarters. But one evening, I remember, we broached an extra jar of rum ; soon there was a party in progress, and as the light hovered and fell, so our spirits were revived.

A memory such as this remains very clear : Paddy Mayne stretched out beside me and speaking little ; David Stirling, George Jellicoe and a few others grouped together further down the slope ; the French in an animated chattering circle ; and the Germans nearby, the two together and the third left with his own thoughts. A memory of the atmosphere of men : the deep jumble of voices ; the sound of a laugh that seemed to hang in the air for a fraction of a second before it was lost in the night ; the yellow flame of a match lighting up a man's bearded face, throwing the features into sharp relief, sketching in the lines with deep shadows ; the brighter glow of ruby red as he drew on his cigarette. The men themselves ; some hunched forward, talking eagerly ; some joking ; some lying back quietly. One huge fellow, bare chested, sitting facing us on the floorboards of the lorry, with his thick legs dangling over the tailpiece—a self-appointed master of ceremonies. Another coming round with the jar of rum, holding it carefully in both his hands, spilling a little into each mess tin or mug, telling us that, " The lime'll be round in a minute."

As it grew darker the men began to sing, at first slightly self-conscious and shy, but picking up confidence as the song spread round to the other groups. The man on the lorry produced a stick, and began to beat time with huge exaggerated sweeps of the arm, as he roared away at the top of his voice. The volume of sound spread until everybody was singing, some shouting the snatches of the words they happened to know and others adding their variations to the tune. It was a mixture of voices that swelled and died away in gusty waves. Then fresh cigarettes would be lit, the smoke would rise in clouds against the pin-points of light, and the voices would be thrown backwards and forwards once more as men in different groups called out to each other. Soon a fresh song would start up and everything else would be lost in it. You would hear the individual voices of those near to you ; you would smile to yourself as they tried to reach the higher notes. But beyond them it was just a wall of sound. And beyond that again it was the blank emptiness of the desert, milky and pale as it stretched away faintly into the silent gloom. We had formed a small solitary island of voices ; voices which faded and were caught up by the wilderness. A little cluster of men singing in the desert. An expression of feeling that defied the vastness of its surroundings. For we might have been in the mess, we might have been in a pub at home, we might have been in a crowd waiting for a football match to start.

It was not the songs or the quality of the singing ; it was simple emotion. Indeed, our efforts were not very harmonious. The French turned to watch us questioningly while the Germans stopped talking and studied us with intentness. After a while we had exhausted our repertoire of good songs, and those with a Highland swing to them gave way to the lewd ballads and the melancholy jazz.

" Ha ! " said the Germans, nodding their heads enthusiastic-ally to the rhythm of the harlot of Jerusalem, " Goot folk song—ver goot ! "

But they were mystified completely by the jazz which slowly spread and took control of the proceedings. The more burly and gorilla-like the individual who got up to sing, then the more love-sick his refrain, and the more pronounced the tremolo over the moving passages. Looking more and more baffled the Ger-mans watched our huskies perform " My Melancholy baby," " I'll never smile again " and so on. Gone were the " Pack up your troubles " and " Good-bye Dolly " marching songs of the last war, and in their place had crept " I'm dancing with tears in my eyes " and the " Don't say it's true " sort of stuff. Why was it ? I wondered. Why was it that the Poles, the Slavs, the Czechs, the Greeks—why everybody, for that matter, except ourselves—could

sing folk-songs and national airs, and sing them well? We
disapproved of too much patriotism, even in war-time, but did
that answer the question? Or was it that we were just too lazy
and too democratic to bother to learn them?

I voiced my queries to Paddy, but he was not perturbed,
" Och, Malcolm, there's nothing to worry about," he said,
" they're happy. That's the main thing."

After a certain amount of persuasion we got the French to
sing and they gave us " Madeleine," their voices sounding weak
and trembling in the open air. It fell quiet for a few moments
after they had finished, until suddenly someone shouted, " The
Germans—you sing ! " There was a second of dead silence and
then the words were taken up and passed along the little groups—
" The Germans ! "   " The Germans ! "   " The Germans—you
sing ! "

In the half-darkness of the starlight we could see them talking
and arguing seriously with each other. Was this an order or a
request? Should they sing? Would the Fuehrer approve? You
could almost read their thoughts.

Then away they went, just the three voices, a little doubtful
at first but gaining courage as they continued. " In Hoffmann
Stat da gibts ein Haus." They sang chiefly in unison but with
harmony here and there, and it was hard not to be impressed.
We applauded them heartily at the conclusion of their song.
" More ! " we demanded, " Sing us some more ! " They did.
They sang " Marlene," the good-night song of the Afrika Corps.
They sang it very well.

And so it was on that starry night, with our voices coming and
going into the darkness ; with Arcturus looking down wisely from
above, while Scorpius rose high and brilliant in the southern sky.
And here we were, half-clad and looking very dark in the milky
light, heavy-shouldered and broad-chested, squatting in tiers on
the rough escarpment slope and sprawling on the softer ground
at the foot of the lorry. A strange body of men thrown together
for a few days by the fortunes of war. Enemies? Yes, we were
enemies all right, but quite happy now in our little truce. Whatever would they say at home? I wondered. Would they condemn? Would they be bitter? Or would they simply shrug their
shoulders and give it up? I did not know and I doubted if it

mattered much. But what I did know was that, for most of us, there was something especial about that night, something we would be remembering, something which we would recall in later years when we spoke of the war and said :

"Ah, yes, the desert war. Now that really *was* a war. Why, I can remember how we had a rum party behind the enemy's lines one night. You just wouldn't believe it if I was to try and tell you . . ."

CHAPTER EIGHT

LIFE AT THE RENDEZVOUS

" 'Here and here did England help me : how can I help England ?'
  —say,
  Whoso turns as I, this evening, turn to God to praise and pray,
  While Jove's planet rises yonder, silent over Africa."
    Home Thoughts from the Sea.   ROBERT BROWNING.

BY NOW our supplies had begun to run low, and David Stirling decided to return to base with the greater part of our men and vehicles in order to refit and collect fresh stores. But a small party would have to remain at the rendezvous so that a quick raid could be carried out if necessary.

" You see, Malcolm," he told me one morning, " what I really want, is to have a permanent advanced base or rendezvous somewhere behind the enemy's positions, so that we can keep our raids going all the time ; and when the boys get tired or desertweary, they can go back to Kabrit for a rest."

We were lying beneath the belly of a three-ton lorry, one of the few places where we could find any shade ; and I rolled over on one side to look at him as he lay on his back, with one leg crossed languidly over the other, sucking peacefully at his empty pipe. He had the makings of a fine black Captain Cuttle beard, I thought, as I listened to him talking about the possibilities of raids on fresh objectives and sounding, for all the world, as if he was discussing the form of an approaching point to point. Two of these objectives, which could be dealt with at the same time, were the escarpment passes at Sollum at Halfaya. If Auchinleck were to attack and advance westwards, then it was absolutely essential that we should be ready to move instantly. For our plan would be to drive north towards the coast, join in by night with the retreating enemy vehicles, and demolish and block the passes as effectively as we could. We had a sergeant who spoke Italian, and two Palestinians, who were formerly natives of Germany, to look after the interpreting side of the business, and it would largely be a question of timing and effective demolition. Certainly the idea was very good as these two passes handled most of the coastal traffic ; and their destruction would result in the utter chaos of the enemy forces caught on the eastern side of the block, without any way of getting up the escarpment.

The other objective that David was very keen to attack was a tank laager, for'he reckoned that tanks were more valuable than aircraft. But it was too difficult, really, for it meant driving round the desert just behind the enemy's front line and trying to stalk a moving prey. We did, in fact, make several attempts, but never with any success. The main thing, however, which David desired, was to keep a permanent rendezvous in existence so that any target could be attacked at a moment's notice ; and if we could not motor backwards and forwards to the rendezvous, then we should have to be supplied by air.

For my part, I decided to remain at the rendezvous and send my medical orderly back with the wounded French officer and a few others who were sick. He could then return with some more medical supplies to keep us going for the next few weeks.

It was a sad day when they moved off, and we climbed up the escarpment to watch their departure. It was mid-morning and they were risking the daylight drive in the heat haze ; once they got into the Qattara depression they considered they should be pretty safe. (Actually it was north of the depression that they were attacked by aircraft—but without loss of life or limb ; only one truck burned out). For now the enemy had extended his forces down to the northern border of the Qattara depression and, by sealing off our track of approach, had obliged us to make a larger detour to the south. The statement that it was impossible for wheeled traffic to cross the Qattara depression, was founded on about as much experience and common sense as the implication that it was impossible to fight in the desert during the summer months. In other words it was merely the opinion of certain elegant gentlemen in Cairo—" Devilish hot, what ! Flies are such a bally nuisance, don't you know ! What ? Fighting in the desert ? Oh, don't be absurd, my dear sir. Why ! Phew ! It's too hot to play golf, dammit."

Yes, at the risk of diversion, one might add that there were quite a few popular misconceptions concerning the desert. Some

thought that it consisted entirely of sand, whereas statistics, for
what they are worth, stated that eighty per cent of it was made up
of rock formations. Or that it was hot in the desert throughout
the year ; while in true fact you might awake on any morning
from December to March, and find it freezing. Lack of protective features made the bitterness of the winter wind seem
doubly penetrating. In this respect, too, there were those who
thought it was unusual to have a breeze or wind in the desert ;
but in reply I would say that it was a sorry day in the coastal
region if there was not a breeze fresh off the sea. Inland, of
course, the breeze might be scarcely noticeable, and hot and arid
in summer if it was. A stiff breeze did not mean necessarily that
the sand would be blowing. This depended upon the area concerned, how much traffic had passed that way and ground up the
dust, and the wind velocity. Thus "sand storms" or "dust
storms" might be differentiated from "khamasins" and were
more frequent in the coastal area where the fighting had taken
place. "A khamasin" was a particular type of southerly wind
which flung up the dust in a rearing wall, several hundred feet
high, along the line of its advance. Frequently, then, you could
see it whirling along towards you before it enveloped you in its
oven-like, stinging embrace. The worst of these which I experienced occurred on May 9th and 10th of 1941, and I well
remember a small party of us groping our way down to the sea
to have a bathe on the first day. It was about six o'clock in the
evening and, as we stripped, the driving sand whipped against
our naked bodies. The visibility was about five yards. Anxious
to get into the water, we did not linger, but made our way
cautiously down the sandy beach. It would be foolish to try and
pretend that it was pleasant swimming ; and, of course, it was
unwise to get out of your depth in case you lost your sense of
direction. Then, all of a sudden, the wind veered round from the
south through the west until it was blowing hard from due north.
Within a minute or two the sand had settled and we could see
again. It was an astonishing sight for, extending out to sea about
half-way from shore to horizon, the water had been coloured
thickly by the dirty yellow grit.

With regard to the brainwave that respirators should be worn
in khamasins, one can only suggest that practise might provide the

answer. Incidentally a khamasin or a severe dust storm usually cried " halt " to battle activities. Aircraft were grounded ; while forward troops huddled together in disconsolate groups, trying to find some shelter on the leeward side of a vehicle, or in its driving cabin. All around was the murky greyness of swirling, driving sand. The sun was blotted out. There was no shade. Instead, the heat diffused everywhere. It soaked into the wind and was thrown back from the ground. At such times it was the little things that assumed importance. The successful performance of the daily rites. Keeping the tent flaps pegged down securely. Finding your way from one tent to another. The consideration of where you would unroll your blankets for the night. The enemy ? Well, you trusted that they found it as uncomfortable as you did. But the average soldier was far too intent on minding his own business in a sandstorm ; the chances were that the guns would not fire anyhow. A " look out " could not see more than a few yards—so why worry ?

It was only when a sandstorm was subsiding that one realised the intensity of the sound that had accompanied it : the crying hiss of the sand as it drove against the hummocks and broken scrub ; the soft smothering noise as it eddied and whirled on the leeward side of an obstacle ; the pelting, beating clatter, like a hailstorm, that you heard inside a tent or a truck's cabin ; the occasional thud as something was blown heavily against the side of your shelter. When all this unmusical accompaniment had died down and silence had crept furtively into its place, you could almost feel the absence of sound. Your ears were ringing ; you did not have to shout to make yourself heard. The quietness appeared unnatural.

The wind could attain a considerable velocity at such times, sweeping in furious gusts across the level plain of the desert. Strapping young soldiers would plod their way forward blindly like elderly women in a gale on the Southend sea-front. Pieces of scrub and camel thorn would bowl merrily along until, of a sudden, they were thrown up into the air with a joyful shout of the wind. I shall not forget seeing a pick and shovel blown off the top of a truck on one of these occasions.

The subject of mirages, too, seemed to be one on which many people at home were misinformed. Presumably the explanation

of their occurrence can be found in the appropriate literature ;
but most of us took it for granted that it was a phenomenon of
light refraction, in which horizon and skyline become interposed.
This would occur with the varying refractive indices of air at
different temperatures, and would explain the apparent reflection
of objects. Yet, despite the factor of heat, it was surprising how
cool it could be when mirages were apparent. The theory that
a mirage was dependent on the state of exhaustion of an individual
was, of course, utter nonsense ; I feel sure that the best fed staff
officer in Cairo could not give credit to that explanation. On the
other hand imagination and exaggeration would account for the
phenomena of oases, palm trees, sailing ships, and so on, which
formed such an integral part of the repertoire of an " old soldier "
in the desert. The heat haze would distort an object at a few
hundred yards' distance ; it was not surprising, then, that at a
further range camel thorn could sprout into palm trees or scrub
into sailing boats. In this connection I can recall an occasion
when we were travelling in convoy, and were passed by another
convoy about a mile or two out to our flank. Looking over in
that direction we could see their trucks apparently floating through
the air. A number of people mistook them for low flying aircraft,
and it was only when they had " touched down " that we were
reassured.

Other minor misconceptions were : that there were mosquitoes
in the desert ; or that we walked about the desert and went into
battle with gasmasks at the alert, gas capes rolled up neatly on
our backs, and tin-hats, just so. In fact there were very few
mosquitoes in the desert, apart from the oases and areas which
had been cultivated. Nor were we very particular about our
appearance (the Guards excepted) when action was imminent.

However, to return to the story.

The men were in great form on that morning when they left
us ; and who would not be, we said to ourselves, as, trying hard
not to show our jealousy and bitter envy, we endeavoured to
make the appropriate remarks.

" Have a beer for us," we shouted, and " Think of us when
you're having a bath."

Ah, yes, it was comparatively easy to joke and to laugh in
reply when there were things to be done, and the eyes of other

people were upon you. Easy enough to think that you were doing your stuff and keeping things going, as you shouted and waved them farewell. But afterwards ? After you had watched the jeeps merge into the shuddering heat haze, become distorted and magnified, and then plucked suddenly from your sight. It was then ; then, in the silence which followed, as you turned back to your cave with an empty aching in the heart ; it was then that you knew the real anguish and the bleak loneliness. For the officers I knew best had gone : Stirling, Mayne, Jellicoe, Bill Fraser and Arthur Sharpe, the Air Force officer. There were just three of us left. And the men too, poor devils, looked very forlorn and disconsolate as they straggled back over the rocks.

Our job was by no means cheerful. For we had to stay where we were and wait—wait for the raid on Sollum pass which never materialised. And waiting is far worse than being employed on active operations, when both food and water supplies are running low. For when you are stationary at the rendezvous and not occupying your time in physical or mental exertion, it was far more difficult to make your water ration last throughout the day than it was when you were on the move. Actually this time of low water rationing probably did us all good, for there were harder times in store. We had our water-bottle filled once a day—that was our great blessing and standby—and in addition we had a mug of tea with our three meals. From the physiological standpoint of preserving a water balance, this was more than adequate ; there was no cause to worry as long as you could urinate. Anyhow, that was the way I looked at it, and I can remember how one of our sergeants never used his water-bottle, sufficing himself simply with the ration at mealtimes. I envied him his severe austerity, for these days in late July and early August were very hot.

His name was Sgt. Almonds, a finely built man and more sensible and intelligent than the average officer. He had the great ability, too, of becoming interested in little things and in this way he helped to pass the time of the day. I recall how we both collected, and argued over, the different types of sea shells that were strewn in vast profusion over the desert in this area. There were snail shells, too, carpeting some of the ghôts. Snails in the desert !

One day he discovered some pottery. " What do you make of that, Doc," he asked, rubbing his finger along the smooth, worn edge. " Must be very old, don't you think, and yet it was just lying on top of the sand."

It was a fragment of a vase, fashioned, apparently, in terra cotta, with its markings and symmetry unimpaired by time or sand erosion.

" Where did you find it ? "

" Over in a little wadi up there. I'll show you. There's any amount of it lying about, but it's nearly all broken up."

Together we walked over to the wadi, and there it was, all in one little group, as if someone had only just put it there. In the main this little outcrop of pottery was made up of small pieces : the tapering neck of a bowl ; a portion of a basin ; a beautifully symmetrical handle, lying by itself—there was nothing whole or complete. It was pottery of the Greek Roman period (as the curator of the museum at Cairo informed me later), that is to say between the third and first century B.C., and it was strewn about the desert fairly liberally. Were these relics of the march of Cambyses' army ; an army, forty thousand strong, which had set out to march to Siwa oasis and vanished completely ? Who could say ?

Then what of the thick oyster-like shells and their negative reliefs which had been imprinted on the surface stones. They must have been prehistoric, yet they were lying about on the ground as if scattered there yesterday. One was left with a feeling of wonder and a desire to know more of the early geographical construction of the Libyan desert.

As I have said before, Sgt. Almonds was a fine disciplinarian over his water consumption. For my part, I do not know what I should have done without a water-bottle from which to take a small sip at occasional intervals, rinsing it round to keep the mouth fresh. By sundown my bottle would be half empty, and then I felt I was free to lust and revel in what remained. Loaning of water was practised by some ; but I always condemned it, and it was never a practice of Paddy Mayne's. He was another person, who, despite his great size, seemed to have no trouble in restricting himself to a low water ration. Of course the whole thing was really psychological, and it was a case of resisting the temptation to drink. You knew the water would not quench your thirst, and yet the knowledge did not nullify the desire. It was a case of forcing yourself *not* to drink, and of making yourself realise that the water was not necessary. But it certainly was the devil sometimes, when you ran your tongue over your cracked lips ; when your watch said it was only two o'clock in the after-noon ; when the heat was fairly blanketing down over you, and you knew there was worse to come ; when you could see your water-bottle tucked away securely in the shade, and you must needs say to yourself, "There's absolutely no use in having a drink now." You had to fight that dreadful desire to gulp at the water, to have one really good drink and not stint yourself. That was the battle which you were waging constantly throughout the long heat of the day.

I think that we were about twenty men strong at the rendez-vous at this time ; but there was the New Zealand patrol of the L.R.D.G. which had settled to the north of us, and Robin Gurdon with his little patrol to the south, so that they, too, were on my medical charge. It would be impossible to praise the New Zealanders too highly ; their rough friendliness, their generosity, and their reliability were beyond that. You could not have wished for better company, and soon we had become very inti-mate. They would come slouching over to me sometimes, in variegated head-dresses, or with kiwi hats pulled over on to the backs of their heads. "Any dope for a crook stomach, Doc ? " they would ask. Or perhaps they would vary it with a " Me guts are crook, doc, d'yer think yer can fix 'em ? " Everything was " crook " with them on sick parades. They had their own " Doc " really, a darkly bearded medical orderly who had done some work in a New Zealand hospital. Sometimes he would " bring a case over for consultation," and on these occasions we would nod our heads sagely, stroke our respective beards, and speak in highly medical language, while all the time the patient's alarm became more and more clearly depicted on his features. This " Doc " of theirs had a fund of medical stories and a wealth of gory surgical material with which to uphold his reputation, and there is no doubt that he ruled his roost very efficiently.

In thinking of these New Zealanders I am reminded of an evening in Kufra, later on in the year, when we had a sing-song.

Some of the New Zealanders came over from their camp to join us. One of them, a great swarthy fellow who was sitting near me, suddenly recognised me during a pause in between the songs.

" Why, hyah Doc," he shouted. " Hyah, yer old bassterd."

" Why, hallo," I replied, smiling a trifle faintly at his dubious form of approach.

" Hyah," he repeated, and then winked solemnly, " oh yes, we've met before. You went on the Benghazi run, didn't yer ? Yer a reglar old bassterd, Doc, that's what yer are ! "

There was a sharp nudge in my ribs and I turned round to find Sgt. Rose whispering in my ear. " When they call you a bastard, doc, that's the hell of a compliment, see. Don't look so worried. Give him a grin."

My mind was relieved. " Why, *hallo* you old bastard," I said, turning back to the swarthy New Zealander ; and nothing would satisfy him then but that we must drain a bottle of beer together.

Then there was the Rhodesian patrol of the L.R.D.G. whom we met rather less frequently ; but when we did, they were more than generous, giving us cigarettes, sharing their water and rations with us, and making up for all our deficiencies. For they knew that our system of supply and organisation was less secure than their own, and they never grudged us anything we lacked. They were a fine crowd of men, and I only feel sorry that we never had the opportunity to repay them for their open goodwill.

So here we lived in our little rendezvous, not seeing very much of one another, only emerging from our rocky caves and crannies for meals and when the sun was falling below the sky line. The days dragged past in all the monotony of their continual routine. The flies seemed constantly to grow worse. They would wake us before sun-up as we lay swathed in blankets, and we would be obliged to cover ourselves mummy-like, in order to avoid their irritating persistence. They pestered us throughout our meals, settling on our mess-tins, crawling over our food and clustering round the tea ; so that these became silent, brisk, and energetic affairs, as we used one hand with which to feed ourselves and kept up a constant waving movement with the other. It was always a bit of a relief to finish the abrupt meal, I used to think, and then to be able to lie back and sip leisurely at the tea and swat the flies.

My God ! How we grew to hate those flies. And what a trial
they became at the sick parades, clustering round the desert sores,
or the exudate that had seeped through the dressings and bandages. Sometimes you would see a man waiting his turn, quite
unaware of the black, rosette-shaped cluster of flies that had
grouped round his sore, until, suddenly noticing their activity, he
would slash at them in his fury and start the ulcer bleeding afresh.
Yes, those sick parades were pretty grim. And the irritating
tickling as the flies ran over your back, up your arms, and round
your lips and eyes, while you were bending over trying to adjust
a dressing or tie a bandage. It is almost too nauseating to recall
now, but it was so horribly true for us then.

In the afternoons three of us would crawl into our cave, and
under a mosquito net—taking great pains not to introduce a fly
as we did so—and there we would lie, body to sweating body, as
we tried to read or fall asleep ; or perhaps we would discuss
the fancies and delights of Cairo and try to forget ourselves,
but always we would be counting the slow passage of the
heat-ridden hours. That little cave became a sort of fly trap ;
and the flies would settle on the net in their hundreds, so that
if you were to give it a sharp flick with the finger, you would
produce a deep unmusical discord as you disturbed them into
flight.

Why did we have these flies ? Obviously they had accompanied us on the lorries, and had bred in the odd little pieces of
food and jam that must inevitably fall to the bottom of the cook's
truck. But I know from later experience that we could have kept
them in check if we had been able to use proper latrines, dispose
of our refuse adequately, and adopt satisfactory anti-fly measures.
Only all those fascinating diagrams which one could contemplate
in *The Manual of Hygiene* were, I fear, of little value to us. For
any trench system of latrines, or newly turned earth, was considered to be too easily recognisable, and hence dangerous, from
the air. Therefore it was up to each one of us—a point which
it was not altogether easy to impress upon the French—to be as
clean as we could in our habits, and to burn our waste whenever
possible. In this way we did keep a slight control over the flies
and prevent our lives from becoming utterly intolerable.

At this time I was reading the *Whiteoaks Chronicles* and, without

a doubt, it was the main thing that kept me going during those
melancholy days. Poor old Finch ! How strange it was, I thought,
that such an ungainly and often foolish character should be by
far the most appealing in the whole book. Why was it ? And
thinking it over it seemed to me that if you could make your
principal character an unlucky sort of person ; if you could make
the reader feel that he was far better off than the individual concerned, then you had made a good start with your character
sketch. That was what seemed to make Finch such an interesting
person : you felt sorry for him the whole time, he always seemed
to be getting into one scrape after another. Anyhow I simply do
not know what I should have done without that omnibus volume ;
it tided me over this period of waiting and the descriptions of the
countryside made me feel very conscious of better things to come.
Even now as I think back on those days—curled up in a little
corner of the cave ; moving round continually as the hot sunlight
crept in after me like a remorseless, hungry animal—I am filled
with the pangs of sick longing, and the sense of unbelieving that I
experienced as I read of horses in paddocks, of musical streams and
placid lakes, of the mottled shadows in the deep green of the
woods. Then, as I looked up from my book at the wavering
expanse of hot yellow desert outside, suddenly I would be wrenched
back into the unhappy realisation of the truth ; or perhaps it
would be the warning cry of " Aircraft " that would whip the
mind away from the fantasy.

We made a rule of having two sentries posted on top of the
highest rock of the escarpment, and we took it in turn to do the
hourly shifts. The signal for aircraft consisted of short intermittent blasts on a whistle, while long blasts denoted that ground
troops had been sighted. On hearing the whistle we remained as
still as animals in danger, frozen into immobility ; and then we
would hear the steady hum, hum, hum, sounding down the wind.
Later we would see the speck of a plane over on the horizon ;
would watch it take shape and grow into recognition as it passed
slowly—God, how slowly !—across the sky. Sometimes we were
caught at meals and, hiding our mess tins beneath our bodies, we
would lower our faces to break up the individual outlines. And
as the plane flew over, you would find yourself peering at it
through the crook in your elbow and wondering—is he going to

turn ? Has he seen us ? Is that his wing dipping now ? Or now ?
Is it dipping *now* ?

But we remained unseen. The planes flew on and passed us
by. We looked up, and got on with our food again. We slashed
at the flies. We returned once more to our monotonous day of
lifeless routine and petty incidents.

One afternoon, as we lay perspiring in our cave, we were
surprised to hear three long blasts on the whistle. That meant
ground forces ; so we bundled out in a hurry, just in time to see
a ᴖolitary L.R.D.G. truck skirt its way slowly along the escarpment edge and draw up nearby. We grouped round it as Corporal
Preston, the navigator of Robin Gurdon's patrol, lowered himself
down wearily from his seat next to the driver. His leg was
bandaged ; a dirty old bandage through which the blood had
soaked and dried in irregular dark patches. He looked as if he
was exhausted, and his eyes were reddened with fatigue. When
he spoke, it was almost with a tired resignation in the very words.

" Mr. Gurdon is badly wounded," he said simply. " Could
you come out, doctor, and see if you can help him ! Although
I am afraid he may be dead now. I left him at about ten o'clock
this morning." He paused for a moment, and then laughed
bitterly. " We were only about five miles away from here, you
know, and all the bloody day I have been searching for this
rendezvous. You see we've had our sun compass shot away off
the truck, and we lost our bearings. But I could swear," he screwed
up his eyes and looked across the blank yellow-white plain, " I
could swear I've been here this morning. Parker's been hurt,
too, sir—nasty one through the elbow—left elbow I think—but
he's not as bad as Mr. Gurdon. He got it through the chest and
stomach."

I clambered up the rocks to my little medical store, and while
I was getting my things together one of the lorries was got ready
and backed out of its hiding-place. Within a few minutes we had
loaded on a couple of stretchers and some equipment. I joined
Corporal Preston in his L.R.D.G. truck and as we jolted away,
with the three-ton lorry following behind, he told me what had
happened.

A few days previously they had set out to navigate a party of our Frenchmen on to one of the coastal airfields near Matruh. As they were approaching, however, they were detected by a C.R. 42 which came down low and strafed them. Mr. Gurdon and Parker were wounded almost immediately. A few of the others were peppered a bit, too, he tapped the bandage on his leg, but nothing much. "We wanted to bring the wounded back to you there and then," Preston went on, "but Mr. Gurdon refused to hear of it. Although he had been wounded badly, he did not seem to be in too much pain ; and, after he and Parker had had their wounds dressed, he insisted that we went on towards the airfield. But the Jerries must have heard us coming or something, 'cos when we got near the drome they suddenly switched on their ground searchlights and opened up. We didn't have a chance of getting in among the planes. Just had to turn round and clear off as fast as we could. I think a few armoured cars came out after us, but I'm not too sure."

He interrupted to direct the driver ; we were travelling over rough stony ground on a bearing just south of east.

"Well," he continued, "we came back on rough navigation, and we were hoping to find the rendezvous soon after it was light. But our luck was right out. It was bumpy, too—pretty hard on the wounded, you know. After a bit we had to give it up. We kept on thinking we had reached the right place—probably we were just a little to one side or the other. Once the heat haze was up we knew it wasn't much good. Mr. Gurdon needed a rest, so we put him and Parker in the shade by some rocks and boulders. He was getting weaker all the time and just as we were leaving, he told us to bring you straight back, or else it would be too late. That's all. We've been circling round here most of the morning—no proper navigation—but I don't know how we could have missed you.

As he was talking in his rather tired dejected way, I tried to realise just what had happened. For however hard you try to convince yourself of the truth, there are times when it is so difficult to accept. That Robin Gurdon—he, of all people—should be dying here ! Surely it was not real ; not tangible fact. That sort of thing would not happen to him. He was too proud, too lordly, to die ungraciously like this in the wilderness. This was not the right ending for him ; for someone else, perhaps, but not for him. For he was nearly forty and should never have been doing this sort of work. Oh, damn you, Robin ! Damn you ! I thought, why the hell need you have done it. But of course I knew the answer : a case of satisfying the insistent conscience, and I knew, too, that he had been completely happy in this work.

I recalled the old days in the regiment—his infectious high spirits ; his temper, which would settle as quickly as it had risen ; his superb authority and self-assurance, and all those little things that had made him very lovable. I remembered one day on Auchinleck's retreat to Gazala ; how we had been surrounded, with German vehicles driving past our flank, in full view and not far away ; how Robin had watched them go past and then had thrown back his head and laughed. " What damned cheek ! " he had said, as if he had been speaking about an impudent schoolboy. Ah, yes, it was a wretched thought to feel that such a man had been shot up by a miserable, dirty little Italian. But then war was the supreme equaliser. . . .

After about half an hour's slow progress we came to a small saucer-like depression, in which were scattered elevations and rocky cliffs. From one of these some figures came walking out to meet us, and almost before our truck had stopped I knew that Robin had died. When I inquired, they just nodded and pointed to two small stony hills to the south, saying that that was where they had buried him.

I turned and walked into the gloom of one of the deep caves in the cliff face. It was dark in there and I thought I was alone. But Vaughan was there, too ; his faithful batman, who had followed him in regiment and L.R.D.G. without a murmur, and, indeed, was happy to do so.

For a minute or two he stood telling me how they had made him as comfortable as possible ; of how he had not been in too much pain for they had given him the morphia tablets and—but there Vaughan broke down. I patted him on the shoulder to comfort him until, of a sudden, I found that I, too, was crying. I hid my face in shame and leaned up against the rock face. Oh, God, I thought, this is too bloody for words. Where is the right in all this ? For, all at once, it seemed as if the joy and pleasure had gone out of life ; and perhaps there was a certain amount of self-commiseration in my tears. Then I pulled myself together.

You would never have seen Robin showing his feelings over some-body's death—that was hardly the form. A friend's death was simply a case of a reference to " poor John " or " poor Richard " when his name chanced to crop up in later conversation. You should never show your true feelings on the subject. Besides, there was Parker needing attention. I wiped my eyes on a dirty rag of a handkerchief, and blew my nose vigorously.

A French officer, Jacques, stumbled into the cave, and stood for a moment, peering and blinking in the darkness. Then, seeing me alone—for Vaughan had wandered out—he discerned the trouble and offered me some water.

" I think 'e was your good friend," he remarked.

" Oh, fairly." I swallowed a mouthful from his flask—it was laced with rum. Then I went in search of Parker. His elbow, I found, was in a bad way. An explosive bullet had opened the joint and laid bare the splintered bones. I considered it wiser to leave a toilet of the wound until evening, so having given him some morphia and dressed the arm, we lifted him out on a stretcher, and loaded him into the back of one of the lorries. Then we drove slowly away, a sorrowful little party ; and looking over at the L.R.D.G. truck at the figures cut out in sharp black silhouette against the bright desert background, I could see Vaughan with his shoulders hunched and head sunk low, looking the picture of utter dejection. Poor Vaughan ! He and Robin had made an ideal pair, for they both held such a high opinion of one another.

That evening at the rendezvous, when it had become cooler, I got a couple of our chaps to help ; and between us we gave Parker a little pentothal for anæsthesia (he did not need much), and set to cleaning up his wound, dressing and splinting it properly. He was weak from loss of blood ; but he came round quite quietly soon after it had grown dark, and passed a restful night. The two men stayed up with him all night, in case of any worries or bleeding ; and as I was dropping off to sleep I could hear them talking in that solemn, homely way of theirs : about how you should treat this, that and the other, and comparing notes of the details of horrible accidents witnessed in " civvy street."

It must have been in the early hours of the morning that we

were suddenly awakened by the shattering explosions of bombs dropping just nearby. With minds fuddled by sleep, and not fully comprehending, we started to our feet crying out—" What was that ? " " What was that ? " But there was only the receding drone of an aircraft to give us answer. We thought that probably it was one of our own Wellingtons, though how he had discovered us, we never knew. Perhaps he had seen a torch or the light of a match from our two vigilants, or perhaps it was one of the men in the L.R.D.G. camp.

I lay awake and looked up at the stars, flickering against the dark blue of the night sky, and thought how strange the desert war seemed : the way we travelled over vast tracts of wilderness in order to search out and kill one another ; the way we fought so bitterly over this little piece of barren ground or that rocky waste. And yet, after all, this was the best place for war ; for here we left few scars, few stricken towns and homelands in our train as the battle swayed and eddied this way and that.

Slowly and silently the stars traced their courses across the sky above. They were wise in their old age, I thought—wise, and probably very cynical as they watched the futile efforts of mankind. For, over two thousand years ago, they had seen the army of Cambyses march to its unknown fate. They had seen the Romans and Carthaginians locked in pitiless battle. They had looked down upon the Turks as they strove to hold the mastery of the desert. They had watched the childish brutality of the Italians as they tortured and drove the Senussi from one oasis to another. They had seen us warring in the desert twenty years ago, and now here we were back at it again. In a fraction of a second in the history of time, they had watched these little dramas of puny man—each, in turn, had strutted across the sandy stage and held it for a fleeting instant—and then the dust had blown over in its caressing forgetfulness, his traces had been conccaled, and his ways had become just a memory.

CHAPTER NINE

" Ah, pray make no mistake,
    We are not shy,
    We're very wide awake
    The moon and I ! "
            The Mikado. W. S. GILBERT.

" ' The night is fine,' the walrus said,
    ' Do you admire the view ? ' "
        The Walrus and the Carpenter. LEWIS CARROLL.

WE HAD DECIDED to give the relief party a dramatic reception
when they returned. We discussed and planned how, when
eventually they did arrive, some of us would come crawling out on
all fours from our cave, croaking, " Water, master, water ! For
the love of Allah, water ! " whilst others would be feverishly
digging holes in the ground with their hands. We would be
scrabbling and inarticulate, with the light of fanaticism in our
eyes and a mad despair in every gesture. We would be laughing
maniacally as each fingered a small piece of dried bully, licking
it, nursing it, caressing and crowing over it with possessive pride.

In truth, I suppose it was a bitterness of mind that prompted
our feelings, for Stirling's party was well overdue. During their
absence, the small patrol which had proceeded to the airfield
south of Sidi Barrani, returned to us with no adventures to record
other than the privations of an acute water-lack. There was little
enemy movement upon which to report. They called in on us and
livened our dull routine for a day or two before they returned to
base and left us, once more, to our dreary contemplations. In the
meantime our supplies had grown short, and we had been obliged
to reduce our issue of food quite considerably, while our water
ration had been cut down to half a mug of tea per meal. Since
I was acting as quartermaster at this time—in liaison with the
perpetually harassed Sergeant Bennett—it was my unhappy task
to try and make the supplies last out.

But they came one morning, and it was marvellous to see them. They brought an air of freshness and eagerness with them, of enthusiasm for the next raid; and by no means least important, they brought food and water. Our jaded spirits were revived.

They had brought many more jeeps with them, and the place began to look like Piccadilly as they drove busily up and down the escarpment edge. We expanded our rendezvous to fit them in, taking advantage of a long shallow cave to the north of our present position, into which about eight jeeps could be packed, head to tail. By letting down a camouflage net from the top and decorating it suitably, these jeeps were quite invisible at a hundred yards. It was as effective a piece of camouflage as I have seen.

I chose a similar sort of cave nearby and draped two tarpaulins over the edge, end to end, with pieces of mosquito netting (just brought up) to cover entrance and exit and render it fly-proof. In this way we had a safe and permanent refuge; safe because it was difficult to detect and more than once I walked right past it, and permanent enough to enable us to detain our wounded with relative comfort. We swept the sandy floor clear of animal droppings, and ran stretchers along those parts that were level. Not very roomy perhaps, but the fact that it was fly-proof made it a paradise on earth, while the little jutting rocky ledges served as racks for the medicines and stores. All we needed, I thought as I surveyed the scene, were a few of those large, coloured bowls which bedeck a chemist's shop window and then everything would have been perfect.

David Stirling was amongst the first of the patients to this new aid post, for his wrist had been giving him some more trouble. I had some plaster of Paris with me and wrapped him up in that pretty soundly—far too soundly for his liking—but judge my feelings when I discovered that the plaster would not set; it was Italian in origin and remained soft and malleable.

David viewed its soggy dampness with concern, " But how long before this sets hard ? " he asked.

" Better give it twenty-four hours," I replied, ignorant, yet determined to be on the safe side. " But what about the whiteness. Won't it make you conspicuous, and show you up a bit ? "

We painted it over with iodine, giving it a mottled and variegated appearance ; but when the next morning had dawned and

the plaster was as limp as ever, we were forced to abandon our
policy of immobilisation. I must confess that I felt a trifle foolish
about that plaster, although, as I discovered later, a great deal
of the Italian stock was found to be useless.

Having a cave like this made the sick parade a far more
pleasant affair. Desert sores could be examined better. " You
could really get down to 'em ! " as the men informed me. Nor
were our tempers tried to the breaking point.

It was disappointing to find that neither Bill Fraser nor Jim
Chambers had come up ; although the former had not been well
when he left us, whereas Jim, apparently, was making such a good
job of training the newcomers that David was loth to take him
away from Kabrit. · This decision must have been hard for
Chambers to accept, but it was a very good thing for the unit,
and the trainees were put through it in the old Jock Lewis style.
There were, however, two fresh arrivals with the relief party : an
Australian Air Force officer, Ginger Shaw, who had taken Arthur
Sharpe's place, and was acting in liasion with his squadron of
Bombays at base ; and Don Pettit, pleasant, honest, and with his
boyish freckles making you feel that you were very much his
senior in years.

On the second evening after their arrival, we held a rehearsal
for the forthcoming attack on the Sidi-Enich airfield. This time
our tactics had changed. For it should be realised that the enemy
were becoming acutely aware of our presence and were doing all
they could to discourage our attentions. At first they had thought
to counter our destruction of aircraft by making a man sleep
beneath the wing of each plane, but the subsequent loss of life
had convinced them that this was not the correct solution : it
had resulted merely in a loss of one man per plane, and presumably
there were quite a few of the ground staff who suffered from uneasy sleep at nights. Then they decided to strengthen their guards ;
that made it more difficult for our men to approach the planes,
but the raids were still successful. Later they fixed up ground
searchlights, and stationed armoured cars mounted with searchlights on some of the important airfields. Finally they began to
prepare strong ground defences round the perimeter of the fields,
and these measures, combined with the constant search of
patrolling aircraft, were making our successes less easy to achieve,

and necessitated adjustments and modification in our methods of attack.

With these factors in mind, David had decided to attack Sidi-Enich airfield with twenty jeeps, relying on the sheer weight of fire power to overcome any defence that the enemy guards might muster. For twenty jeeps meant eighty machine-guns firing in tight concentration as the cars drove, this way and that, across the aerodrome. It was a formidable prospect, I thought, as we drove out in the darkness, and practised positioning in the box formation in which the attack would be made. Situated thus we made up a square, with five jeeps to each side, and the fire would be directed outwardly as the jeeps drove on to the field. In the centre of the square was one solitary jeep belonging to Mike Sadler, a navigator attached to us from L.R.D.G., who later became commissioned in our unit. Once the jeeps had got on to the airfield and had silenced the enemy fire, they would, on the given signal, extend out to each flank in line abreast, driving across and round the field, and shooting up every plane within range. Then, having done as much damage as they could, they would leave the drome, splitting up into small parties as they did so, and make for the rendezvous. They were to lie up during the day and drive in to the rendezvous as it grew dark. Mike Sadler himself, who would be accompanied by my medical orderly, would not be driving on to the airfield but would be waiting just outside it, ready to pick up any stragglers or wounded and get them straight back to me. For my part, in view of the fact that the raiding force was splitting up into little groups of two or three jeeps, I deemed it wiser to remain at the rendezvous.

Practising changes of formation in the darkness necessitated a good vehicle control. I remember that I was in Paddy's jeep during the rehearsal, sitting perched between him and the front gunner, while the rear gunner took up most of the room behind. David was in the centre of the front row, while we were out on the right flank of the square. At the given command we moved off across the scrub-scattered plain, little dark shadows lurching and bumping, with the drivers trying hard to maintain their correct position. Suddenly a Verey light arched up from David's jeep, throwing us all into a garishly green electrical sort of relief. Immediately the machine-guns barked out with their deafening rattle, shaking the jeep with each shuddering burst and sending the tracer flying and bouncing along the ground on every side. The noise was deafening. Soon another Verey light—a red one this time—flew up from David's direction. We answered it from the flanking jeeps and ceased fire to form up in line abreast, before we opened up once more, scathing the ground before and behind us with a vicious spray. " It looked deadly—definitely it did ! " as Sergeant Bennett soliloquised afterwards ; and we improved with every repetition until eventually we had come to change position and direction without a hitch. At last David was satisfied and we turned for home.

Paddy leaned across me and addressed the front gunner. " What direction are we driving in ? " he asked.

The man scowled up at the stars, obviously uncertain and thinking hard, " North-east, I should say, sir."

" Ha ! You wouldn't get far if you had to walk back from Benghazi." Paddy revved up and changed gear. " Mind you're certain of your direction by to-morrow night."

We tucked our jeeps away into their hiding-places and went to bed early ; and as I was dropping off to sleep I could hear George Jellicoe and Sandy Scratchley (who had just returned to the unit after a bout of sickness) laughing at the way we had held this rehearsal behind the enemy's own lines, and speculating on the surprise of the Germans if only they could have seen it.

The following morning was spent in preparation and the raiding party set off just before sundown : a long line of vicious looking jeeps, each with its attendant plume of dust, standing out sharply against the evening sky. I felt sorry I was not going with them but I could not doubt the correctness of my decision. After their departure, the rendezvous seemed lonely and empty. We, who were left behind, set to work in tidying up the place and camouflaging the remaining vehicles and off-loaded stores more carefully than ever, for we expected considerable attention from aircraft on the following day. The Australian and Pettit made very good company, and we sat up till quite late that evening talking about the relative merits of our peace-time governments.

The next day passed slowly. We ate our meals cold, lest aircraft should discriminate the smoke from our cooking fires, and we passed the time reading and in leisurely speculation on the success of the raid. It must have been about four o'clock in the afternoon when we heard three long blasts on the sentry's whistle, and to our surprise we saw Paddy come driving in along the escarpment edge with a couple of jeeps. He looked as massive and unconcerned as ever, hunched up and dwarfing both driver and vehicle. After their jeeps had been hidden away we walked over to the main cave. There were a hundred questions racing through our minds and, for my part, I was very anxious to know about the position with regard to casualties. We found him lying down beside his jeep, reading the inevitable Penguin. His fingers were heavily bandaged—for he was susceptible to desert sores—and in one hand he held a fly swat, with which he made an occasional lazy swipe at a fly.

" Hallo, Paddy—how did things go ? " we asked.

" Och, it was quite a good crack." I might have known that would be the answer.

" How many planes did you get ? " " What happened ? " " Anybody hurt ? " We pestered him with questions, but he had little to say in reply.

" How many planes ? " he queried in return. " It's hard to say. Forty maybe. I doubt that we'll be claiming more than thirty (in fact we claimed twenty-five), you couldn't really count them properly. Some, we probably only damaged—they didn't all seem to catch fire. Casualties ? Rowlands was killed outright —shot through the head—but I don't think there was any one hurt badly. Just a few got nicked. Would you like to dress these sores for me ? " he added, with a glance in my direction. " They've got stuck to the bandages and the flies are after them."

As we walked over to the aid post together I asked him why he had come in to the rendezvous by daylight. At this direct question he raised his eyebrows and gave me a searching glance. Then : " I got bored with waiting," he replied briefly, " there were no planes about." And with that the subject was dismissed. I never got the full story of the raid from him, but the others gave me a rough account of what had happened.

There were few incidents, they said, in their drive towards the coast, but their course had taken them over an old battlefield, and in the dim glittering light they could make out the charred distorted figures of the dead as they lay huddled together and sprawled out across the stony ground. They got down the escarpment without any difficulty and made their way towards the airfield. It looked as if they had caught the enemy completely red-handed, for, as they drew near, they could see that the flare-paths were lit up. Some aircraft were being loaded whilst others were awaiting their turn to take off ; and others still were circling low overhead watching for a clear runway and the signal for them to come in and land. The raiding party approached cautiously, and then, when they had drawn close, they accelerated and opened up with everything they had got. It must have been a terrifying experience for the enemy. At one moment the airfield had been a hive of German efficiency, with everything running to schedule—at the next, there had been utter chaos and confusion. Sudden hell had been let loose. Tracer and incendiary was whipping past in every direction. It is true that the ground defences opened up in reply, but they were overwhelmed and quickly quietened—save for one solitary Breda, that is, which kept on firing, persistently and accurately, throughout the action. It was at this time that Rowlands was killed. The machine-guns were turned on to the Breda but were unable to silence it. However, there was no time to spare so the party were obliged to ignore it and drive on to the field itself.

As they did so, they opened up on one plane after another. An aircraft landed and came taxi-ing in down the runway. It was blown to pieces before it had drawn to a halt. Within a few minutes there were fires and explosions everywhere. Aircraft were burning like matchwood. Each one was riddled with incendiary bullets until it burst into flames ; then they drove clear to avoid the blast of the explosion. They saw one pilot lying between the wheels of his Heinkel. His plane was on fire. The flames were racing up the fuselage towards the bomb racks. They could see the bombs quite clearly. The pilot lay there, too frightened to move. As they drove away, there was a huge explosion.

They drove on. Now the flames were lighting up the field, illuminating the targets. The noise was appalling. The roar of aircraft blowing up drowned the din of the machine-guns. Yet still that one Breda fired back at them.

David sent up his Verey light. They changed formation. Then they wheeled, skirting round the airfield, looking for further planes. There was a halt. Paddy caught sight of a plane a little way off. He ran over to it and placed a short-fuse bomb in the cockpit. Then he dashed back to the jeep, only to find the raiding party was still halted. For a second or two he waited in an agony of suspense. Then he shouted the warning. A moment later the plane blew up, and they had to get away fast from the flaming wreckage. There seemed to be fires on every side. They could see the twisted skeletons of the planes burning furiously as David continued to lead them round the field until, satisfied that there was nothing more to be done, they moved off in a southerly direction under the protective fire of the rear guns. The attack had been a success. Mishaps had been scarce. A few jeeps had tip-tilted into slit trenches ; one had had to be left behind.

No sooner had they left the airfield than they began to separate out into their little prearranged groups. Mike Sadler, however, remained near the 'drome for the next hour or so. His comments were interesting. It had been a remarkable spectacle to watch, he said, "But you've got to take your hat off to those Jerries. Soon after the rest of you boys had left the 'drome," he was talking to the men who had been on the raid, "Well, within about ten minutes anyway—they had the airfield working again, with planes landing on the runway ; and before I pushed off, they had started to tow the wrecked planes away."

This came as a douche of cold water and served to sober our judgment effectively enough, but it did not alter the number of aircraft that had been destroyed.

Shortly after Paddy had left me and walked back to his jeep, I heard the shrill blasts of the whistle which I had been expecting, almost subconsciously, throughout the day. I waited, listening for the faint drone of the engines. But this time it was different ; it was not the usual solitary note. Instead there came the sound of several aircraft which soon swelled into a deep, heavy roar, and the cave was filled with noise. Pushing back the flap of the tarpaulin, I peeped out. Six Junker 87's were flying straight down the wadi, about one thousand feet up. In front of, and behind them were two M.E. 109's, weaving and zigzagging across the line of their path. They looked dark, aggressive and full of foreboding. Looking through the field glasses (a foolish thing to do in case the reflected light had attracted their attention) I could see the bombs loaded up neatly on to the racks. It was with a sigh of relief that I watched them pass by and recede into the blue—there was something very satisfactory in seeing German planes obliged to carry their bombs back with them!

That evening, soon after sundown, two more little groups returned and we were happy to see David Stirling back with us. The men were in high spirits, laughing, and telling their stories over and over again.

" Did you see that Iti try to dash across in front of our jeep? "
" Did you see that Jerry lying under his plane and the bombs all loaded up? One minute later—whoom! bang! " They shook with laughter.

" Did you see Captain Mayne blow up that Heinkel? "

" Yeah, I reckon that's how we shoud've attacked. Now if we'd all gone in on foot we might've blown the whole place to blazês."

In a way this raid had provided the men with novelty; but without a doubt most of them, especially the older hands, preferred to blow up the planes with time-bombs. Their reasons, of course, were entirely egotistical: with bombs each man could keep a tally on the number of planes which he, personally, had destroyed; there was a healthy rivalry over it; but with a machine-gun attack they were obliged to share the credit, for there were three men in each jeep, and frequently more than one jeep would be firing at the same plane. Nevertheless they were very happy, contented and tired; and catching sight of me as they trudged off with their blankets they shouted, " Done you out of a job again, Doc! Better luck next time! "

The remainder of the party came in at first light the next morning. Some rode in on jeeps while others limped in, footsore, weary and blear-eyed, for one or two of the jeeps had been hit by Breda fire and had been unable to complete the return journey to the rendezvous. Jellicoe's jeep, for instance, had kept going to within a few miles of our position before it had finally failed.

David Stirling had a few remarks to make about the raid. He called us all together soon after breakfast; and when the men had formed up round him in a silent cluster, he gave them some straightforward speaking.

" It's pretty plain," he said, " that you think you have done jolly well. But if you want to know what I think—I'll tell you. It wasn't good enough ! It wasn't nearly good enough ! Some of you were out of position. Some of you were firing at planes you could only just see ; and a lot of you were firing wildly. You must shoot low rather than high. I told you that before we started. And you must save your ammunition for the targets you can hit for certain ; other people will be shooting up those which are outside your range." He looked round at us. I had not seen him as angry as this before and I wondered what had upset him. " How many of you ran out of ammunition ? " he demanded. There was a show of hands. " There you are, you see ! It was quite unnecessary, and anyhow there's no disgrace in leaving the aerodrome with ammunition to spare. It's quite likely that you will need it on the return journey." He paused for a moment and then continued, broaching the subject which evidently had annoyed him. " And don't let me hear any of you say that you could have done better by going in on foot. You couldn't ! Get that quite clear in your minds. There were far too many sentry posts and ground defences about. You would never have got anywhere. All right ! That's all ! "

He nodded a curt dismissal. Some of the men, however, remained behind to talk with him, and I could hear his voice repeating and emphasising the points he had made. Others made off in thoughtful groups, but their spirits were too high to be depressed seriously. This was one of the few occasions that David made a speech—so to speak—and it came at a very good psychological moment, for it stopped the men from becoming too conceited or thinking that this sort of work was all plain sailing. From this raid we claimed twenty-five aircraft destroyed, but I was told later that our reconnaissance planes had confirmed many more.

The truth of David Stirling's words concerning the husbanding of ammunition was very apparent to some of the returning parties ; for, on the morning after the attack, there had been a ground mist and more than one little group had driven in and out of a German camp as they made their getaway. This gave us to realise that the Qara Matruh track was being used far more than we had previously suspected, a fact which was of some importance to us since our rendezvous was situated only about five miles to the west of it.

There was another strange incident which deserves mention. As one of our parties was racing back in the early morning, a German Feisler Stork aircraft suddenly appeared over them, flying very low. They scattered and got the guns ready for trouble when, to their surprise, the plane proceeded to land on the level ground beside them. No sooner had it drawn to a standstill than two figures jumped out of the plane and started to walk over towards them. Our men let the Germans get clear of the aircraft and then opened up on it. Notwithstanding this, one of the two men dashed back into the plane and reappeared, waving a Red Cross arm band over his head.

" You can't shoot me," he cried as he was taken prisoner, " I'm a doctor ! "

But doctor or no doctor, he and his friend were bundled unceremoniously into one of the trucks, while the plane was shot up and set on fire. Then, not wishing to remain anywhere near so conspicuous an object, they made off at top speed.

And that was how we came to have two doctors in our camp.

CHAPTER TEN

VIEWS OF A GERMAN DOCTOR

" So every bondman in his own hand bears
The power to cancel his captivity."
Julius Cæsar. SHAKESPEARE.

" And I know not to this day
Whether guest or captive ! "
World Strangeness. SIR WILLIAM WATSON.

THE DOCTOR was a good chap. At any rate that was the conclusion I reached after he had been with us for a few days. But whatever had he been doing in an aeroplane at such an early hour of the morning? He, himself, told me about it as we lay back, smoking our cigarettes after supper the next evening.

" Oh ! " he said, in his pretty good English, " we were going to Siwa. It was a sort of um—joy cruise. You understand? Yes. But you see what has happened. We start for pleasure, and we end——" he left his sentence unfinished, but, with a curiously " un-Teutonic " gesture of the hands he gave satisfactory expression to the swing of fortune's pendulum. " C'est la guerre ! " he added unexpectedly as he sat up, removed his spectacles, and breathed on them preparatory to cleaning them on his jacket.

" Where are you from ? " I asked.

" From Hamburg. You know ? "

No, I didn't, but I thought I had seen it from the sea on approaching the Kiel Canal. He nodded. Wasn't it at the Hamburg museum, I asked, that they kept a glass case covered up in a black cloth and on the outside, a notice reading, " The most dangerous thing in the world."

Again he nodded, smiling at the recollection. "You know what it is inside ? " he asked.

Yes, I did. It was a big water-lettuce.

" We have many cases of tropical diseases in Hamburg, you

understand," he said seriously. "Very many cases, because so many seamen always are there."

Our conversation veered round to medical subjects. I gathered that he had been to Abyssinia after qualifying, and had worked there for eighteen months. A curious job, I thought—the sort of appointment our "chiefs" at hospital would have dissuaded us from accepting—but perhaps he was going in for tropical medicine as a specialty. Anyhow the war had recalled him and he appeared to have spent most of his time in Germany since then, having arrived in the desert only comparatively recently. Despite this, I saw that he boasted the coloured ribbon of the iron cross on his lapel, and could not help but wonder what class it was. What a strange method of decoration it seemed, to have the distinction divided up, like railway compartments, into three classes. Could you feel really satisfied with only a third-class to your credit? Why, the very appellation, third-class, seemed to detract from any sense of achievement!

He had little information to give me on the subject of desert sores, which, it transpired, was as much a source of worry to them as it was to us. But they had isolated a spirillum in many of their cases which was something I had not heard of before. Their routine treatment consisted in the application of sulphonamide and vaseline, already made up as dressings and carried about by their soldiers; a typical piece of German thoroughness.

"Where have you been working in the desert?" I asked.

"In Bardia. You know? A small hospital, it is, with tents. That was before I go on my air journey." He smiled. "Now I wonder where I go."

"Probably to a prison camp, where you will be the medical officer. Or perhaps to a little hospital. We have got some in Egypt for prisoners."

"You think so? And I go there for the rest of the war?" The prospect did not seem to appeal to him.

"Well, that rather depends on the war." Once on this topic I could not refrain from asking his opinion. "Do you think you are going to win?" I inquired.

"Yes. I think so."

"Soon?"

" In about two years, I think."

" What about Russia ? She will not be easy to beat."

" In Russia, we shall reach the Volga this year. Then next year we shall go on and Russia will be defeated."

" You are sure ? " I queried. " Because, to me, fighting Russia seems to be like fighting some fatal disease. You can advance here, and you can make improvements there ; but all the time the disease is waiting, and once your efforts begin to flag—you know, begin to slow down—then the enemy closes in on you."

He did not seem impressed with my simile. Attentive, certainly, but I could see that I was not cutting any ice. " We shall win," he said emphatically.

" But look at the size of Russia ? Look at all the country behind Moscow ! The war will not be over as soon as you have captured Moscow, you know ! "

" We shall win," he repeated, " because we hate them so much. They are not—civilised. We find the bodies of our soldiers badly um—what is your word—mutilated, yes ? And our prisoners we find have been tortured."

I changed the subject. " Well, how about Egypt, now ? Do you think you will conquer us here ? "

He nodded. " Yes," he said quite quietly, without a hint of a swagger, " I think we take Egypt in two months."

" If it was not for the war," I replied, " I wish you would take it. I think you would clean it up for us very well ! "

He blinked at me seriously from behind his spectacles, " But Cairo is a nice place, I think. Much green," he waved his arm around vaguely, as if to summon up a picture of lush pastures, milk and honey, " and you say it is—um, dirty and the Egyptians not clean ? That is strange. We hear it is a very good place to go to."

I was sorry to have to disillusion him.

" Anyhow," I went on, returning to the war in general, " suppose you beat Russia in two years, and suppose you conquer Egypt and Palestine. What next ? What about England ? "

He thought this over. " We conquer Russia and Egypt. Yes. And then we take India. No, I think the Japanese take India ; they are very good fighters and——"

" Why do you say they are good fighters ? "

" Because they fight until they die. They do not give up or surrender when——"

" The same as the Russians. They don't surrender much either ! "

" No. That is not the same. The Russians are—fanatics. Yes? Not good."

" But you can't praise the Japanese and condemn the Russians on the same score," I said. " Anyhow, I hate the Japanese, don't you ? "

At this directness, the ghost of a smile flickered over his face. " Ah, I do not know the Japanese. But we hear that they fight very well."

" All right, then," I continued remorselessly, determined to see this argument through. " You beat Russia, you conquer Egypt, Palestine and the rest of the Middle East and you share India with Japan. What then. What about invading England and winning the war ? "

Silence for a few moments.

" And what about America, for that matter ? " I added.

" I do not know," he remarked eventually, and then paused again. " I do not know. England will give in, you understand ? Yes. England will give in. The blockade. Yes." And then, not feeling very satisfied, I suppose, at the way things were going, he turned the tables round. " And you say you will win the war ? "

" Yes."

" Then how are you going to beat Germany ? " again that suggestion of a smile.

" Well," I started off. " Well, you see, it's like this." And then, when I thought of our present situation—of the way we were just hanging on for our dear lives to a little strip of desert in front of Alexandria ; of how we seemed to have our backs to the wall everywhere—I became very much aware that I had not got the vaguest notion as to how we would win the war. Of a sudden the situation struck me as being very humorous and I rolled over on to my back and laughed.

" I haven't the slightest idea," I said, and at that he started laughing too. But I do not think he really understood what I was

laughing about, and for the life of me I could not have explained
it to any one.

In view of the increased amount of traffic passing up and
down the Qara Matruh track and the consequent insecurity of
our position, David Stirling decided to move the site of the
rendezvous. The fresh location that he chose was some fifteen
miles west of the present rendezvous, where the uneven ground
denoted on the map would probably afford us satisfactory cover.
Accordingly, we busied ourselves in packing up the aid post,
while the stores were made ready to load on the lorries at nightfall. For we were doing nothing until it grew dark since,
of late, hostile air activity had been sufficient to make David
issue the order that we were not to walk about in between mealtimes more than was necessary. Thus it was not until after sundown that we emerged from our hiding-place, ran the lorries over
to their respective loading points and heaved the stores aboard.
Looking back on it now, one is struck by our remarkably good
fortune in remaining undetected at this rendezvous. For we were
situated about thirty miles south of the coast and about five miles
from a track which was in frequent use. Further, our jeeps by
now must have made a sufficient number of tracks running up and
down the escarpment edge to attract the attention of any inquisitive low flying aircraft. These considerations, together with
the fact that we were moving away from a fly-ridden area, were
sufficient to make us all welcome the change of air.

Glancing round in the half-light, as we waited for the signal
to move off, I was pleased to see the German doctor travelling
on our three-tonner. He saluted me as correctly as ever, and took
the opportunity to inform me that if, at any time, I should require
any medical assistance, I had but to let him know and he would
be only too happy to be of some use. His companion, the sergeant-
pilot, looked a morose sort of fellow, I thought, but then it was
difficult to judge when a man could not speak your language.
Two Palestinians, Karl and Joseph, served to make up our mixed
complement, and we were not kept waiting long before it was
time to start.

Fifteen miles on the map is little enough. But when you are
travelling by night over rough desert, with occasional halts to

check on your position, and very frequent halts for reasons which you can never ascertain, then a short journey takes up an incredible amount of time. After one such night drive you are left with the impression that you have spent as much time in halting as you have in moving. So it was on this occasion, and the only feature of the drive that I can recall was that the German doctor was suffering from a severe attack of " Gyppy tummy " ; and, possessed with the necessary articles, he would dash forth into the night, pursued closely by his guard, at every available opportunity. It was bitterly cold, travelling in an open lorry, and we huddled together, drawing the blankets tight over our heads and shoulders and trying, with little success, to snatch some sleep.

Daylight found us in a shallow hollow of ground, surrounded by rough undulating rock to the west and extending away flatly to the east. To the north and south were bare conical hills while in the centre was a large circle of thick scrub in which we dispersed our jeeps. The three-tonners were run into the little narrow wadis and concealed fairly well by camouflage nets, stretched across them from the adjacent rock surfaces. The next procedure in camouflage consisted in pulling up large tufts of camel thorn and scrub from different parts of the ghôt, and throwing them over the camouflage net in order to break up the outline of the vehicle underneath and render it indistinguishable from the air. I had to smile as I watched Karl helping at this work, for he was arranging his tiny little pieces of scrub and dry thistle with all the fastidiousness and delicacy of a fine craftsman. Looking rather like some superior flower shop assistant in the West End, he would place one little tuft deftly over the corner of the three-ton lorry, and step back to admire the artistic effect. " Goot," he would say as he arranged another little piece to his evident satisfaction, and then smiled round at us with happy pride in his handiwork— " Goot ! "

" Come on, Karl," I said. " For Heaven's sake, let's get a move on ! " But nothing could disturb his equanimity or his daintiness of pattern.

They were strange chaps, these two Palestinians, and what surprised me as much as anything was the way in which they would chatter away with the prisoners. Have the Jews got no pride ? I asked myself, as I heard the guttural German pass backwards and forwards. If I was a Jew, I could never reconcile myself to a German. Yet here they were, apparently on the best of terms ; and one afternoon Karl said to me, " I have been talking with the pilot and he is not such a bad man. He says that he hated the English before, but now he realises that he has been told a lot of lies about them and that the English are a good people." For a moment I felt like telling Karl that if I was a Jew, I would slit a German's throat as soon as talk to him. But somehow Karl was such a kind old chap (for he was by no means a youngster) that I had not got the heart to say anything.

We remained at this rendezvous for about a week, during which time several little patrols went out on raids. Once again our water supplies had grown short, so short in fact that we had to send Paddy out to obtain fresh supplies from a secret water dump near the Matruh Siwa track. In the meanwhile, our daily water-bottles were withdrawn and we were obliged to suffice with the tea at meal times. There was little for us to do and our time passed correspondingly slowly. In the morning we would lie in the shadow on one side of the lorry ; in the afternoon we would be under its belly, gazing up at the massive framework and feeling the suffocating strength of the heat ; in the evenings we would crawl round to the lengthening shade on the other side. It was interesting to note the symmetry of the white sinuous lines which had formed on our backs, thighs, and legs from the evaporation of the small trickles of perspiration. But there were some days when it seemed almost too hot to read, and I can recall one afternoon when, unable to take much interest in Jane Austen, I found myself involved in another heavy argument with the German doctor. Somehow or other, I cannot remember how, the subject had turned on to the Red Cross.

" Why is it," I asked, " that you attack the Red Cross ? "

He looked surprised. " The Germans ? " he queried.

" Yes. You have sunk several of our hospital ships. Once, I went on, " I was in Tobruk—when it was surrounded, you know. Three Junkers planes bombed the hospital in the town and three bombed the beach hospital. One of the planes was shot down but the pilot jumped out. He said it was as a reprisal for the British bombing of hospitals in Germany. Soon afterwards some more planes attacked a hospital ship in the harbour. Then at other times some of our hospital ships have been sunk by submarines."

It was a silly question to ask, I suppose, for how could he have given a satisfactory reply? Yet that was the feeling these German prisoners provoked in me. They had started the war and I found myself wanting to bully them and make them answer for their misdeeds.

This doctor did not attempt an explanation. "But," he remarked, "we, also, have had hospital ships sunk. How? Usually by torpedo, I think. Also they say that when the sun is bright and, um—shines off, you know?—shines off the water, it is hard to see the marks of the red cross. I do not know. In Germany, of course, we have many hospitals hit by bombs. Goebbels says on the wireless that the British aim for the hospitals, but we do not believe that."

I was interested to hear him criticise Goebbels, "Would you have dared to say that in Germany?" I asked.

"Please?"

"Could you criticise—would you talk like that in Germany?"

"Yes." But he did not sound convincing.

"If you were on a train in Berlin, could you say 'Hitler is a fool'?"

"That would not be good—to say that. But we do not think that."

"In England we can say Mr. Churchill is a fool. Nothing would happen."

He looked unimpressed, and somehow it did not sound very impressive the way I had put it. "What of your King?" he asked.

"Well. Nobody would want to say it of the King."

"In Germany nobody wants to say it of Hitler."

"Yes, but we *could* say it if we *wanted* to."

"Ah!"

This was becoming rather childish.

"What about the wireless?" I asked. "Do you listen to the British wireless stations?"

"Yes. Sometimes," he nodded his head, "in the desert."

"A lot of you?"

"Five or six, perhaps."

"What would happen if you were reported?"

At that he smiled and there was almost a twinkle in his brown eyes. "We are very careful," he said, "when we listen to the British stations."

By a curious coincidence Jellicoe had met this doctor's wife at a luncheon party in Hamburg during the middle 'thirties. What a strange place and what peculiar circumstances in which to meet her husband! This was an unlucky rendezvous for Jellicoe, as it turned out, for it was while we were here that he twisted his knee badly. It was not the first time that this accident had befallen him since he had previously had trouble with it when he had been ski-ing in Switzerland. A strained ligament, he had been told, was the cause of the repeated injury. Looking at it on this occasion I decided that he had torn some fibres of the internal ligament of the knee joint, and bound it up accordingly with strict instructions to rest. These, of course, were ignored, and he could be seen, not infrequently, hobbling backwards and forwards from his jeep.

"Ah!" observed the German doctor as he watched Jellicoe, pipe in mouth, lurching along through the scrub with a grim, determined expression on his face, "Ah! The cartilage is hurt, yes?"

"No!" I replied firmly. "The ligament is hurt."

"Ah!" he repeated, and, as if by common consent, the subject was not broached again.

Later on, when we arrived in Cairo, the English doctor who met us had soon noticed Jellicoe and his limp.

"Ha!" he remarked briskly, rubbing his hands together, "looks like a nice cartilage!"

I gave him a sombre look. "No," I said, "a torn internal collateral ligament."

"Ah," he opened his mouth as if to say more and then catching sight of my face, he desisted, "Ah, yes," he remarked blankly.

As a matter of fact it was both a ligament and a cartilage!

However, to return to the scene at the rendezvous. David Stirling was in frequent touch with base by means of wireless communication, and it now appeared that there was going to be a really big raid in the near future. It would be a raid that would necessitate our return to Kabrit in order that we might refit and re-equip. Consequently we were going to move back eastwards to our old rendezvous, wait there a day or two for any patrols which were out, and then some of us would return by plane, while others brought the transport back through the Qattara depression.

I shall never forget the evening when we moved back to the old rendezvous. We had loaded up the lorries quite early but were waiting till about one o'clock for the benefit of a waning moon. Sergeant Almonds, the German doctor and myself were smoking a final cigarette before we retired to bed. I think it was Sergeant Almonds who started talking about the stars and I know I soon took him up. Between us we pointed out Arcturus, Deneb and Vega over to the east and then Antares in the south. We looked round for some more.

" Der Milchestrasse," came the solemn voice of the doctor. Oh, yes—the milky way. We agreed, it was looking very fine. In Austria, the doctor said, they used sometimes to go for walks across the country by starlight. "And there," he continued, pointing to the north, " the little pole star—very small but very important, I think. You understand ? "

We nodded agreement, and, having finished my cigarette, I turned to go.

" Good-night," said the doctor as I was walking away.

" Good-night," I called back over my shoulder.

A fine time to be saying good-night, I thought. Good-night, indeed, when, in three hours' time, we would be bumping and jolting back on one of those ghastly night drives ! Thinking along these rather dismal lines I had just unrolled my blankets, when I heard someone running towards me in the darkness. To my surprise it turned out to be Sergeant Almonds. He was short of breath.

" The Germans," he panted. " Have you seen them ? "

" No. Why, what's the matter ? "

" They've gone, sir."

" Gone ? "

" Yes, sir. They've vanished all right ! "

" But what was the guard doing ? "

" Well, it was like this. One of them—the pilot, I think it was —just walked round the front of the lorry to get his blankets. But he didn't come back ! The guard got a bit suspicious and went round after him to see where he was. There were some of our chaps nearby, but none of them had noticed him. Then, of course, when he went back he found the doctor had gone, too."

" Hell ! " I said, " and there we were, talking about the stars ! "

" I know, sir."

We walked over to Stirling's jeep, only to find that he had already dispatched search parties which were moving out in a widening circle with the ghôt as the central point. They had orders to stay out until they were recalled to the laager by a Verey light. Feeling that this affair had a certain personal touch about it, I decided to go out myself and join in the hunt ; and as I loaded my dusty, neglected revolver, I began to consider just which was the most likely direction that they would have taken. Now if I were in their shoes, I thought, what would I have done ? Why, I would have made off to the north of course— following the doctor's little Pole star ! Or was that too obvious ! Would they break away first into the rough country to the west, before they turned north towards the coast ? In all probability, they would ; but I could hear search parties moving out in that direction, so I decided to make for two small conical hills which jutted up blackly against the northern night sky.

What a strange situation for a doctor to be in, I thought as I padded along, peering this way and that and clutching tightly at my revolver. Whatever would my parents say if they could see me now ? This type of thing was all right in the whiteman v. redskin sort of game, but here it was so very serious and yet, at the same time, you had to keep nudging yourself to realise that it was not just a schoolboy prank. If I saw them, I knew I would have to shoot, doctor or no doctor ; and I sent up a little prayer that someone else might catch them, and that no unhappy duties would fall on me.

Having arrived at the nearer hill, I circled round it cautiously and then climbed up the steep incline, inspecting each little cave and boulder as I did so. At any moment I might hear a voice, " Don't shoot. We surrender. We are your prisoners ! " But nothing occurred. It was all dark, shadowy and very empty ; and I seemed to be making a most appalling noise as I dislodged clinkers and stones and sent them rattling away down the slopes to the level ground below. I searched the other hill but with no better success, so I decided to sit up there quietly, peering down into the darkness below, ready to pick up the faintest movement or the slightest sound. In fact it was a situation to which the Saint or Bulldog Drummond might have done adequate justice—but hardly the one for me, I considered as I laid my revolver dowu awkwardly. For the thrill of the chase had begun to wear off as far as I was concerned. It was as silent as the grave sitting up there in the middle of the night, and I felt I might well be a hundred miles from the next human soul.

Suddenly I heard a low mumble of voices. I was on the alert immediately and picked up my revolver. The voices stopped. Noiselessly I flicked back the safety catch and crouched down low. So far so good. I was doing fine! But then one of my feet slipped, dislodging a stone ; and for the next few seconds I was painfully conscious of the noise it made as it leaped and bounded right down to the bottom. I cursed it freely for it seemed as if it would never hold its peace. Then I heard the voices again ; they were closer now and I could just make out the words.

" There 'e is, Nobby—up on the 'ill—don't you see 'im ? "

" Where ? Where ? " There was far too much eagerness in that interrogation for my liking.

" Up there. Look ! "

" Hoy ! " I shouted. " It's me."

" Who's that ? "

" It's me. It's the doctor."

" What yer on, matey ? " a voice sang out, and I knew it was Sergeant Hardy. " We nearly had yer then."

There was a clattering of stones as they came running up the hill. " We could 'ave drilled you like a sieve, sitting up there so nice and pretty," he remarked as he sat down beside me.

" Thank you," I replied, a little coolly.

Somehow, we felt, if the prisoners had made their escape in this direction, there would be little chance of our catching them now ; and it was with a certain amount of relief that we saw the green Verey light arch up, tremble, and then fade away. What little thrill there had been at first, had by now given way to a sense of disappointment and sullenness at the thought of the cheerless night drive ahead. We arrived back at the laager to find that the prisoners had not been caught ; and after a brief sleep we set off back to the old rendezvous, leaving Jellicoe behind with two jeeps in order to continue the search on the following morning. It was most improbable that they would be found, but it was worth our while to make every effort. For we considered that it would take them only two days' marching to reach their own troops on the coast, and then our position would be compromised. We did not grudge them their escape—they had both refused parole. But it did put us in an uncomfortable position ; and the only saving grace was that, in two days' time, we should be making tracks for home.

It was with such thoughts as these to keep us company that we made the dreary return journey to our old rendezvous.

CHAPTER ELEVEN

WE RETURN BY AIR

" For solitude sometimes is best society,
And short retirement urges sweet return."

Paradise Lost. MILTON.

WE CAMOUFLAGED up especially well when we arrived back at the old rendezvous, and spent a very long day in trying to sleep or read. In doing anything, in fact, rather than allowing ourselves to realise how near the time had come for our return to base, for last minute disappointments were too frequent to make pleasant speculation worth while. And, of course, the chances of enemy interest in our location were increasing with every hour, not to mention the nice distinctive tracks we had made between the two rendezvous ! Any pilot flying over and noting these tracks running east-west in the middle of nowhere would, if he had any intelligence, become extremely suspicious.

Towards the evening Jellicoe's two jeeps were seen approaching us across the plain from the west, and as they drew nearer we could see that they were grossly overloaded : there appeared to be about six men in each jeep. Very mystified, we came out from our caves to meet them and found that they had, indeed, brought back quite a number of strangers ; but there was not a sign of the missing prisoners. The newcomers were a mixed bunch with an R.A.S.C. officer in charge, a voluble South African sergeant who could not be accused of restraint, and about eight more, some of whom were plainly unwell. While the jeeps were being run away out of sight, Jellicoe introduced the newcomers by explaining how they had chanced to meet.

The two jeeps, he said, had been driving round the area west of the rendezvous and had seen nothing of the German doctor and his friend when, quite suddenly, they caught sight of a stationary lorry in the distance. As they got the guns ready and approached they could see that there were men in the lorry ; so

without wasting any time they opened fire. To their surprise,
however, far from there being any answering fire, the figures had
leaped out of the lorry and disappeared from sight on the far side.
But they were even more surprised when the figures came out
towards the jeeps with their hands up, and when, apart from two
miserable Italians, they had turned out to be British troops. In
fact it would be hard to say just who were the more surprised,
Jellicoe's party or the newcomers. as they discovered each other's
identity and exchanged their rather inadequate greetings. The
account given by the R.A.S.C. officer was quite straightforward.
He and his party had escaped from Tobruk prison camp and,
despite the handicap of one man suffering severely with dysentery,
they had kept together, and were making tracks eastwards towards
our own lines when they had sighted and captured an Italian
Lancia lorry, complete with driver and passenger. Thinking that
Siwa oasis was occupied by British troops, they had ordered the
driver to take them down the Matruh Siwa track. But things had
gone wrong—the driver had lost his way and the petrol had run
out. Hardly a pleasant prospect for a group of men, already pretty
exhausted, with low water and food reserves. It was while they
were considering just what to do next that Jellicoe had interrupted
their thoughts so briskly.

However Jellicoe's patrol did not remain in the vicinity for
long, and having given sufficient food and water to the cringing,
fawning Italians, with adequate directions to the nearby Matruh
Siwa track, they left the pair of them to walk the distance, loaded
the others on to the two jeeps and trundled slowly back.

At this stage it might be pertinent to remark on the extremely
good performance shown by these jeeps. They were as reliable
as anything on four wheels and their only drawback for rough
desert work was the low setting of the sump. On account of the
relatively large number of " holed sumps " we were getting, we
found it worth our while to construct a protective underplate ;
but, apart from this disadvantage, one can only say that we put
them through every conceivable form of hard driving and they
emerged from the experience apparently none the worse. Later
on, we added an extra petrol tank below the passenger's seat and
this gave each vehicle a greater range of action. Jellicoe's patrol
provided an example of the load a jeep could take over rough

country, and there were other occasions when they were obliged to carry as many as eight men each.

In retrospect, then, we considered that we had done well enough on the exchange of prisoners, the only drawback being the fact that the site of our rendezvous had been compromised. With regard to our return, David Stirling explained his plans. The majority of us would be returning by air, and he had arranged over the wireless that three Bombay planes should land by night and pick us up at an old disused landing field to the east of the Qara Matruh track. Ginger Shaw had already driven over to inspect it and had vetted it as being serviceable, but first a runway would have to be cleared of stones and boulders. Accordingly he and another officer were setting off after supper ; they would clear it during the night, hide up nearby throughout the day, and guide us in by torch flashes at about ten o'clock on the following evening. We would then make a flare path and await the arrival of the aircraft which were due to come in at midnight.

In addition to this Paddy was going to take back a lorry and jeep convoy through the Qattara depression, heading south for the depression itself but driving warily in the vicinity of the Qara Matruh track which we knew the enemy had mined, in places, for our especial benefit. Paddy, in fact, was taking most of the transport, with an allocation of one driver per vehicle—a tiring proposition for a long desert drive. That left a small party—a handful of men with two or three lorries—whose orders were to remain at the rendezvous until the two small patrols, at present engaged on operations, had come in ; then the whole lot would follow in Paddy's footsteps. It would be a wait of not more than a day or two so the prospect was not as unpleasant as might be supposed.

That evening Ginger Shaw left us at about eight o'clock, heading eastwards for the landing ground ; and the next morning Paddy set off with his convoy, trusting to the cover afforded by the heat haze. We lingered on through the tedious hours of the day, and happy indeed we were to see the red sun dip down, and no evidence as yet of aircraft or ground forces in search of us. Then we packed up our few belongings and bundled them together on the three-tonner. As we rumbled away along the escarpment edge, I watched all the little caves, inlets and boulders

that I had grown to know so well ; and as they receded I bade
them all good-bye. For I had come to hate the sight of them, as
we seldom can hate the inanimate, and yet, as I left, I realised
that this was another chapter ended. And I thought how fortunate
we had been, living here between these two tracks as we had done
throughout the past five weeks ; for we had come here early in
July and now it was August. So I was grateful, too, for the cover
and concealment these crannies had afforded us, and for everything we had learned in this place. It was a feeling that was
accentuated perhaps by seeing Sgt. Almonds as he stood, a lean
brown solitary figure clad in shorts and sandals, waving farewell
from the foot of the escarpment. Then he turned back to his
hiding-place in a way that made him seem infinitely lonely, and
made me feel unhappy to be leaving him. The next moment we
had climbed the uneven ridge and were bumping along the open
stony desert towards a darkening Eastern sky. Behind us was the
dying flame of colour in the west, and in front was the track and
the little landing strip on which we were placing all our hopes of
withdrawal.

By this time to-morrow, I thought, we would know the
pleasures of water and food without limit ; we would know the
restful security of a mind without apprehension and anxiety ; of
drinks, and maybe a girl or two. Was it too early yet to permit
ourselves to imagine what beer tasted like ? Or the thought of a
John Collins ? Could we now, and without heart-rendings, consider the sound of running water and a bath ? Ah, God, a bath
and the smell of soap ! Just these next few hours and we would
be able to sleep in a tent ; we could walk inside a building ; we
could rest in the coolness of shade. Real shade ! We could get
most gloriously drunk. . . .

After some hesitation we found the track and crossed over,
heading towards the Bir Chaldee that adjoined the flat stretch of
desert which had been used as a landing ground. Here we found
Ginger looking very pleased to see us all and shivering in the night
wind as he showed us the strip he had cleared for the planes. We
had no time to waste so we got busy at once, filling empty petrol
tins with sand and then soaking the sand thoroughly with petrol.
When we had laid out a sufficient number of these in a long row
we put matches to them, and, in less time than it takes to record,

we had our flare path ready to guide in the planes. With a prayer in our hearts that it might not be difficult to recognise from the air, we waited patiently for the incoming aircraft. Over to the north of us, Matruh and Bagoush were being bombed by the R.A.F. ; we could see the orange flares hanging in the sky like Christmas lanterns ; we could see the occasional sudden flash of an explosion, followed, a few seconds later, by a little shudder which touched the earth like a mother's sigh.

If we could see *them* so clearly, then what, I wondered, were the chances that night fighters or other enemy aircraft might become interested in our night's welfare. It was a sober thought and did not bear too much reflection. I walked over to one of the flares beside which a group of Frenchmen were standing and, as I did so, became aware of the drone of an approaching plane. A minute later and it could be seen, winking down a light to us as a recognition signal while it circled overhead. Ginger Shaw replied with his Aldis lamp.

" Which side of the flares do you think it will land ? " I inquired of the French.

They turned to me with cheerful faces. " We do not seenk eet matter so much, provided 'e do land all right." They laughed merrily at their humour.

Well, maybe not, I said to myself, but it might be wiser to get away from the flares since it was evident that the plane must run in just beside them. I started to walk away and, at that moment the plane came in very low, about fifteen feet from the ground. I just caught sight of it in the darkness as it came rushing towards me like a huge bird, and then as I fell down it roared past with a swirl of air. However, that was only the trial run and after one more circle it came in straight over the flares, straddling them, and leaping and careering along the ground like a live thing. By the ruddy light of the flames, I could see the men—little black figures in silhouette—tumbling and falling away to either side like lively ninepins. It was a remarkable spectacle and I imagine the plane must have come very near to crashing. I began to appreciate the courage of those men in landing their aircraft under such impromptu conditions. Sandy Shaw, who was busy signalling them in, suddenly had his Aldis lamp knocked out of his hands ; and with a stream of curses he pursued the pilot who, by now, had turned his plane round and was uncertain where to park it. These men were fellow members of Sandy's squadron, and for the next few minutes there was a lively flow of Australian language as the repartee was thrown backwards and forwards in the best of humour. David Stirling, too, had been obliged to get down quickly while the plane bounced over him ; but he reappeared, sucking quietly at his pipe, as if it was the most natural thing in the world to have happened.

Well, that was one plane anyway, and we were glad to see it taxi away into the darkness and out of the light of the flares. Soon afterwards the second plane came in and made a better landing, although on this occasion the pilot was not harassed by seeing people dart away from beneath his wheels. It drew up beside the other plane and then we waited for the third ; but after a time our hopes began to fall and we douched our flares lest we should attract undue attention. The plane never came ; and later we found out that it had missed its bearings some while before and actually, while we were waiting, was on its homeward run.

We hung on until three o'clock, however, and then decided that it would be foolish to delay longer, for the planes were un-armed and it would be preferable to return in darkness. By now the bombing of the coast had quietened down, and in order to avoid any flak or night fighters, we were going to fly south and then eastwards over the Qattara depression. The next point to settle was : who should now be left behind ; and after some con-sideration it was determined that we should all try and get into the two planes. It meant overloading, but it was very necessary for us to get back as soon as possible so that we might prepare for the next raid. Therefore we all bundled inside, very close together, body to body. There was some shouting in the dark-ness outside. The door was slid across. Soon the port engine had stuttered and broken into a shattering roar. A minute later and the starboard engine had joined in the din, rocking the aircraft with the violent vibration. It was very close in there, and we seemed to be jammed together tight and with no means of exit. Through the dusty window I could see the flares being lit up once more—a little row of yellow beads. For one fleeting moment I saw the blurred shape of the other plane race past them as it headed out into the blackness beyond. Then our engines were

tearing madly as they were revved up and tested out. We turned
slowly and taxied over to one end of the flare path. The engines
revved up again and we began to move away ; we could feel the
jerk of the acceleration. Outside the flares were flicking past one
after another at an increasing speed, and we could see the figures
standing by them before they were suddenly snatched from our
sight. We lifted off the ground—up—then down again. We
bumped. Up once more, and again down. Then we had lifted
clear, with not too much room to spare from the uneven hummocky
ground beyond.

I found myself sitting next to Jellicoe, his heavily bandaged
knee showing whitely in the darkness, but apart from that I
could see nothing inside the plane. It was simply the tightly
packed, closed-in atmosphere that one could sense. Outside the
desert was faint and milky white, with dark irregular shadows for
the patches of scrub. We settled down and prepared to go to sleep.

Suddenly the plane fell. It was a dreadful sensation. Unable
to do anything, we might have been in a lift whose support has
given way and sent it dropping down a pitch-black lift-shaft. In
fact, of course, we had merely struck a down current, and had
fallen a matter of five hundred feet in a vertical " bump." It
seemed that we were falling through the darkness for an age. Then
came the full impact of the shock as we hit the " firmer " air
below ; there was a lurch and a crash ; odd pieces of kit came
bouncing down on our heads in animated packages. For a few
moments more, the plane was reeling and out of control. Several
of the men jumped from the seats in alarm.

" Sit down ! " It was Jellicoe's voice coming through the
blackness above the roar of the engine. We could see the white
patches of one another's faces sufficiently well to be able to detect
movement. " Sit down," he shouted, " and give the pilot a
chance ! "

A moment later and everything was under control ; we droned
on monotonously through the night. But there was no sleep for
some of us after that incident. I sat awake, listening to the steady
throb of the engines, feeling the lift and fall of the plane in the air
currents, and watching the slow spread of the luminous half-light.
On the opposite side of the plane I could just distinguish the men,
sprawled out in all the strange, unguarded attitudes which sleep

had given to them. Then as dawn brightened and each detail slowly emerged, I could differentiate and recognise them—the furrowed lines across the forehead, the expression on the face, almost innocent despite the biblical appearance of the thick mass of tangled hair and the heavy growth of beard, while those others who had not grown beards so readily seemed almost puerile in comparison.

I turned and peered out of the window, looking through the gaps in the cloud banks and trying to recognise the grey patterned fields of the delta below. Once or twice we passed aerodromes with their flare-paths shining up at us like the bulbs of a seaside pier. We circled over one of them several times and then made off in a fresh direction. Now what on earth is the matter, I wondered, as I tried to fathom this fresh mystery, and then resigned myself to the unknown. It was the sand, I discovered later, which was blowing across the landing strips and making them impossible to use. Soon the sun had come up, fringing the clouds with blood as they stretched away to a dull horizon. We flew low over the Nile with its ships and feluccas looking like a child's playthings, and shortly afterwards we touched down for a perfect landing.

What a sigh of relief! Solid earth once more! Jumping out we could see Ginger Shaw wipe a bleary eye, swallow several times at the taste in his mouth, and peer down at us from the cockpit window. David Stirling laughed up and ragged him for, when the plane had fallen, Ginger had wakened up very suddenly indeed and had taken a keen interest in what was going on ; but as soon as he had seen that everything was all right he had relaxed and yawned with exaggerated casualness. Then he had stretched out his legs and started to rub his right knee vigorously. " My knee ! " he had shouted to David who was next to' him. " My knee. Cramp ! Woke me up ! " A piece of guile which, it appeared, had deceived nobody. And now he was obliged to reply to tender inquiries about " the old gentleman's gout."

" Yer bassterds ! " he shouted down at us, " wait till I get hold of yer."

CHAPTER TWELVE

OBSERVATIONS ON CAIRO

" Nothink for nothink 'ere, and precious little for six-pence."
Punch, 1869.

THE first feeling that followed the relief of a safe arrival, was one
of complete anticlimax. We felt foolish. We felt that we looked
foolish : that our beards, our ragged dirty clothes and our sandals
were out of place. There were so many charming, clean-
uniformed Air Force people about ; there were so few of us.
Voices sounded so cultured, remarks so irrelevant. Nearly everyone stopped to stare at us in what appeared to be a pitying sort
of way, as if we were a group of unclean beggars ; and having
been so careless about our appearance over the past weeks, we
were now acutely self-conscious of our deficiencies. However,
Peter Warr and Bernard Schott had the transport ready and,
after a rapid breakfast in a very polite mess where the occupants
just *looked* at us, we hurried away and drove fast down the desert
road to our camp at Kabrit.

We drew up outside the office and, pushing aside the flap of
the " post tent," collected our mail. How strange to see the
same handwriting on one letter after another and read our news
in serial form. There were a dozen letters for me, I found, one
or two parcels and a few magazines. Feeling very satisfied with
my haul, I gathered them together and made my way towards
my tent.

" Why ! If it isn't the old apothecary, himself, once more
amongst us ! How about a beer, Doc. ? "

Of course it was Bobby Dodds—you couldn't mistake that
greeting—and looking round I saw his moustaches poking out of
his tent entrance. And then, of a sudden, Eric Parten had
appeared quietly from nowhere with a remark to the effect that
a drink was not such a bad idea, at that. Soon Jim Chambers had
joined them. He was looking fitter than ever and demanded that
I should give him all the latest " gen." So, having put my letters

aside for a quieter occasion, I walked over to the mess with them. We had our own mess now, a very posh affair, with Corporal Leitch greeting me with a twinkle in his eye and a "Guid mornin', doctor, it's fine to see ye back again " as he whipped the caps off the bottles. It was not long before Bill Fraser, and Forceps and Fangs, the two dental lads who messed with us, had got wind of our arrival and had popped in to see us. They kept pestering us with questions and, before I knew where I was, I found that it was *I* who was telling the tales and spinning the yarns, and beginning to feel quite an old hand as I did so—and possibly a bit of a daredevil, too, as I glossed over some adventure or hardship with a few airy phrases and ordered another drink all round. . . .

After the lingering enjoyment of those first few drinks I was happy to get under the shower and scrub my body hard, revelling in the luxury of water slipping down my face and over my shoulders, listening to all the musical liquid noises as it drained away, rejoicing in the soap and the clean smell of the rough towel. Happy to see my tent once more, the old camp bed, the books stacked neatly on the blanket-covered table, the hurricane lamp : everything that seemed to be familiar and permanent welcoming me back. Thank God the inanimate does not change, I thought, as I sat down and picked up the first letter. It was from home and had been posted in June. In it were all those little items of news which could make you feel so terribly home-sick. . . . The roses in the garden were coming on nicely. . . . The lawnmower was not working properly and it was such a job to get someone to mend it these days. . . . Something would have to be done about that patch at the bottom of the garden. There was so little sun down there that it was difficult to get anything to grow properly. . . . The tortoises were becoming very frisky now that the weather was getting warmer. The cats were still as quarrelsome as ever. . . . Mr. Howden had passed away quietly one night during the week. What a blessing there had been no pain. . . . It was very quiet on the sea front these days compared with the summers before the war. . . . They had taken their books down the other day and sat reading. . . . The sea had looked so tempting. . . . Some of the old stagers had been playing bowls on the lawns behind. . . . It had seemed so peaceful in spite of the barbed wire. . . . Did I want any socks because they were knitting some ? . . . How nice it was having the longer evenings ! . . . They were hoping the fine weather would keep up. . . . Last week the cricket match had had to be abandoned. Sudden squall of rain . . . weather so changeable. . . . Rotten for the farmers. . . . How were things in the desert ? . . . Someone had been talking about it on the wireless an evening or two back. . . . Situation looked pretty black, but they were hoping for the best. . . . Good luck. . . . Love from all.

With my thoughts far away I slipped it back into its envelope. I could see everything so clearly : the garden, the sea front, the dancing waves, the beautiful green of the lawns, the fleecy white clouds. My reminiscences were interrupted by Griffiths, my batman, poking his homely face through the tent flap.

" I've brought you some hot water for shaving, sir," he said as he added it to a little cold. " I expect you're real glad to be back again, aren't you ? "

" Yes, Griffiths, I certainly am ! "

" You've been away a longish stretch, sir. Quite a few weeks it must be. I think you'll find that water about right," he added as he sorted out my shaving things.

" O.K., Griffiths. Thank you very much."

" What time will you want your water this evening ? "

" About sixish."

" Very good, sir."

He walked out into the bright glare, and a few moments later I was trying to remove my beard, piece by piece. It had never seemed impressive until now ! Then, feeling very clean and not a little girlish in my smoothness, I wandered over to the mess once more, promising myself the privilege of an uninterrupted afternoon with my letters.

The following morning I went up to Cairo to try and obtain some fresh medical supplies for the next operation. I had no set inventory and my equipment was woefully short ; it was not even up to regimental standards. I required an adequate supply of pentothal, and satisfactory plaster of paris ; I wanted some blood plasma (for it seemed to me that this was very important), and first aid sets which I could issue out to each jeep that went on

the small patrols—a set which would contain rather more than
the first aid packet. Further I had been asked to get·another
doctor ; it appeared that we might be needing two for the next
raid ! But even if this was not the case, a second doctor would be
most valuable. For by now the unit had expanded to the strength
of·three hundred men and fresh volunteers were still coming in.
It was evident that soon we should be splitting up into sub-units,
each with its own headquarters, and, in view of this fact and of
the long distances over which we were operating, it would be a
great advantage to have more than one doctor. But would this
be appreciated in the superbly industrious offices of headquarters ?
Apparently not.

For the methods of medical headquarters are immeasurably
slow ; they can think only in terms of Army Forms and routine
procedures. Anything that falls within these bounds they can
comprehend, but anything outside is entirely foreign and alien.
The written word is their law, the signature (in triplicate) their
code, and the verbal inquiry for immediate action their greatest
despair. They rejoice in such expressions as " through the usual
channels," " results will follow in due course," and " attention
will be given to the points you have raised." If they are very
dashing and anxious to create an impression they will stamp the
word " Urgent " above their communication.

It was hardly surprising, then, that my demands should be
met by the uplifted eyebrows, the open mouths, and the looks of
hurt indignation in which these gentlemen specialised. Why, here
was a case of a man who was stupid enough to think he could
obtain something quickly ! Here was a man who wanted something at once ! The folly of it ! Such inquiries as mine were not
only a waste of time but also tended to upset the running of
headquarters.

In such torpid backwaters one can readily appreciate the
difficulties of obtaining stores at short notice ; and it was with a
sigh of profound relief that I stepped at last from those dismal
corridors into the bright sunlight outside. It had taken me more
than an hour to obtain the necessary sanction for my fresh
supplies.

You could obtain a very pleasant and fascinating air of detachment in just sitting quietly on the terraces outside the big hotels, sipping at a long iced drink and watching the life that eddied and flowed around you. If ever you wished to see Artificiality with a capital " A," then these were the places to go to ; for every one was so aware of the surroundings and environment, that he or she began to act straightaway. Officers, always trying to look dignified and never perturbed ; moustaches on the most unsuitable faces ; boys trying to behave with the culture, decorum and worldly knowledge of early middle age ; and the older men attempting to act like boys. There was something pathetic about the continual sustained effort to create an illusion, to get away from reality ; the endeavour at substitution ; the constant pretence and make-believe.

I suppose that the women were, if anything, rather worse than the men ; for never before had the majority of them been paid so much attention, or had menials to dance to every tune they cared to play. Since every woman acts her way through public life, the reaction to this eutopia was quite the most natural thing in the world, and one had scarcely to turn the head to observe the film gestures materialise : the arched look ; the coy glance ; the delicate shrug of the shoulders ; the expressive gestures of the hands ; and the hundred and one tricks of the eyes. These were the concomitants of female life in Cairo, and, of course, ill manners and gross behaviour flourished exceeding well in such a fertile soil. For the Middle East had developed into a glorified marriage mart with every woman anxious to snap up the best bargain that she could, and every officer striving hard to obtain the most for the least without committing himself in undue measure. Cairo, itself, was merely the Oriental stage—one watched or was watched. Privacy had had become a foolish old-fashioned word that had long since passed out of current use.

The best hotels, it might be mentioned, were, as can well be supposed, out of bounds to other ranks. But a new problem arose when service girls came out to Egypt and were escorted to the hotels by officers. The law, however, was adamant : British girls must seek their food and shelter elsewhere. Everything then continued to go according to plan until the South African girls refused to play, insisting as they did so, that if an Egyptian or any other form of native could dine at a fashionable hotel, then they jolly well did not see why it was too good for them. Eventually there came the master stroke of appeasing British diplomacy—the touch of genius that ever reaches out the hand of assistance to the under-dog—and it was permitted that South African girls could enter the distinctive portals while British girls must remain without. Which showed the better character, I wondered, the disciplined or the self-sufficient ?

Cairo was very sultry on these hot August mornings ; the streets were thronged with all varieties of natives (so adequately described by Major C. S. Jarvis) while Americans, guide-book and camera in hand, inquired their way from the mosque to the sphinx and back again. Gezeira resembled nothing so much as a suburban swimming pool on a bank holiday. Bodies were littered everywhere, bodies of every shape and hue. There were the white, the pink and the brown ; you could take your pick : those from G.H.Q., those who had recently arrived from home, and those on leave from the desert. Dotted around sparsely here and there, were British and native women, engaged, as usual, in an industrious pantomime of flirtation. The demand exceeded the supply ; it was merely a case of exploiting it to the full. And who should say that they were backward ?

One evening I was sitting up on the roof garden of a hotel with a nurse, Joan Gardiner, whom I had known in London training days. It was quite agreeable up there, after its own particular fashion, with such coolness as there was to be obtained ; the garish lights, the occasional hoot of a taxi and the jingle of a gharri came to you from the dark, stuffy streets below. We were both drinking rye highballs ; they were iced and very good. All around us was the continual buzz of conversation from the grouped tables, with every now and then the interruption of a chatter of laughter. After a while the cabaret commenced. A coloured girl sang a song, not well, not badly. She received vast applause, some people clapping because they liked it and others because it was the done thing to like it. Then came a dance from a white girl ; it was pathetic and her reception was due to our sympathy. After that some more dances—efforts with little skill and less grace —with the performers summoning up a futile endeavour to shed their years and look as if they were enjoying themselves. And if you watched them closely as they walked off the stage and out of the glare of the lights, you could see the way in which the artificial smiles vanished, the way the faces fell and the hard lines of their natural expressions became so markedly evident. For them it was now a matter of a quick change, and then the rest of the evening must be spent in trying to entice the British officers to buy as many drinks as possible. There was a reasonable percentage for them on each drink ; they lived by their wits ; they must store up now for the lean days ahead for, after all, wars were not so frequent.

I suppose Joan must have seen the expression on my face. " A penny for your thoughts ? " she questioned brightly.

I gave a sheepish grin—" I'm just feeling cynical. You know. Don't you get that way sometimes ? "

" Often."

" And bitter ? "

" Yes. But what's the *béte noire* to-night ? "

I liked Joan. She did not seem to have changed much : still very pretty with her dark hair and steady brown eyes. Not affected : no drawl had yet appeared in *her* voice. In fact she remained very much the Joan I had known at hospital, friendly and attentive, and a very able nurse with it all. I offered her a cigarette, and we sat for a moment in silence.

" Well," I started off, " I was just thinking of the way the war seems to alter us all, and the way artificiality thrives at the expense of sincerity. I really can't understand why it should be, because in war we are suddenly thrown up against so many of the real things that matter. No, that's not what I want to say — that's the hackneyed sort of stuff one reads everywhere. What I mean is this. Before the war most of us were escapists : we avoided the things that we did not want to meet ; we were afraid of a contact that was too intimate ; there was always another path leading round. But we can't do that now ; and yet we don't seem to have improved as a result. We have to think for ourselves, we have to think quickly, we must become self-sufficient and so on—you know the routine formulæ—but instead of getting better, we get worse.

" The answer's obvious, Malcolm," her voice was as steady as her eyes. " It *is* obvious and don't think I'm being sentimental when I tell you. What you lack is your family life ; that's a loss which is greater than most of your fresh experiences. All you men without your families and homes are like a lot of overgrown schoolboys. Oh, yes, you are ! No. Don't interrupt. You are just like school kids, only instead of a sports blazer you've got a uniform ; some of you get your colours, others don't. And you come back on leave just like you did from school : full of talk about what the regiment has been up to ; boasting and bragging sometimes, depressed at others. Oh, yes, I'm looking after an officers' ward at the moment—it's always the most unpopular ward to work in, you know—and the things I hear said every day remind me very much of my brothers on holiday : the rivalries and the little petty jealousies. You talk about women—I know what *you* think about them—but you are every bit as foolish with your pompous manners and the way you ape your superiors."

" Me ? "

" No, silly ! " she laughed. " Not you personally, but just you collectively," she waved her arm round to include everyone. " What you all need is a bit of common sense from your homes and hearths, and the natural atmosphere thrown in with it. You don't act at home ; you would soon have it taken out of you if you tried to ! Every one knows you properly for what you are at home. No bright buttons and clean belts needed there : they know what you look like in your braces ! But here you saunter around behind the protection of an assumed indifference and a smart uniform. Am I right ? "

" Well, it's hard to say all at once." I was hedging, knowing full well that she was right, " But I think there's more to it than that. In civil life most of us are aware of our position and status without being conscious of it. We are subconsciously aware. If we are made to feel foolish or insignificant, we can always compensate for it mentally and overcome it by associating with people who are our inferiors.

" I don't get that."

" No, I am afraid I have put it badly. But in peace-time there is always a way out, an escape. A man can escape from a feeling of inferiority by associating with people whom he knows to be his inferiors. In so doing, he restores his self-respect. The duffer is always a popular person because he gives other people a sense

of superiority, and they like it. They go to him for a mental and
moral buck-up. Psychologists talk about the ego and the super-
ego—but that is roughly what they are driving at. If a number
of people jeer at me, it may upset me for quite a while until I
have associated with people who respect me and so restore the
balance. In the army, it is very different. You are branded as
an officer or a man. If you are an officer you will often find that
you are the subordinate ; or perhaps there are a number of you
who are subordinates, all of whom are in competition. You might
think that you could obtain compensation by taking it out of the
other ranks, but only a few are sufficiently unintelligent to be
able to do that. The majority of people know that their commands
are obeyed only because they have the authority of uniform ; they
cannot restore their egos in that way. Since they cannot restore
their feeling of self-importance by associating with their inferiors,
then they are obliged to act in the competitive manner which you
see going on all round you : a constant effort at preservation
failing the opportunities of self-restoration."

"Malcolm, old boy, I haven't got the vaguest idea *what* you
are talking about." She looked at me in such a way that I could
not help laughing at myself. "Anyway I *still* think it's the
braces."

"It would be rather funny," I admitted, "if our wives, or
mothers or aunts were to appear beside each one of us now. Look
at that major over there—on your left—the one with the bald
head drinking with the wog girl. I would love to see his expression change, wouldn't you ? "

"Ah ! Now you are just being malicious," but she chuckled
all the same. Then her voice grew serious again and I wondered
what was coming next. "There's another thing which you've
got to consider," she said, "when you glibly criticise our girls—
or rather our British nurses. Perhaps you don't realise that we
have to serve the same length of time overseas as you do before
we are eligible to be sent home."

"What ! Nearly five years ? "

"Certainly," she nodded, "but that is only for British nurses.
Other nurses get paid more and serve less time abroad. The girls
in the R.A.F. and Navy only do two years. Well, look at the
men in the R.A.F. and Navy. They only do two years, don't

they? Just you listen to all the homesick R.A.F. boys grumbling after thay have done two and a half years. It's silly, isn't it? We are women but we have to serve the full male army sentence—Iraq, Persia, the Sudan, Burma—anywhere. Now you take the case of a girl of twenty-five who has qualified in her training as a nurse. She joins the army. Although she has spent four years in being trained, her pay is less than that of some unintelligent officer in the A.T.S.—or in any of the other services for that matter. She is in the army and is under their regulations, but she is not even paid at army rates. If she is sent abroad, as she almost certainly will be, she knows that she will be about thirty by the time she gets back to England. Now can you blame her for getting the best she can out of this sort of life, and for making the most of her opportunities? "

" No. I agree. But because I agree, it does not mean to say that I like to see our girls behaving as they so frequently do. Surely you have never seen such atrocious manners in either men or women as you have done here, have you? "

" No. I haven't. It's a result of the general atmosphere."

" With regard to the question of pay, of course, well you could argue about that for hours. Why is the British tommy paid less than any dominion soldier? How do you think our tommies feel when they see Australians, say, throwing money around and buying things that they can't afford to buy. Once you start talking about relative rates of pay, you begin to hear grievances on every side. Look at the Americans.

" Yes, but why can't they have a standardised rate of pay for all the Commonwealth troops? "

" How should I know? The British are always putting up with far more for far less than anybody else. We take a sort of pride in it. It's something to be able to grumble about. It's something to fall back on. And grumbling is the life blood of the British soldier. We make a great deal of our grumbling. Because we can grumble, we say, we have got free speech. It's an argument that is fostered by those in authority, but it doesn't mean as much as it is made out to mean. How could we right a grievance or a wrong if we wanted to? By grumbling? No! That is just an appeasement of the conscience. There is only one thing we could do and that would be to strike. But that would be unjust to others. Our conscience would not allow it ; we would not be happy in our action. Of course we couldn't very well strike out here, but we could make our feelings felt quite unpleasantly at home where there is no true fighting front. Still there you are : we prefer to submit to wrongs and grumble over them, than to alter them and feel that we may be doing the country a disservice. It is all a part of our British make-up."

At that moment the band struck up and there was an immediate movement and scraping of chairs in response. Our thoughts and arguments were interrupted ; perhaps it was just as well.

" Good show ! " I remarked. " It's a slow fox-trot. We can dance without getting hot."

Joan danced very well, I thought, never reminding you that your feet were at fault, but always making good your mistakes. We were dancing in silence until I heard her voice close to my ear.

" You know, Malcolm—don't laugh—but I would like to see that brought up in parliament at home—our length of service abroad, I mean. Somehow I feel it should be brought to the public notice that we are forced to stick out here for over four and a half years. I would really. The public at home have no idea about those sort of things."

" Why don't you put your complaint through the official channels ? "

" Ha ! Ha ! Through the matron ? What a hope ! She wouldn't dare to forward it. It might cost her her job."

" Wait till we get to Singapore ! Then we can grumble."

" Beast ! If we weren't being watched now, I'd pinch you hard."

" Ah, but in Cairo ' we are not alone ' as Paul Muni once remarked."

" No," she sighed and looked up. " Isn't it a lovely night ? Black as velvet."

Yes it was indeed a lovely night and I think we both felt better for having aired our grievances. It seemed a little cooler, too, as we hooted our way back through the streets in a taxi. How strange ! I thought. It was only a few nights ago that we were out, prowling after the German doctor. It was just about as dark as this, then. Yet looking back on it now was rather like watching a number of animated figures in a peep-show. It was a different life in another world ; something that had slipped out of a dream and was not tangible. I wondered what the German doctor was doing now. Working in a tented ward ? Drinking with his colonel ? Had he been interviewed by the high officials ? Had he received a second decoration ? Anyhow I bet he gave us a good write-up. And what of our patrols ? Had they left the rendezvous yet ? What was it like there to-night ? I wondered. Was it still and quiet or was the wind flicking the dust viciously from off the broken rocks ?

" You know you really are most unsociable." It was Joan's voice rousing me from my thoughts. " Here we are at the hospital and you have scarcely uttered a word. What are you thinking about now, you mystery man ? "

" Well, Joan, my dear, I would love to tell you, only I don't want to behave like one of your school kids."

" Damn you ! " she said, and then, " Good-night, Malcolm. Thanks so much for the evening. You know we must go out one evening and start an argument, a proper argument this time. How about it ? "

" Rather ! " I said, " but you have been warned. Can we make it pretty soon ? "

" Please."

" Good-night, Joan."

She turned and walked to her billet ; and as I watched her pass under the lamp and then beyond, her shadow thrusting out beside her, I could not help feeling sorry, so very sorry, for some of these British nurses.

CHAPTER THIRTEEN

WE TRAVEL SOUTH TO KUFRA

" The Walrus and the Carpenter
  Were walking close at hand
They wept like anything to see
  Such quantities of sand :
' If this were only cleared away,'
  They said, ' it would be grand ! '

" ' If seven maids with seven mops
  Swept it for half a year
Do you suppose,' the Walrus said,
  ' That they could get it clear ? '
' I doubt it,' said the Carpenter,
  And shed a bitter tear."
    The Walrus and the Carpenter. LEWIS CARROLL.

WHEN I returned to Kabrit I discovered that all our patrols
had got back safely ; and this in spite of their being sharply
attacked by one of our Wellington aircraft as they were making
their way south near the Qara Matruh track. But we had run it
finely enough ; for, according to R.A.F. intelligence, a few days
after our departure a whole regiment of armoured cars had been
seen scouring the desert in the vicinity of our rendezvous areas.
So much, then, for the operations which were carried out during
the months of July and August, in which, I believe, well over one
hundred enemy aircraft were destroyed.

    But we were busy preparing for the next raid, and it looked as
if we were going to do things on a large scale for we had numerous
jeeps and three-ton lorries being camouflaged and especially
fitted at the workshops. I had been allocated a Red Cross jeep
and found that there was little difficulty in accommodating a
blood-plasma transfusion box between the two front seats ; while
fresh fixtures and the removal of the back seats enabled the various
panniers to be strapped down firmly behind. One stretcher was
slung along either side of the body and, by the time my driver

and I had added our bedding and personal kit, the jeep was definitely overloaded. Consequently we had to travel light on food and petrol loads, and even so we looked rather like a mobile Christmas tree. Our main satisfaction was that we were more or less self-sufficient. We had packed our equipment so that there was a little of something in each pannier, and if one pannier was destroyed then we would not be at a complete loss for, say, sulphonamide. Similarly there was a reserve of everything in a pannier packed away on one of the three-ton lorries.

At this time I had only one medical orderly with me, a well-trained man called Ritchie who had been out on the last series of operations. Two fresh orderlies, I thought, should put us in a strong enough position with regard to personnel. Accordingly (in military parlance) I was instructed to proceed to the R.A.M.C. Base Depot where I spoke a few halting words, feeling extremely foolish the while, to a group of apparently highly uninterested medical orderlies. From this visit I obtained Shotton, a fair-haired Yorkshire lad whose sound common-sense came to our rescue more than once, and Johnson, a spectacled Londoner, who soon earned the nickname of " Razor-blade " through his evident surgical skill with this implement.

There was something very satisfying in being able to take blood-plasma with us. In this sort of work, where it was so difficult to obtain shade, shelter, and sufficient fluid, I felt sure that plasma was worth its weight in gold ; and the kind-hearted generosity of the blood transfusion department at the Scottish General Hospital did much to offset the official attitude at G.H.Q. It seemed that Colonel Buttle, the head of the department, could not do too much for us although, Heaven knows, he must have had his hands very full since he was organising the supply of plasma to the whole of the Eighth Army. No army forms were needed here, thank goodness ; it was simply a case of come and get it, and there must be many medical officers who have happy memories of that little block of rooms on the ground floor.

From an operational point of view, it appeared that we were setting out on " the next job " in three convoys, each of these consisting of about a dozen jeeps with half as many lorries to carry the supplies. Only one or two people knew where we were going ; the rest of us were obliged to wait until we had struck the open desert, and then we were told that the convoys would be assembling at Kufra oasis prior to moving north and. attacking Benghazi.

About mid-way through August Paddy Mayne set out with the first convoy. His course took him down the Nile as far south as Assyut where he branched off, following the old camel track to Kharga oasis and thence westwards to Kufra. Two days later the second convoy under Sandy Scratchley followed the same route, while Bill Cumper, our engineer, brought up the rear party. Jim Chambers and myself were on the last convoy ; and since it was such a happy journey, it might be as well to give the reader some impression of Bill Cumper, who was largely responsible for the good spirits and the successful organisation that attended it.

Bill had joined the unit at some time previous to my arrival, and when I first met him he had just been making up some of his portable time-bombs. " Lovely little bombs, they are," he said with a proud nod of his head. " Made 'em with me own 'ands, so don't you go wasting 'em ! " His injunctions were addressed to Jellicoe before he set off for his raid on Crete ; and I can remember his opening remark to me after we had been intro-duced : " Blime ! " he said in an aside to Jellicoe as he shook my hand, " A sawbones ! What's going on round 'ere, George ? 'Cos if things are going to start getting rough, I'm 'opping it."

After that I used to watch him quietly in the mess and try to make what I could of him. But if I was uncertain about him, at least I had the satisfaction of knowing that he shared the same feelings with regard to me. One evening, however, he got me aside. " Were you in the Wavell retreat ? " he asked me. " You were ? Where ? Derna ? I was there too, my lad. Yes, I was there all right, blowing up things all over the place. Fair made me 'eart bleed, it did. Shockin' waste ! " He shook his head at the recollection. " Were you in the Wavell push ? No ? I was." He jerked his thumb towards his chest. " Yes. Bill Cumper was there all right. 'Course I was only a sergeant then, you know, but I was workin' like a black, I was. Doing the work of a dozen officers really. Those were the days ! Were you in Tobruk when it was surrounded ? You were ? So was I. Yes, I was there ! "

I offered him a cigarette.

" No thanks, Doc."

" A drink ? "

" No. I don't touch the poison. I'll 'ave a lemonade though.
Oy, China ! " he turned suddenly to Corporal Leitch who did
not look in the least surprised at being accosted in this manner.
" Nice long lemonade, China, there's a good soldier ! You see,"
he said turning back to me, " there aren't any vices about Bill
Cumper, and I want to keep clear of your little medical business
if I can."

That was roughly how I first came to know him, with his
animated talk and his little bright brown eyes which peered out
at you from a puckish and almost monkey-like face. He was one
of the most humorous people I have ever met. Darkish and of
medium height, there was no such thing as restraint about
Cumper. He would step in where angels feared to tread and carry
it off every time. Then, too, with his shrewd cuts or blunt
attacks, he could make you feel uncomfortable more quickly than
any one else I have met : for there was no beating about the bush
or marking time with him. At the first meeting you did not know
what to make of him, at the second you reckoned he was someone
to keep a careful eye on ; but it took you a good while before you
got to know him, and, even then, you never knew *quite* what he
was going to say next. For he could bring a blush even to the
cheeks of the most superior as he hit upon a tender spot ; and
some of the things he said and did just weren't done, don't you
know !

I can see him now, coming in to tea and sitting down next
to a delicate-looking Guards officer, accosting a waiter with a
" Come 'ere, China, yer lazy rat ! " and, when the waiter had
come, " Cup o' char, please, same as the officer," with a jerk of
a dirty thumb in the direction of the rapidly colouring guardee.

Bill came from the ranks ; he knew it, rejoiced in it, and
pushed it straight in front of your face to see how you would
take it.

I can remember him entering the mess with his battle-dress
all awry, pulling off his cap and reading the legend under the
badge. " 'Oo cares 'oo wins ? " he recited loudly, and slinging the
cap up on the rack he proceeded to order a lime juice—a stiff one.
This was at the time when he was doing his parachute jumps ;
and we would inquire tactfully how things were going as he

lowered himself warily into a chair, giving his tail a little sympathetic rub when he had done so.

"You can call me ' one jump,' me lads," he replied, looking round at us boldly. "Remember that. One jump Cumper. That's me."

The next day the dignified clerk in the orderly room was rather startled when he answered the telephone.

"This is two jump, two jump Cumper speaking. . . ." Came the voice from the other end.

Then, too, he took great pains to divide his parachute badge into five equal parts, and after each jump he solemnly pinned one more portion on to his left shoulder.

Or again, perhaps, of an evening, when some new officer had entered the mess with immaculate uniform and tunic just so, you might have heard Bill's rough voice raised in cheering greeting : " 'Allo Buttons—'Ows tricks ? "

No air of superiority or disdainful demeanour ever affected *his* irrepressible spirits ; and any form of rudeness was quickly met with better and blunter replies.

"What an uncouth fellow ! " commented a freshly arrived cavalry officer ; but unfortunately for him, Bill overheard the remark. "Me ? " he shouted, and every one could hear him. "Me ? Uncooth ? D'yer hear that ? What's biting yer, Cheddar ? Me, wot's bin in the army man and boy for twenty years ! Ain't I good enough for yer ? "

For the next few days he proudly styled himself " Uncooth " ; and it was " Uncooth speaking " on the telephone, and " Uncooth to you " in the mess. I think that officer could have bitten off his tongue ; people soon became very sorry when they got on the wrong side of Bill Cumper.

There was another amusing incident which stands out quite clearly in the mind's eye. It occurred on an evening when David Stirling had dashed down from G.H.Q. to see that everything was running smoothly at the camp. We were due to move off in a day or two and consequently the conversation was full of figures concerning rounds of ammunition, the numbers of tyres required, the quantity of petrol to be carried in reserve ; and so it went on throughout dinner, rather like a business meeting.

"How many rounds of ammo ? " David turned to Jim

Chambers who had been working like a slave to get everything laid on.

" About two hundred thousand."

" Good ! How much tracer ? "

" Fifty thousand." .

David nodded. " And incendiary ? "

" Forty thousand."

" Hmm ! Are you all right, Bill ? " He turned to Bill whose head had been bobbing, birdlike, this way and that as he tried to keep up with the rapid fire of conversation.

" O.K., Maestro."

" Detonators ? "

" Trezz Beans " (Tres bien).

" Bombs ? "

" Kwayis Ketir ! Just the job ! "

" Good ! "

David looked at his watch. He wanted to get back to operations branch in Cairo by midnight. He would have to step on it.

" What time does the moon rise ? " he asked suddenly, looking round at us.

" Sorry, sir," replied Bill as promptly. " Forgot to lay that on."

David looked so completely nonplussed that we had to laugh.

In conclusion I may add that Bill Cumper was nearly forty ; that he had been married recently ; and that he was coming out on the Benghazi raid to perform an extremely hazardous task.

That was Bill Cumper who took our section to Kufra— " Cumper of Kufra to you ! " The men loved him and would have done anything for him.

We set out in late August, when the morning heat had turned the road into a dark trembling band that wound its way between the irregular sand hills ; and all around us were the colourless pools of mirages, receding and spreading up anew as we drove to Cairo. Bill was in the lead, with his jeep driven by a rotund cockney known as Busty ; and a strange pair they made as they proceeded, solemn and dignified, through the crowded native streets. It was a quieter procession through Cairo this time, for Bill had informed us that there was to be " no nabbin' of things off barrers " ; and consequently we went on our way with only the usual songs, catcalls and ribald remarks echoing in our wake. I remember Sergeant-major Riley and Sergeant Phillips were in the jeep behind me, and after we had crossed the Nile and were heading south down its western bank they broke into song with a vengeance, one cowboy tune following another without a break until we had halted in the shade of some palms for a quick lunch.

It was pleasant driving through the rich luxuriant delta, if only because it was all so new to us ; it is true that the dusty patches were trying enough and necessitated our wearing goggles, but for the greater part of the journey this precaution was not necessary. The river flowed, slow and brown, between its dark banks ; while on either side we could see the sails of the large flat-bottomed ships which, since the waterways they traversed were out of sight, appeared to glide evenly across the flat fields.

Only one incident served to break the even tenor of a long day's run, and that took place after we had drawn up at the side of the road for a welcome rest. The jeep in front of me contained two men whose relative variations in height had earned them the names of " Lofty " and " Shorty " respectively. I think that it was Lofty who was at the wheel, for he was taking advantage of this journey to learn to drive. As the convoy moved off again he pulled his jeep out from the side of the road, where it was halted, to pass a stationary native cart when, all of a sudden, he saw a vehicle approaching in the opposite direction. He must then have got mixed up with the different foot pedals for, to the surprise of those of us who were behind, his jeep accelerated briskly in a semi-circle across the road and took a neat dive over the bank and into the Nile below. Had it been performed for a feature of a comic film it could not possibly have been more effective ; but as it was we found ourselves anxiously scanning the dark muddy waters below, and especially the little patch where a swirl and an eddy denoted the site of their abrupt departure from our sight. Then up came a stream of large bubbles, followed soon afterwards, by two red puffing faces ; and looking very wet and bedraggled, the victims pulled themselves up out of the water. The problem of the missing jeep, however, was not so easy to solve ; but soon we had obtained a tow-chain, one end of which was attached to a lorry, while it was considered

only fitting that " Lofty " should submerge once more to attach
the other end to the rear axle of the submerged jeep. This having
been done, there was much shouting of directions, interrupted
with loud curses for the benefit of the lorry driver, and the jeep
was slowly and jerkily dragged from the river bed. The appearance of the dripping vehicle from out of the depths of the Nile
caused the utmost bewilderment and alarm amongst the garrulous
natives who had gathered around. Deep cries of "Aah ! . . .
Aah ! " heralded its appearance above the water level ; jaws
sagged and eyes grew large and round, as many a trembling dusky
hand pointed with wonder to this new River God. Doubtless
their high esteem of the local " gully gully " man felt pretty sharply
after this exhibition of super-witchcraft by the white stranger, and
we left them still expostulating and pointing out the exact spot of
the miracle to the newcomers who were fast swelling their ranks.
Following this incident, " Lofty " and " Shorty " were known
collectively as the " Mermaids."

At noon on the second day we left the dark-green fringe of the
delta life ; the winding dusty roads and paths ; the natives who
came up to us at each halt, eager to bargain over their liquid
water-melons. We left the flat-topped houses, mud-covered, straw-
covered, dung-covered. We left the winding ramifications of the
Nile, dark with pollution and abundant in mosquitoes ; the dirty
children with their innocent, wondering eyes and their obscene
mouths as they ran and danced before us, and cried shrilly at
our departure.

All these we left where the desert reached out suddenly with
a yellow arid hand, eager and clutching, and the green fertility
of the Nile dwindled down to its very banks. And we were alone,
alone once more with our thoughts and shadows, as we set out
across a wilderness which stretched away evenly to empty
distances of whose immensity the mind could hardly conceive.

From Assyut we headed off west of south following the old
Arab track, marked out by wind-eroded cairns and smoothly
polished skeletons, that led its sinuous way to Kharga. For this
was the course which the native caravans had taken long centuries
ago, and every now and then you caught a glimpse of something
that made you realise just how short was the human span of life.

" We went into a cave," said Sergeant Lilley afterwards, " and we saw three skeletons. One looked like a man, another was smaller like a woman, and the third was a child. There was hair on the child's scalp and the fingers were still covered with flesh, quite white and dry. There was another skeleton, too ; it looked like a donkey. What do you make of that, Doc ? "

We were in trouble from the very start, running into deep stretches of treacherous soft sand and having to dig ourselves out continuously. As one truck after another fell behind, the convoy became stretched out in a widely-spread single-file ; it was not a race exactly, but whenever there was a definite course to follow and no need to group together, it developed into a form of obstacle competition ; and of course there was a certain satisfaction in feeling that you were somewhere up in the front. Each jeep was self-sufficient and every driver competent enough to remedy the smaller breakdowns ; at the rear of the column came the fitter sergeant, abusing each laggard with cheerful expletives and making good the defects.

That evening, as it grew dark, we halted beside the smooth slopes of a cluster of massive rocks. Soon the whole convoy was in, and a bright crackling fire had sprung up near the cook's lorry. Already the breeze had grown cool, and you began to feel that life was really good once more as you tramped around in your shorts and sandals.

For this was the hour when each man became a specialist. The drivers checked up on the maintenance of their vehicles ; and it was not long before the air had become loud with clatter and clanging as wheels were unscrewed and metal rims removed in order to mend the day's punctures. Every now and then, in the brief intervals of silence, you might hear the voices of the navigators as they took shots of the stars ; one of them would be peering through the eye-piece of the theodolite calling out : " Three . . . two . . . one . . . Now ! " and the other would read off the time, exact to the second from wireless checks, by the light of his torch. Then jumbles of figures would come to your ears as they drew geometrical lines across the map and plotted our exact position.

Men came trudging across to the medical jeep, unrolling their stained bandages and joking as they showed me the red, angry sores. In fact they always ragged on the sick parade and laughed at the pain, if only because some of their mates were looking on, and they were not going to have any jokes made at their expense if they could avoid it.

So we were all busy, each in his separate capacity, knowing that the work must be finished to-night so that we might make an early start on the next morning. Then, on the cry, "Grub up!" we would form an eager, noisy queue by the cook's lorry, and, at the appropriate moment, hold out one mess tin for the grub and the other for the steaming brown tea.

Ah, that was the best part of the day without a doubt! Eating with the healthiest appetite in the world and not talking much, but just watching the flames lick and hiss round the black cooking pots. It was a great feeling : that sense of satisfaction as you lay back with your belly pleasantly full, and blew out a cloud of cigarette smoke in your complacency. Your thoughts would wander far away as you basked in the feeling of contentedness and lazy peace. As a rule it would not be long before someone had risen to his feet with a rough "Good-night all"; and the answering voices, "Night, Joe," "Night, Joe. Dream o' Blighty, lad," would come in return as he moved off, a dim shadow in the darkness, towards his truck. Yes, those few moments as you lay between the blankets and felt the fresh caress of the breeze on your cheek ; you looked up, and there were the stars so friendly and familiar, and seemingly so close in their trembling brightness. You felt wonderfully sleepy as you drew the rough blanket round your chin, and with a little wriggle of your arm and shoulder to scoop out hollows in the soft sand, you were provided with a bed that lacked no comfort. . . .

We started early the next morning ; and in a short while the country had changed, with sand giving way to barren outcrops of black rock with jagged and serrated edges. The track became more bumpy as it wound in and out among them until, quite suddenly, it took a downward slope and we found we had reached the edge of an escarpment. Below us—I suppose at least a thousand feet below—the flat Kharga depression stretched away like a vast mottled plate, shuddering in the commencing heat haze. Our track led down aslant the precipitous slopes, with frequent hairpin bends, twisting and turning between the black conical peaks and traversing ledges where the rocks fell sheer on either side. It was a case of first gear, four-wheel drive, and all brakes in good working order, as we clung to our narrow track like cautious insects.

Once we had arrived in the depression itself it seemed as if a sun-glass had been laid over our heads, and the only respite was to drive on fast and catch the breeze, hot though it was. Semi-naked, with goggles fixed firmly in position, and the bonnets of the jeeps burning to the touch, we ran along the even ground, threading our way through the several small oases.

My driver stopped the jeep at one of these oases and, since the convoy had become well scattered and there was no one in sight, we thought we might as well get into the shade for a while. The natives seemed very friendly and unusually active as they climbed up the palms and threw dates down to us ; " definitely a good type" as my driver remarked with firm conviction, munching away contentedly as he did so.

The remaining part of our run to Kharga was quite uneventful, save for a barrier of a thick long drift of sand which lay near the single track railway as it led into the oasis. It was a remarkably good piece of driving that got the lorries across it, for even the jeeps became overheated as they churned their way along at no more than a walking pace, throwing up great clouds of smoky dust and leaving deep tracks in their wake as they did so. Eventu-ally, however, like Christian in his progress, we had all overcome this obstacle ; and so, after driving up a short rise in the firm ground beyond, we found ourselves entering the well-kept roads of the oasis village of Kharga.

I suppose that Kharga must be pretty modern as these habitations go. Certainly it boasted a railway station of its own, and two-way levelled roads with a dividing floral piece down the centre : signs of civilization which, I believe, were directly dependent upon the medicinal effect of the sulphurous springs which are peculiar to the oasis. I dare say I shall stand corrected by some Oriental expert or other, but they definitely smelt of sulphur to us on that hot August afternoon, as we stripped off our clothes and jumped into the open tank through which the water ran away to open irrigation ditches and channels. Running water in the desert !—and fairly gushing out at that ! To us, ruffians and ragamuffins, with our faces, hair, ears and bodies coated thickly with yellow dust ; to us who looked like a troupe of painted clowns at a circus ; to us whose lips were already beginning to crack with the dry heat of the desert, this sound of gurgling water seemed as unnatural and unreal as it was surprising.

Nevertheless it took us next to no time to get into the warm clear water and drink bellyful after bellyful as it came cascading out ; and all the while we did so the natives watched us in little silent wide-eyed groups, wondering at the way in which the white man displayed his body with such attractive unconcern. As soon as we looked round and pointedly returned their gaze, the girls averted their eyes and hid their faces as if they were ashamed or embarrassed about something !

At Kharga we learned that Paddy and Sandy Scratchley had already passed through, both of them well up to their time schedules, and the former picking up two Honey tanks which had come by rail as far as the oasis. We, too, completed the loading of our lorries here, piling on more oil, petrol and food supplies, and then driving them over into the shade in order to check up on the vehicle maintenance.

That evening some of us drove over to the club—a building that reminded me of a suburban cricket pavilion—and here we sat in wicker chairs, sipping daintily at lamoons and indulging in polite conversation with our hosts. It made a pretty exercise of our water discipline for, as the time went past, we became aware of an increasing thirst which, presumably, was due to the spring water, Under such conditions, pleasantries and gracious remarks came slowly to our tongues, and I fear a few of us were indelicate enough to request a " third helping " of the drink.

We inquired about the oasis. " Yes," said the local doctor in reply, " this was quite a health resort in peace-time, a sort of Harrogate to which the fashionable Delta practitioners sent their wealthier patients, and where bathing and partaking of the waters was the correct treatment for all rheumatic and arthritic complaints." " Hence," he informed me, with a wave of a dusky hand towards the dirty native huts down the road, " the evident prosperity of the oasis." I noticed that he carried himself very well and was plainly a man of consequence in the community.

" What of malaria ? " I asked. It appeared that there was indeed a certain amount ; but he had found that his methods of treatment gave exceptionally good results. He spoke with such a superb satisfaction concerning his medical arrangements that I only wished I might have had the opportunity of visiting his hospital.

We returned to the springs for supper only to find that thousands of flies had come to join us, and, in fact, they were so bad that we were obliged to crawl under our mosquito nets to eat our food ; while the swarms of them round the cook's lorry reminded one of a humorous Oriental cartoon. After supper we smoked for a while but the atmosphere was so warm and close that few of us could resist the temptation of another bath. So we sat there in the darkness, with the shadowy outlines of the palm-trees around and the bright stars overhead, feeling the running water play round our bodies and revelling in the luxury. It was so delightful that we found it difficult to drag ourselves out and go to bed.

How best to describe our journey to Kufra ? For mere description of the country or of halting places would be as bare and lacking in essentials as a diagram or chart. How to recapture the spirit which radiated from Bill Cumper and Jim Chambers, spreading down to every single man until the whole trek had become one glorious rag, as well as being an efficient piece of work in covering the distance in less than the scheduled time ? For it was in the nature of a happy adventure or exploration to those of us who had not travelled as far south as this before ; we did not know what sort of a journey it would turn out to be nor what kind of " going " was in store for us.

We started off, then, letting the solemn three-ton lorries rumble ahead, while we in our jeeps jockeyed about for position in the rear. In this respect it was our policy to give the lorries clear room for manœuvring in the front, so that when they did run into difficult going they would not be put off by jeeps zig-zagging across their paths. It was a form of courtesy towards the lorry drivers, for every one realised that they had by far the hardest job of work to do.

I can picture the convoy now : the little navigating jeep in front, the solid three-tonners rolling along steadily, and the jeeps scampering about at the back. I can remember the long cloudless days when we drove on for mile after even mile over desert that stretched out around us as flatly as an unruffled sea ; the way we would pull the throttle out so that the needle stood up straight at the figure forty, and then would laze back with our legs stretched out across the bonnet. Looking round at the scattered convoy it seemed that we stood motionless. For all the vehicles were travelling at exactly the same speed, and there was no alteration of their relative positions. Yes, we might have been perfectly stationary had it not been for an occasional boulder or a little chocolate-coated hillock which drifted past to the right or to the left and served, momentarily, to break the illusion. We were like a convoy of ships, save that our horizon was a trembling yellow band, and there was not even a wake to indicate our movement. Behind us we left our parallel tracks, like railway-lines, spinning them out effortlessly over the firm sand ; while all the time the milometer figures revolved in steady rhythmic sequence. Those were our only constant reminders of movement and of distance covered.

Was it boring ? No, rather not ; and I'm afraid that we in the jeeps were rather like boys in bumper-cars, ragging and chasing each other round the place out of sheer good spirits. Then there was an American who came with us on this raid, and his jeep, as one might expect, was heavily overloaded with any number of gadgets and knick-knacks. Sometimes, as he drove along seriously, with his eyes fixed away out on the wide open spaces, Jim and I would take advantage of him and be childish enough to approach him quietly from behind. As we drew close we separated a little, coming up abreast of him, one on either side, with no more than a foot to spare between the vehicles. All of a sudden the American would become aware of one of us, and with a jump he would start to swing the wheel over, until, seeing the other partner, he would be forced to straighten out his course again. Then his head would jerk rapidly from side to side as he pursued a wavering course between us. We could see his lips moving as he hurled execrations at us, and we would smile and laugh in reply. So it went on ; he could not get rid of us for we were an inseparable trio : when he accelerated then we accelerated, when he slowed down then we

did likewise. It finished up by the three of us halting, while the
rest of the convoy ran rapidly away to the west. We waited to
hear the satisfaction of his words.

"Why, what's the matter with yew fellers?" he shouted at
us. "Do yew think that's funny or sumpin'?"

"No, why, do yew?" we chorused.

"Why no!"

And then, before the argument became any more involved,
Jim and I would race ahead to see who could catch up with the
convoy first.

From time to time we passed great jagged outgrowths of rock,
standing out in sullen, naked contrast to the dull yellow, and
mottling the sand over large broken areas. Occasionally we ran
fast and unsuspecting on to long patches where the sand had blown
into fine hard sinuous wrinkles, and we would find ourselves
bouncing about like peas in barrels, with all our work cut out to
keep the vehicles under control and to prevent them from tipping
over. But the events which stand out most vividly are those when
we had to cross the great heavy drifts of sand, so soft that we sank
in ankle-deep as we stood, and with no distinguishing features to
give us any warning of their locality. It was amusing to watch a
jeep driving along peacefully at, say, forty miles an hour and then
to see the lower half suddenly disappear as if it had been sliced
off by an invisible hand, and the jeep come to an abrupt halt.
Yes, it was comical to see the upper half of the jeep apparently
resting in the sand, with hardly a sign of a wheel anywhere. As a
rule it was not very difficult for a jeep to extract itself from such
a dilemma, and there was no need for the convoy to halt. For each
jeep had its sand-shovel and sand-mat, and it was usually a case
of a little digging and then backing out slowly along its tracks of
entrance. Of course there were times when other jeeps had to
stop and help, when the radiator of the jeep that was in trouble
had pushed a little pile of sand along in front of it like a snow-
plough, when it was impossible to "ride" it out and when, in
fact, it was thoroughly "bogged down." On these occasions the
wheels would have to be dug clear of the sand, sand-trays or sand-
mats would be laid down, willing hands would take the weight
of the chassis off the wheels of the jeep while the driver backed
out very slowly. It was fatal to try to accelerate out of such a

position : the spinning wheels simply churned up great sprays of sand and the jeep would begin to settle, or " submerge," even more deeply. The men got a great deal of fun out of all this " crash-diving " and " periscope work," and soon a friendly rivalry had developed to see who got into difficulties least. I remember, too, how we used to indulge in a little practise of driving in a complete circle round someone who had just " submerged," shouting out epithets and catcalls as we did so—a piece of heavy humour which was intended to inflict humiliation on the victim concerned.

When, however, the three-ton lorries became stuck, as they did of course far more frequently than did the jeeps, then it was a very different matter. Bill Cumper set the example by halting and helping with the spade-work, laying down the sand-trays beneath the massive wheels, and getting us all to shove hard as the lorry trembled and staggered forward in slow jerks like a stricken monster. There was something so life-like about these lorries ; the way they would struggle on, panting and groaning, until at last they had reached the far side of a long sand-drift, or the way the engine would falter and cough before it broke down completely and left the lorry resting back helplessly on one side. On some of these days our work became well-nigh back-breaking ; and there were periods at a time when the men would walk by the sides of their vehicles, carrying a sand-tray between them, ready to throw it in front of the wheels as soon as they began to sink. At such times we fell back heavily on our daily mileage, and patience and hard work became the two main factors responsible for our progress.

On one such occasion, I remember, a lorry was unable to climb over a large sand-drift that had been blown in an incline against a layer of rocks. The driver was changed more than once but without effect. There was no way of circumventing the drift for it was only with great difficulty that we had reached it, and to turn back would have been as hard as to go on. It was Jim Chambers who started us on unloading the lorry and carrying the heavy tins, boxes, and panniers up the drift. He set the example, his stocky figure bowed down beneath the weight of a large sack ; and soon there was a little chain of men, their backs glistening with perspiration as they trudged up and down,

" portering " the load to the rocky ground above. Then, when the
lorry had been lightened, we got to work with the digging and
sand-trays, while others stood by ready to shove the moment it
was required. " O.K.," we shouted to the driver, " take 'er
away." There was a grate as the gear-lever slipped in, and a
grinding protesting roar from the engine as it tried to lumber out.
We rushed round and heaved like fury, with arms straining, thighs
tense, and body hard against sweating body.

" Push you bastards ! What the bloody hell are you playing
at ? "

" Shove you ——s, shove."

And away it would go, shaking all over like an old woman,
lurching its way along while we, bare-backed and panting, chased
closely after it with the sand-trays, throwing them in front of the
heavy slipping wheels. Breathless and dry-mouthed we returned
to our jeeps, fell back into the hot seats, wiped the sweat off our
faces and toiled off in pursuit once more.

Those are the two figures that I recall, the two who were
able to make a pleasure out of that work : old Bill Cumper, down
on his hands and knees, scooping the sand from beneath the long
wheels, running the back of his hand across his brow and saying
that if ever his nippers wanted to play at sand-castles, he'd give
them sand-castles they wouldn't forget in a hurry and then, with
the exhortation of, " Now have a shot at the next hundred
yards," signalling the driver to go ahead ; and Jim Chambers,
sturdy and honest, as he kept the men going, when quite a
number, like myself, felt far more inclined to rest and take things
easily.

So we proceeded on our course, driving just south of west,
covering a good mileage one day and only a short distance on the
next. At midday we would halt, sprawling in the shade beneath
the lorries' bellies, eating our lunch of tinned fish or bully and
biscuits, sipping the tea, cleaning out our mess tins with the fine-
grained sand, and then lying back to fall asleep for an hour or two.
All around us the desert shimmered in the heat ; we were
encircled by a vast mirage which faded into the hot blue sky ;
we were alone in an empty saucer of yellow. By resting now—
undisturbed by flies—we found that we were fresh and ready to
move on again in the late afternoon. We would brew up some

tea and smoke a cigarette and then, with Bill gesticulating and shouting to " the land crabs " to get a move on, we would drive until after nightfall.

Our shadows became longer behind us as the sun drew low and stared us straightly in the face ; the black and white turned slowly to softer hues, and gradually the western sky became a vast sea of red and gold, tinging the desert landscape with an infinity of colours. And we were simply dark shadows, little toys cut out of black paper, as we moved slowly—so slowly it seemed—towards the western blaze of colours. How puny and frail we were in contrast to nature's handiwork ! Yet this kind colouring of a colourless world provided a balm to the senses ; it soothed our minds and nerves, it served as a reconciliation for the day and set our hearts at ease. Then came dusk, timid but quick, and the first stars looked down shyly until they were joined by their myriad companions ; and we had become merely dull outlines against a darkening background. As night crept over we switched on our lights ; and there we were, pools of gleaming yellow, and seemingly motionless once more as we ran over the flat unbroken sand. Only a shudder as the jeep passed a slight irregularity, only an occasional stone that showed for a second and then was lost, and only the ruby-red glow of a discarded cigarette told us that we were moving at all.

Soon after dark we would halt for our supper and then, if the going was good, would motor on for a few more hours. It seemed very quiet when we had halted on these nights ; in choosing a sleeping-place, in scooping out a little hollow, and in laying out the blankets, one became aware of the completeness of the silence ; a completeness which was made all the more evident by the occasional mumbling contrast of the sentries' voices.

In such a way we came to Eight Bells—eight coal-black conical hills set out in a row like halma-men. Climbing up one of these slopes I watched the laggards of the convoy approaching our halting place at the foot of the hill ; they looked like little black dots crawling with painful slowness across the mottled, lifeless landscape. To the west of us the country changed suddenly to rough rocky ground with ragged cliff-faces. How long had it looked like this ? I wondered, as I sat down and lit a cigarette.

How strange it was to think that early nomadic man had left his imprint on some of the caves in this vicinity and that, in former days, this wilderness had been a rolling pasture-land over which he had grazed his flocks. It was a thought that left me speculating upon the immensity of space and time and the very reason for life's existence.

Past Eight Bells to the cliffs and narrowing gorge through which our track led in a wandering defile to the more open country beyond. Past huge rocks and boulders that reminded one of the old western films ; with ourselves crawling ant-like in and out, round and between, until we had turned northwards to the cool shadows of Wadi Sura. On either side of us the rocks, coloured by furrowed mixtures of interlacing violets, reds and browns, swept up to nearly a thousand feet. They had been weathered by sand and wind and fashioned into fanciful shapes ; one of them looking like a cathedral dome, another like a lion's head, and another, again, resembling a vast sugar loaf ; and all gave one the same stern impression of their own timelessness and of man's callow modernity.

In such an imposing theatre of silent grandeur we halted and brewed up our tea. The metallic clatter of tins being opened and the voices of the men were echoed and thrown back from the lofty walls above. The shade was refreshing, and the irregular contours made a relief from the barren openness to which we had grown accustomed. After a brief meal we left these huge shapes ; left them as they looked out far across the approaching plains, and drove on late into the evening. And so, on the next day, we had reached the jagged white outcrops of broken limestone, which threw a continual aching glare into the eyes and set our tempers continually on edge. Then west again to where the occasional scrub threw a thrifty existence from the soft sand dunes, and where a solitary desert lark came to share our meals and follow our tracks. This was the first sign of life, and we knew now that we were close to Kufra.

On the following morning, soon after breakfast, we drove over a slight rise in the ground and caught a glimpse of the oasis in a hollow some ten miles further on. A dark olive-green smudge, that was what it looked like, with here and there a neighbouring satelite oasis ; while through the glasses we could make out the palm-trees standing out sharply against the yellow, like little tufted matchsticks.

So this was Kufra ! A minute colony of existence set apart in the desolate wilderness ; one little spot on the map where God had placed his finger and said, " Here ! Here only shall there be life ! "

" Oy ! " came Bill Cumper's voice, " what's yer waitin' for, quack ? It ain't goin' to come out and meet yer ! " And with that abrupt interruption of my thoughts, I let in the clutch and dashed helter-skelter in pursuit of the others down the soft sandy slope. It was not long afterwards that we found ourselves bumping over the hummocks that fringed the oasis itself.

" Blime ! Niggers ! "

" They ain't niggers ! "

" Oh, no ? And what are they then, since you seem to know all about it ? " (Heavy sarcasm in the voice).

" Natives. That's what they are. Natives." (Confident note of authority on the subject.)

" Oh, really ! Perhaps you wouldn't mind telling some of us just exactly what the difference between a native and a nigger 'appens to be in this particular case ? "

" A nigger's black. These are only dark brown. That's all. See ? "

" Well of course if you're colour-blind, there's no point in going on arguin' ! "

" Who's colour-blind ? "

" I didn't say anybody was colour-blind. I said *if* you're colour-blind, same as *if* you're deaf, or *if* you're stoopid, or if you got no brains and . . . "

. The voices came drifting across the still hot air as our convoy stood drawn up by the side of a little road on the outskirts of Kufra, waiting for information as to where the rest of the unit had camped. We had come in along the uneven path that skirted the airfield ; and from our present position by the water pumps we could see the fort set up on top of the northern scarp while the main oasis stretched away and below it to the west. We did not stay here long, however, for soon Bill Cumper had returned and, wheeling his jeep round, he led us along a white dusty track which ran between scattered areas of cultivation, and beyond to the flat salt-caked ground where the date palms and occasional cacti grew and thrived.

It was in a clearing amongst these palms that we caught sight of the men and camouflaged vehicles of the previous two convoys. There was Paddy Mayne lying on a blanket in the shade of arching foliage as he read a Penguin and every now and then picked out a date from a large cluster which was piled nearby. With him were Don Pettit and Bill Fraser, both in the best of spirits, while Sandy Scratchley was wrinkling his brow in perplexity as he argued out some problem of navigation and supply with Ginger Shaw. Yes, most of our boys seemed to be here all right, including even Ken Sculthorpe, our parachute instructor who, now that he had been commissioned, seemed to be far less formidable and fearsome ! Then there was the Fighting French party ; and by the time David Stirling (now a lieutenant-colonel), Maclean, and a few others had arrived by plane we must have been about a hundred strong.

One of the great features of Kufra was the circular pool which was shut off by a reed fence and supplied by a windmill-driven bore-hole pump. The sides of the bath were built of stone ; and although it was only a dozen feet or so in diameter the sight of water was too much of a temptation for us and, without any delay, we threw off such clothes as we happened to be wearing and began splashing around merrily. The water was about three feet deep, and we quickly discovered that the bottom of the pool was slime-covered and very slippery, so that it needed considerable skill to maintain one's balance. The first man who leaped in with joyous abandon found that his feet shot away from under him and that he had immersed himself more rapidly and more completely than he had expected. His companions followed him rather more cautiously ; but within a very short time they had gained complete confidence, if not equilibrium, and a free-for-all ducking competition was in progress. Soon the quiet air of Kufra was resounding to shrill discordant whoops and cries, while the pool had become simply a mass of thrashing arms and kicking legs. We were as naked as God had made us, and it was amusing to see the way each one of us possessed a lily-white bar round his loins in contrast to the dark-brown tan that covered the remainder of the skin. Our aquatic exercises continued throughout the afternoon ; and natives, attracted by the girlish screams and whoops, peered over the reed enclosure and were, I think, utterly mystified by our behaviour.

I was informed that these natives were made up of three different races. Firstly, there were the Sudanese who originally had been captured by Bedouin slave-drivers and brought over to Kufra to be sold by auction. Since then, however, they had been granted their freedom and now they seemed very cheerful as they farmed their cultivated plots and tended the irrigation ditches. They lived in their own communities of reed or dome-shaped mud huts, in contrast to the Arabs whose rectangular huts were surrounded by courtyards. Second and third came two different types of Arab, one Zwaya and the other Majabara, although I must confess that I could not differentiate between them. But, lest the reader conjures up a picture of swarthy, bright-eyed, hawk-nosed Arabs picking their way silently across the moon-lit desert, with lean brown hands ever ready to draw the flashing blade ; lest he pictures them leaping upon their fiery steeds and dashing off into the sunset glow looking as clean, athletic and romantic as only P. C. Wren, Messrs. Metro Goldwyn Mayer and the touch of a painter's brush would have them be ; lest, indeed, a completely wrong picture of these men should be construed, I might as well remark that in appearance they were as dirty and as harmless as the majority of Orientals I had chanced to meet. Naturally this may have been a wrong impression, but as a rule if they rode at all it would be at a jog-trot on their donkeys, while their women walked beside them and, incidentally, did most of the work into the bargain. Their houses—usually single-roomed—opened out into the adjoining courtyards which were surrounded by low walls ; the whole dwelling place being constructed of puddled brick. Since this was soluble in water it can well be imagined that on the very rare occasions when it did rain heavily in Kufra, the results were quite calamitous. Rain, therefore, was regarded as a symbol of the wrath of the deity.

Yet despite their innocent appearance and friendly manners, the history of Libya reveals that they were good enough fighters, and certainly they put up a creditable resistance against the Italians. For it was to Kufra that the Arabs came after they had

been harried from one oasis to another ; and it was only in 1930
that the Italians mustered up sufficient energy to attack them in
their place of refuge. To-day, every one knows of the fine feats of
arms of the Italian forces, of their dauntless courage and indomit-
able bravery, of their dogged persistence and their knightly chivalry
to wounded and prisoner alike. Every one, as I say, knows of these
things ; so that I need only add that it was with these fine
attributes behind them that the matchless Italians marched forth
to Kufra to give battle. And by this of course, I mean—and the
reader will understand—that the Italians merely flew over the
oasis, bombing and machine-gunning the native dwellings as hard
as they could. If they did not use poison-gas one can only assume
that it was because they had no supplies readily available. However, they did their best against Kufra and, having garrisoned the
place, they seized the chieftains who had been criminal enough to
defend their families and possessions, and proceeded to throw
them out of aircraft in full view of the inhabitants of the oasis
gathered below. Such was the noble justice of the white Italians ;
and if I might sound a trifle dubious about their qualities, I trust
that it will be borne in mind that the events which helped me to
form an opinion of them took place before they had become our
gallant allies and glorious co-belligerents.

So much for Kufra with its flourishing date-palms, olive-
presses, and colourful community. With regard to our forthcoming operation, we were informed that it was only a part of a
combined scheme and not one isolated raid as some of us had
supposed. The scheme appeared to be made up of a series of
independent patrols, as follows :

We, of the Special Air Service, were going to raid Benghazi
and, if possible, occupy the town. With us we had some naval
personnel who would assist in capturing the port and its shipping,
after which they might be required to sail the enemy ships to
Malta. One of our main objectives inside Benghazi was the
prisoner-of-war camp ; we intended to attack this swiftly and
liberate our troops who could then be armed with enemy
materials.

How was it possible for two hundred men to capture Benghazi,
the town, airfield and the port ? Only by complete surprise, good
planning and rapid action.

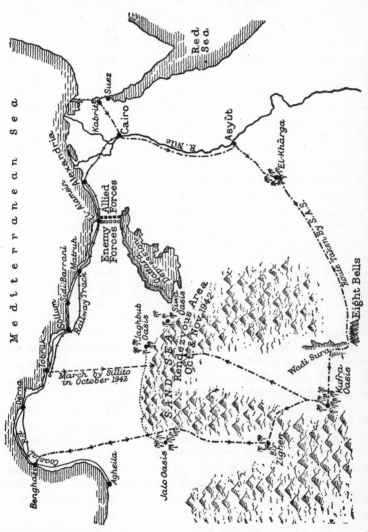

THE ATTACK ON BENGHAZI AND RENDEZVOUS IN THE SAND SEA. SEPTEMBER, OCTOBER, NOVEMBER, 1942.

In addition to our force the Rhodesian patrol, some twenty men strong, were going to attend to the outlying airfields ; while the New Zealand patrol for their part would be raiding Barce and its airport.

We were due to attack Benghazi on the thirteenth of September. Two days later the Sudanese Defence Force, with artillery support, were going to assault the Italian-held oasis of Jalo which lay some four hundred miles to the south of Benghazi, and which we were obliged to pass as we moved north towards our rendezvous in the Jebel district.

On the same night that we attacked Benghazi, land and sea-borne troops were going to attack Tobruk with the object of capturing it and liberating the few Allied prisoners-of-war who were imprisoned there.

If these attacks on Benghazi and Tobruk were to prove successful, our forces in these two areas would consolidate their positions and proceed to converge on the small coastal town of Derna. Allied troops would then hold one long strip of coast line from Tobruk to Benghazi.

Mersa Matruh, also, was being raided by sea-borne troops, although we did not know the details of their plans ; but if our forces could hold long stretches of the coastal road in the rear of the enemy's position, it would be of great assistance to Auchinleck's army attacking at El Alamein.

When first we heard of this operation our chances of success seemed pretty small ; but after a short explanatory talk by David Stirling not only did the whole scheme appear quite feasible but, with a fair amount of fortune, the future looked almost rosy. One of our sergeants, I recall, was reckoning that he stood a good chance of getting a passage to Gibraltar on a German destroyer, and from there he was going to make certain of returning to England. Spirits, then, were fairly high, and individual hopes were far from gloomy as the separate patrols worked out the details of the attack. Beneath one of the date-palms near the track there had been placed a model of Benghazi, and with it were large-scale maps and numerous low-level air photographs of the town. Throughout the day officers and men were grouped round them, each studying his own little area in an effort to make himself memory-perfect. David, himself, was as eager and as full of confidence as ever, explaining away this and that difficulty and somehow imparting his enthusiasm to every single man.

My own plans would, as usual, have to be improvised as circumstances dictated : but it seemed that I would be able to evacuate the wounded by air once the airfields had been captured ; and in any case I was told that I would be in command of Benghazi hospital (a humorous thought !), so there should be little difficulty about disposal of casualties. My first-aid post was a nice-looking villa situated, if I remember correctly, near the Berka aerodrome ; and as I gazed at the little square on the map which represented my future abode I could not help wondering if I should ever use it : that particular house, and not one nearby. In the hurry and confusion of a night battle I could not easily imagine myself stepping out of my jeep, firmly grasping my medical bag in one hand, and walking up the garden pathway to knock on the door and demand my admission. I was to have a small guard posted round the house so that I might work in peace and security, and I was assured that no swarthy Italian would be allowed to sneak up through the back entrance and quietly lob a grenade through my surgery window !

During our short stay in Kufra, my medical life was comparatively idle ; there was the usual sick parade every morning, after which I would conduct a sanitary inspection and endeavour to work out some satisfactory method of latrine construction and disposal of excreta. For the ground here was so hard and salt-encrusted that digging was futile and we were obliged to resort to the ubiquitous if uncomfortable petrol tins, and to burn everything that we could.

Kufra was a bad place for mosquitoes, and soon after darkness had fallen each night we would be plagued by their attentions. Fortunately we all possessed mosquito nets ; consequently there were no cases of malaria—which was not uncommon in the oasis —amongst our own men. The atmosphere was humid and unhealthy, the night air close, and there was no relief of a cool desert breeze. Ants, too, were numerous, and it was necessary to tuck in the flaps of our nets very securely after we had retired inside them. As a result of all these shortcomings we were by no means unhappy to leave the oasis.

Paddy took charge of the first convoy, driving up northwards towards the great Sand Sea—which was shaped like an inverted horse-shoe—crossing over its western limb and running up between this and the oasis of Jalo. Then, heading slightly west of north, he continued towards the Jebel country to the south of Benghazi where our rendezvous was to be situated. With him he took " Razor-blade " Johnson as medical orderly to the convoy ; and he should also have taken on the two Honey tanks which had reached Kufra without mishap, but as soon as this " tank force " —quoted so freely by the papers and periodicals—had reached the oasis, their misfortunes commenced. One of them was " bogged " securely in the salt marsh on the far side of the track which ran past our camp, while the other, although it set out bravely enough, broke down after about fifty miles of the journey had been completed ; so that, in fact, we made our attack on Benghazi without the aid of the journalistic " tank force " let alone the " artillery " !

Bill Cumper left on the day following Paddy's exodus ; and the final party, to which I had been allotted and of which David was in command, pulled out on the next afternoon.

CHAPTER FOURTEEN

WE APPROACH BENGHAZI

" But at my back I always hear
Time's winged chariot hurrying near.
And yonder all before us lie
Deserts of vast eternity."

ANDREW MARVELL.

CLIMBING up the escarpment to the north of the oasis we left the
road, and taking the track which wound past the fort, soon found
ourselves amongst the rough, tumbling hills beyond. But these
were not extensive and we drove on steadily until, by nightfall,
we had reached the first little scattered sand dunes which gave
warning of the Great Sand Sea which lay some fifty miles beyond.

The Sand Sea !

There was a romance in the very name : a nebulous halo of
adventure woven round it by the early exploits of the L.R.D.G.
And here it was, emerging over the flat horizon, ridged and
toothed and white as ivory. Slowly it grew larger, coming
forward to meet and engulf us. Yes, it was a sea ; a sea of white-
grained sand whose waves were shaped and fashioned by the
wind. Here they rose and fell in great, easy, breast-like undulations ; here they had been whipped up to sharp-edged crests of
razor-backed fineness ; while a little further on they would tower
up steeply as if ready and waiting to break over the smooth cupped
hollows which lay beneath. And all the time the Sand Sea was
slowly changing ; the outlines of the waves' crests altered overnight as the wind veered round and blew from a fresh direction ;
in one place the margins of the sea crept slowly forward, in
another they receded. I remember how at its southern fringe we
found old tracks of L.R.D.G. vehicles which had suddenly been
interrupted by a great crested sand-dune that had rolled forward
in the interim ; and on its far side we could see the same tracks
emerging and continuing. These impressions would persist on
firm ground for years, and I think it was in the neighbourhood of

Siwa that the tracks of armoured cars used in the last war were discovered.

The Sand Sea was beautiful in early morning or late evening, when the low glancing rays made every peak and sinuous dune stand out with geometrical clarity. But once the sun was well up there were no shadows, and hence no contours or perspective. You drove along in a sea of blinding white ; and when you felt the jeep rise beneath you then you knew you were climbing a dune ; when you saw the bonnet of the jeep level off you knew you had reached the summit ; and when you noticed it tip down and felt the subsequent acceleration you knew you could let the vehicle coast down the opposite side of the dune. It was almost uncanny the way you were unable to see the dunes as they rose, one behind the other, in a continual sequence and in the same intensity of glaring white. You would see part of the convoy disappear quite unexpectedly away to the right, while a moment later some jeeps over to your left would become tip-tilted as they climbed a dune of whose proximity you were completely unaware. It provided a sensation reminiscent of the dentist's chair as you felt yourself rise and fall over the waves and hollows ; but there were other discomforting occasions when you felt the jeep cant sharply sideways, and you knew you had to alter course suddenly to preserve the vehicle's balance and prevent it from falling over. I saw men thrown out of their jeeps on one occasion as they accelerated fast up a sand dune and reached the top without realising, until it was too late, what had happened ; whereas the danger of razor-backed dunes was made fully manifest later on, when the jeep which Don Pettit was driving somersaulted over one and he was killed immediately. These " razor-backs " were developed by the wind blowing hard up against one slope, packing the sand tightly and building up a fine crest until there was a sheer drop of anything up to two feet on the softly-packed leeward side. It was advisable, therefore, to keep an intent watch on the other vehicles in the convoy, noticing especially what was happening to those in front of you, and slowing down rather than accelerating as you approached the crest of a dune.

It can well be imagined that the Sand Sea made very difficult " going," not so much for the jeeps, tearing about the place like kiddy-cars, as for the poor old lumbering three-ton lorries which groaned their way up the successive slopes. There were, too, the usual unpredictable drifts of soft sand ; and it was by no means uncommon to have to unload a lorry and " portee " the contents over the treacherous parts. I can remember once following a lorry as it bowled cheerfully along a firm level piece, when all of a sudden it half-jumped into the air, almost falling over sideways as it did so, and equally suddenly spun round so as to face me directly. It was most dramatic, and, seeing the large deep tracks which had formed beyond a certain point, I banged the jeep into four-wheel drive and swung it out to avoid a collision. But my luck was little better ; and after the jeep had pushed a small hillock of sand round in a vast semi-circle, the engine stalled, we came to a halt, and then had to back our way out slowly. That error cost us the better part of an hour in delay.

It was, however, the " soft " dunes that proved to be the most serious obstacles. They would form ridges which were almost impassable, stretching out far away to either side of the line of approach so that there could be no question of going round them. At these barriers the lorries would halt while the jeeps held a competition to see who could get up first, and soon the dune would become scored with jeep's tracks ending at different levels up the slope. Eventually one jeep would crawl over, and from his lead the best crossing point could be judged. Sometimes, too, the sand would be so soft on the far side of the dune that vehicles would slide down it broadside ; a fact which should give the reader some idea of the gradient as well as of the loose packing of the sand.

Nevertheless, the crossing of the Sand Sea, although laborious, was extremely enjoyable ; and night would find us early abed and happily tired. Within two days we had reached its western border and had come out on to a completely flat plain, carpeted in places by weed and small flowers, and without a sign of any cover. It was not long before we had located the old Arab track, which had been recently beaconed by the Italians, as it led northwards to the Jalo oasis. This we followed, branching off later on a more easterly bearing in order to skirt the oasis itself, and so drove up cautiously between it and the Sand Sea.

I well remember the evening when we passed Jalo. We could see the little, fragile palms standing out clear and naked against

the dying flame of the western sky, while close to the east of us
was the toothed whiteness of the sand glimmering in the fading
light. Jalo was held by the enemy ; so we crawled past it, through
the twenty-mile gap, and then halted in order that we might cross
by night the track that linked it with the other enemy-held oasis
of Jaghbub. Here we brewed up a hot supper to fortify ourselves
against the cold night-drive that lay ahead, and soon after it had
grown dusk moved on again. But hardly had we started when
one of the lorries ran over a hummock and tossed its occupants
overboard. Looking back on it now, it seems nothing short of a
miracle that this did not happen frequently on our night-drives.
It was the only instance that I ever witnessed, and on halting to
see what damage had been done I discovered that there was only
one serious casualty. This was Wilkinson, a fitter-sergeant who
was looking after our transport ; and as he lay on the ground,
shocked and in considerable pain, a cursory examination revealed
that he had fractured the upper part of his femur. David
approached, obviously anxious to cross the track as quickly as
possible. " How long will you be ? " he asked, after he had
expressed his sympathy and regret. Knowing that we would take
up most of our time in assorting and assembling our equipment
in the dark I demanded an hour ; and within that time we had
anæsthetised him with the invaluable pentothal, splinted him as
best we could, and loaded him up on top of a camouflage net on
the back of a lorry.

We continued on our way. The " going," however, was so
bumpy and slow, and the risk of a repetition of the accident was
so obvious, that we were forced to switch on our lights. Having
crossed the track without any mishaps, we halted at daybreak
for breakfast and a short sleep before proceeding any further. We
had passed the dangerous zone, so now we accelerated and moved
on north as fast we could. The country was rough-coated and
furrowed with small branching depressions ; beneath the dark
gravel-surface lay thick, yellow dust, and this we churned up in
a huge drifting cloud which spread like smoke as it followed in
the wake of our convoy. Any aircraft could not have failed to
see us from a considerable distance, betrayed, as we were, in such
a characteristic tell-tale manner. But our fortune held, the only
drawback being the pain which Wilkinson was suffering ; and

this presented a very real problem. Bumping over the desert in a lorry is never comfortable, but when you have broken your thigh into the bargain, the continual shaking is well-nigh intolerable. Try as he might, Wilkinson was unable to suppress an occasional cry and groan. These sounds of pain upset the driver, who slowed down in order to take the bumps the more easily and thus delayed the whole convoy. I was doing the best I could with injections of morphia, keeping Wilkinson as drowsy as I dared ; a blanket had been rigged up over him to afford protection from the sun ; he had as much water as he could drink ; and the only other thing to do was to explain to the driver that, by driving fast over the bumps, no more pain was inflicted than by taking them slowly. This was very probably correct and certainly it diminished the travelling time ; but Austin, the driver, a man who looked rough enough to perform any task with equanimity, said that this was something he could not do. We sympathised with him—he had a heart of gold—but we had to get to the rendezvous in time, and this we could not do at our present rate of approach. Sandy Scratchley took a turn at the wheel ; and for a while we made better speed—with Wilkinson borne along in litter-like state in our midst—but soon he, too, began to lose ground and fall back. He confessed afterwards that it was a most unhappy experience. We changed drivers for the second time. On this occasion it was a small, inoffensive-looking Cockney who took the wheel—a man, you might have judged, who would not have said boo to a goose—and from then on the lorry kept up well with the convoy and never lagged behind. I do not think that the patient suffered any more as a consequence.

By now we had once more reached dangerous country since the enemy, knowing that the L.R.D.G. and previous S.A.S. patrols had operated in this vicinity, had scattered thermos bombs and various other types of anti-personnel explosives over wide areas. Also, of course, the risk of our detection was increasing as we drove further north, and consequently we were driving more and more by night as well as by day. On the other hand we were taking advantage of the level country to increase our speed, and frequently we would be driving through the night at thirty miles an hour, only halting for a rest during the latter hours of darkness.

Two days after Wilkinson's accident we were sitting round the trucks eating hungrily at our breakfast, when quite suddenly we caught sight of a puff of smoke on the northern skyline. It looked more like the explosion of a mine than either a bomb or a shell, and there was something very ominous about it. Whatever the cause, we decided, after questioning one another concerning the possibilities, it could only mean bad news. There were no planes in the sky ; there was no sound of action ; everything looked peaceful and quiet in the early morning light. What could it be ? With that worrying feeling which is born of uncertainty we returned to our meal ; but before we had finished it we had detected a spiral of dust approaching slowly from the direction of the explosion. As it came closer we could distinguish the out-line of a jeep, and a minute or two later Bill Cumper drove in along the narrow track which ran past our laager. But there were no smiles or jokes from him this morning as he announced briefly that a " job of work for the Doc " was at hand, since two of his men had been blown up by a thermos-bomb and severely wounded.

There was little for me to pack and get ready so, having seen that Wilkinson was comfortable, Shotton—the Yorkshire medical orderly—and myself set off in the jeep. " Follow the track," shouted Bill over his shoulder as we pulled out of the laager, " there's bombs about."

We did our best to do as we were told, but it was difficult to keep up with him and follow the track carefully at the same time. For he was fairly rattling over the ground, in and out amongst the clumps of bushes, whichever way the little path turned ; and as we chased after him I prayed that the ampoules containing the pentothal might not be broken.

After about twenty minutes we reached the convoy ; and as we got out of our jeeps and made our way towards the wounded men, Bill told us what had happened. The casualties, it appeared, were a gunner officer new to the unit and his corporal driver ; they had driven up to inspect a derelict truck and in so doing their jeep had run over a thermos-bomb. It was not an uncommon accident, for the enemy delighted in surrounding any abandoned vehicles with such anti-personnel devices. In the explosion that followed the jeep was set on fire and the officer badly burned.

Cox, the driver, jumped out and ran round to pull the officer out, but as he did so he stepped on another bomb which exploded and shattered his leg. By this time the others had realised what was happening and a few of them dashed over and dragged the wounded men away to a place of safety.

As we approached the wounded, the little group of men who were standing by them turned round and their faces brightened. " You're O.K., now boys," they said, " the Doc's here " ; and I could sense the relief in their voices as they transferred the burden of responsibility over to me.

I took a look at the two men. They were both in pain, but whereas Cox was severely shocked and had the typical feeble running pulse, the officer seemed to be very strong and his pulse was full and bounding. Well, we could only inspect the wounds and do our best ; but before proceeding to any treatment I wanted to be rid of the crowd. Bill was anxious to be on his way ; so, having made quite certain there was nothing he could do, he got his vehicles lined up in a single file and led them away down the track. We busied ourselves in unpacking our medical supplies, and as I made up the pentothal solution I considered what our procedure should be. Cox's leg was broken badly, with the fragments of bone lying open in the wound ; moreover there had been considerable damage to the soft tissues and at first glance it seemed unlikely that the leg could be saved. As for the officer, he had been burned severely ; and, despite the difficulty of estimating exactly which areas were second and which were third degree, the very extensiveness of the burns made the prognosis extremely grave. Yet, strangely enough, not only was he fully conscious but he was even making an effort to crack some rather grim jokes at his own expense. I explained to Shotton how I wanted the burns cleaned and dressed with sulphonamide and vaseline ; but in truth I think he knew the routine as well as I did, for he had done a good bit of field work in the past. In a few minutes he was ready ; there was never any wasting of time about Shotton ; he was keen, sensible and practical. I gave the injection of pentothal and left him to carry on.

Turning to Cox I found that he did not need much pentothal ; quickly and gratefully he passed into unconsciousness. A second inspection of his leg confirmed my earlier impressions. There

were, however, the following points to be considered before
deciding on any form of treatment ; we had another seventy or
eighty miles to travel before reaching the rendezvous ; there was
the period of the attack on Benghazi when I should have to leave
him ; and if the attack was not successful then we would have
to bring him over the eight hundred miles of rough country back
to Kufra. I thought he would recover more quickly if his leg
was amputated ; both bones were already broken into splinters
and lay tangled in the charred skin and clothing. What of the
risks of infection ? And what of gangrene ? To amputate was not
a pleasant decision ; but surely it was not justified to try and save
such a limb at the increased risk of life.

Shotton's voice came over to me, rousing me from my
deliberations : " 'Fraid the officer's stopped breathing, sir."

" Oh, damn and hell ! "

I left Cox and found it was as Shotton had said. We started
off on artificial respiration and slowly his breathing picked up,
automatic and shallow, but at the same time he began to regain
consciousness.

" 'Ello, boys ! . . . Where the 'Ell are we ? " he spoke drunk-
enly, slurring his words. " This is a fine kettle of fish . . . God !
. . . The pain in my eyes.. . . It's my eyes. . . . Can't you fellowsh
do sumshin about the sun ? " He raised his head out of the dust,
trying to orientate himself, peering round at the stones and scrub
as they shimmered in the morning heat. " My head, Doc . . . the
sun . . . it's my eyes."

And all the time we were fumbling clumsily with the anæsthetic
ampoules, trying to get the powder to dissolve quickly, and yet
realising that there was danger in its use. But surely it was right,
it was so very right, that if a man was to die then he should die
without pain. Whoever put us into this world, if He had good
reasoning and kind logic, would say that there was no wrong
in this.

" Quiet, now ! Just keep still a minute."

Quickly he lapsed back into unconsciousness. I looked up to
find that Cox was beginning to talk and move his legs, whereas
his wound had become covered with a thick layer of blown dust.
We dissolved up some more pentothal and deepened his anæsthesia ; it was not very easy working in such an interrupted

manner with these half-gramme ampoules, and it appeared that we would have to speed up our efforts.

That September morning was hot, very hot, and the sun was beating straightly down on to the backs of our heads as we toiled and laboured. There were just the four of us—and all around the silent lonely emptiness of the desert. The sweat ran down our foreheads and we had to shake it off clear of the wounds. Kneeling down I found that my legs became cramped and stiff, so that constantly I was obliged to alter my position. My back ached and I longed to stretch myself.

A desert-lark flew close and came running jerkily along the ground nearby ; his eyes were bright and inquiring as he watched us toiling. In truth I am afraid that it was crude, unskilful work, far removed from the niceties of technique and collaboration of an operating theatre. The dust blew suddenly on the hot wind, forming a dirty film on the antiseptic solution, coating the instruments, and fouling the raw wounds. Every now and then a sand-devil spiralled up and reared its way along, sweeping past with a hissing sound and fading away into the shuddering distance.

There was a slow rumble on the air and soon afterwards David Stirling drove up with his convoy. He halted and walked over to me, anxious to have news of the wounded and find out more about their condition. Were they badly injured ? Yes, they were both very gravely ill. Did I think they would pull through ? I hedged, saying that I could only hope for the best. Could he help ? I shook my head. How long did I think I would be ? Perhaps an hour or so ; I would be as quick as possible.

He looked at Cox as he lay in the sand with his eyes gazing up vacantly at the sky and his mouth dropped open. " Poor devil," he muttered. " Are you taking his leg off ? "

I nodded. " How about a lorry to get them up to the rendezvous ? " I asked.

" Well, Malcolm, I'll leave an empty three-tonner. That's the best I can do, I'm afraid. And one jeep to navigate you there."

He detailed Ginger Shaw to stay behind ; and then, with an encouraging pat on the back, he left me and returned to his jeep. A few minutes later and the little party of trucks had begun to file away down the track. Looking up I caught sight of Wilkinson being borne along on his lorry, and then I turned back to Cox.

Shaw, the Australian pilot, came up to me, " Can I help you, Doc? " he asked. " Not that I've had much practise at this sort of thing yer know, but p'raps I can lend a hand, eh ? "

There was something inexpressibly kind in his rough offer ; and he knelt down on the opposite side of the body, watchful and eager, and ready to do the smallest thing that might be of assistance.

Then, suddenly, quietly, and with no sort of fuss or warning, Cox stopped breathing. Putting down the instruments we got to work on artificial respiration. Up and down, up and down, up and down. Pushing on his chest so that the air blew in and out of his dry throat with mechanical lifelessness. It was exhausting work and the sweat ran down our bodies in little sinuous trickles. After ten minutes, we ceased, Nothing happened. His pulse was not palpable. We set back to work again. How long should we go on with this ? After a while we stopped again. Our efforts seemed to be of no avail.

" Well, it looks like the end." I got to my feet and stretched my legs. " That's that, I suppose ! Now we'll have to find somewhere to bury him."

" Bit stony round here, Doc." There was perplexity in Ginger Shaw's voice, and all at once I wanted to burst out laughing. God, what a life this was !

" Say, Doc—look ! " I felt him gripping my arm tight. " Look. He's breathing ! "

I turned and looked ; and there, slow, faint and uncertain, life and breath seemed once more to have come into being. We set to work again with urgency ; and when it was all over, the skin flaps secured, and the dressings firmly in position, we got busy with the plasma transfusions. Both the wounded were still asleep, and leaving two men from the lorry to keep an eye on them, Ginger, Shotton and I walked over to the navigating jeep and opened a tin of sardines. By now it was past midday and we were grateful for the shade under the lorry. As soon as the transfusions were finished we transferred them on to stretchers and loaded them on to the floor-board of the lorry. Already they had begun to show signs of returning consciousness : the gunner officer boisterous and incoherent, but Cox very weak and quiet. We tied the stretchers down to the floor-boards with rope, and then set off with the navigating jeep in front, the lorry second— with Shotton aboard to look after the wounded—and finally the medical jeep to bring up the rear. It was a sorry little procession.

Following the bumpy winding track as it led in and out of the scrub clusters, we found ourselves passing derelicts from the retreats of both armies in previous campaigns. Here a Hurricane had landed and stood, pathetic and tip-tilted, with its propeller bent and dug into the sand ; while there was a burnt-out German tank, silent and rusted and trackless as it leaned half over on one side. I wondered what the occupants were doing now, for there were no signs of nearby graves.

The " going " was very bad, for the track was covered in places with an inch or two of fine white dust which filled the deep irregular hollows, making them appear level, and which rose like an angry cloud at our approach. We bucketed our way on ; at each hollow the dust flew up like spray from a destroyer's bows in a heavy sea, falling with a soft hiss over the bonnet and blinding us as we strove to keep to the track. ·Soon we had become thickly coated ; the dust was in our hair, rimming our bleared eyes, caking our lips and beards. We looked like a party of grotesquely powdered clowns.

We found it hard to drive behind that lorry and watch the wounded men rolling and bumping about. Somehow it did not seem fair to the sensibilities of the mind and imagination that we should have to suffer such mental torture. For at each irregularity in the ground the lorry would bounce up like a live thing, bumping and shaking the patients ; and from where we were we could see the three legs and one stump fly up into the air and fall back asprawl the stretchers with a sickening jolt. We stopped our vehicles and bound the men's legs down to the stretchers with some more rope. The officer was delirious, rambling in his speech, yet seemingly free from pain. I can see him now, as he tried to prop himself up on his elbows, blinking the thick dust out of his eyes and peering over the side in an endeavour to make out what was happening. Soon he had given it up and was lying back, singing away at the top of his voice. The song was " When I went into Benghazi harbour," and I dare say it was original ; the tune was that of " O'Reilly's daughter " ; and as he roared away he made an effort to beat time to the tune with his bandaged hands. Beside him lay Cox, silent, in pain, and conserving all his resistance to win the personal battle of life and death. You could see it in the expression of his eyes as we washed the chalky dust away : " I'm going to live ! Yes, I *am* going to live ! "

We sponged their faces with water, gave them some morphia, and proceeded slowly on our way. Every half-hour or so we halted to wash away the fresh dust that had settled on them, and allowed them to drink in little sips from the bottle. Shotton was magnificent. " Stick it, lads," he said, " keep it up a little longer and you'll be O.K."

" Hold on, me hearties ! " bellowed the officer. " Water ! Give me water for God's sake ! "

We propped them up against our shoulders while they sipped, but it was almost too much for Cox and he lay back panting with the effort. The water trickled down their faces, drawing little smudgy lines of cleanness over their cheeks and running on to their dirty shirts.

Shortly before sun-down, we met a jeep travelling in the opposite direction ; it had come back to find us and lead us into the rendezvous. We followed it over country which was becoming more and more hilly and fertile, and finally joined the other parties soon after it had grown dusk, when bushes and lorries had become faintly contrasting blurs on either side of the track. It had seemed a long journey ; but now we could make the wounded really comfortable and give them something hot for the night. I wondered if Cox would be alive by the morning ; for on examination by torchlight he looked so grey and weak, while his pulse was racing fast and scarcely perceptible. I decided to give him some more plasma before he settled down. The officer, on the other hand, seemed remarkably strong ; he was rational now and talking sensibly as he recognised his friends, but every now and then he would lapse off into confused speech. Paddy Mayne brought over some of the renowned " hot sweet tea " and supported them as they drank. I thought this action was typical of him, for on these occasions he was always ready to help, and, without obtruding or getting in one's way, he was available whenever needed. " Your grub's ready for you over by the cook's lorry," he told me ; so I wandered over only to find that, despite the fact that I had eaten little throughout the day, I was more tired than hungry.

After supper I paid Wilkinson a visit ; he appeared to be free from pain and happier than I had expected, so I did not spend long with him but returned to our own lorry. There was little change in the condition of the two men. They were both sleeping quietly and, feeling that there was nothing further to be done, I left Johnson to keep a watchful eye on them and laid out my blankets nearby.

I was wakened at about three o'clock the next morning by Johnson shaking my shoulder. " The officer's just died," he said.

I rubbed the sleep from my eyes, trying to recollect the circumstances. " The officer ? " I asked.

" Yes, sir."

" Why didn't you tell me before ? "

" He's only just died, sir. He died in his sleep. He was breathing quite strongly one minute—then he stopped."

I clambered to my feet and walked over. Yes, he was dead all right. It was foolish of me, I suppose, but all the time I had been thinking that Cox was the more dangerously ill ; yet I must have known that burns such as these are nearly always fatal.

I took a look at Cox ; he was hanging on, just doing that and no more. I prayed that he might not die too. It must not happen. We would fight every inch. And yet there was nothing that we could do, absolutely nothing. That was the devil of it ! It was simply a case of maintaining the " cat-like observation combined with masterly inactivity " that the text-books delighted in quoting. Patience. That was it ! How easy, and yet how difficult it was to apply it to one's own practice.

I returned to my bed and fell asleep almost instantly.

CHAPTER FIFTEEN

WOUNDED MEN IN THE JEBEL

" O ! I have suffered
With those that I saw suffer."
The Tempest. SHAKESPEARE.

The next morning dawned fresh with a warm sun and a fine
mackerel sky—the first clouds we had seen for a long time—
and it was kindly in contrast to the continual powder-blue that
we had grown to know, day after changeless day. We were up
early, and buried the dead officer quite simply and with no
ceremony in a small nearby hollow where the soil lay deep. By
the time we had returned to the others it was to find that the
Arabs had already discovered our rendezvous and had come along
to visit us, with their hoods drawn tight over their heads and their
cloaks falling loosely from their shoulders. Their beady brown
eyes were alight with the pleasure of barter as they traded their
fresh eggs and meat for our sugar, salt and cigarettes. Then, when
they had completed the transactions, they would sit down on
their haunches and watch us with puzzled expressions on their
dark wrinkled faces. Or perhaps they would wander down the
branching wadis exchanging salutations and greetings with one
little group after another.

At first I was surprised to see them mingling amongst us like this,
but I was assured that their friendship was genuine and that they
had helped our patrols frequently in the past. The British used a
few intelligence officers who, dressed like Arabs, lived with them
in the Jebel ; and the natives had proved very helpful in obtaining
information for them about military and naval activities in
Benghazi. Naturally the enemy kept a very close watch on the
Arabs, and if one of them was caught helping us he paid for it
with his life. Further, they bribed some of the natives to inform
upon the others, thus forming a sort of Arab Gestapo so to speak,
and consequently causing considerable trouble amongst the Arabs

themselves. In the Jebel, however, the Arabs were loyal to us and when, after this raid, they were told that any members suspected of helping the British would have his whole family killed, they let us know of the circumstances and asked us to withhold our activities in that particular area until the conditions became safer. On the other hand the Arabs in Tripolitania were far from friendly and this, I believe, was accounted for to some extent by enemy propaganda, which had persuaded the natives most effectively that if the British won the war they would hand the country over to the Jews in the same way as they had done with Palestine after the last war. The controversy and incompatibility between Arab and Jew needs no description here ; but this is an example illustrating the far-reaching effects of a decision which concerned but one small group of such a widely-scattered race.

Arguing this problem over with myself, I wandered over to Cox who, I found, was looking very weak and tired, but without a doubt he had improved. If he survived the next twenty-four hours, I thought, his chances of recovery should be good. I asked him how he felt, and he replied that there was not much pain, only an occasional twinge and ache in his foot—" the phantom foot "—which made him want to alter its position. I did not tell him we had amputated the leg below the knee, deeming it wiser that he should remain in ignorance until he was stronger. One of his main interests concerned the welfare of the burned officer, but we satisfied him with our answers and told him that we had moved him further up the wadi to be with his friends. I had noticed before how attached men became to one another when they had been wounded together. All that day he lay on his stretcher in the shade of the lorry, dozing off quietly most of the time ; and when he awoke he seemed quite cheerful and more rested. We kept him out of pain with morphia, made him drink as much as possible, and were well pleased when he took a little arrowroot at midday. On the following morning we started him on a course of sulphonamide by mouth.

As I explored my way around the camp, I found that it extended up a long winding wadi which led away at right angles from the main track. From the top of a small hill I could see the surrounding Jebel country where the rolling green and brown slopes were broken with rocks and boulders. There were thick bushes scattered along the valleys ; and among these we had run our vehicles, camouflaging them well with thick branches and scrub. All the way down the wadi were little groups of men kneeling or squatting as they pored over the maps ; while the officer in charge of the section was making certain that each man knew the part he had to play in the raid.

" Looks as if you're going to be kept busy, Doc," Sergeant Almonds hailed me as I made my way down. What a fine figure he made, I thought, with his dark tan, broad shoulders, narrow waist and Raleigh beard. What a good tobacco advertisement he would have made if he could have been pictured now, as he stood drawing at his pipe and looking at me in that half-amused way of his !

Having paid my respects to Wilkinson who was fast recovering from the strain of his upsetting journey, I returned to my jeep to sort out the medical kit and share out part of it to Shotton. For it was obvious that someone would have to remain with these two wounded men while we were away, and I thought that Shotton most deserved the rest and could best take the responsibility. We were going to leave the greater part of our heavy transport here ; but I was taking a three-tonner forward with me in case we had any more wounded, and the other two medical orderlies would be going with the raiding parties.

When this little job had been finished, I lit a cigarette and pulled out a dirty old copy of *The Forsyte Saga* which I had brought along with me. How strange it was to read the descriptions of London streets, and of Richmond Park with its bracken growing thick and inviting in springtime, a veritable haven for lovers. How well I knew it ! The reality of Galsworthy's characters and the beauty of the descriptions took me far away from the Jebel with its September heat and flies ; far, far away to the green countryside of England ; to those places which I knew so well, still much the same, only now others were there instead of me, and fresh feet trod the leafy footpaths that once had been my private realm. It is strange how we think of these refuges as being our very own : they remain intimate in our memories until we feel that it is ourselves who are indispensable ; yet no sooner have our backs been turned than we might never have existed. Here, where Irene and Bosinney had met and wandered,

I too had followed ; and to me these pages recalled pictures of laughing hazel eyes against a patterned background of leaves and sky. Memories now that were doubly dear ; and, bridging time and space, they brought with them a colour and a reason for living, and left an aching longing in their train. . . .

That evening, on joining David Stirling and Paddy Mayne after supper, I was introduced to a new officer, Captain Melot. He was a very old friend of the unit since he had helped previous S.A.S. patrols in the Jebel. He was about fifty years of age, married, with a wife and children in Alexandria where he had been working before the war. In the last war he had served with distinction ; and this time he offered his services as an intelligence officer, since he was closely familiar with the Arabs and their language. His offer was accepted and he had spent a considerable time living with the Arabs in this Jebel country, obtaining information about the enemy and wirelessing it back to head-quarters. It was in such a capacity that he had come to know and help our previous raiding parties. On this occasion, I recall, after we had been introduced he continued with his interrogation of a rather timid looking Arab and, following a minute or two of animated conversation, he turned to us and explained the position.

This Arab, with whom he had been working for a considerable while and therefore accepted as trustworthy, had just returned on foot from Benghazi after spending the whole of the previous day in the town. He had brought back depressing news, which seemed to indicate that the enemy had long been aware of our raid and were ready to meet it ; they were cognizant, even, of the approximate date of the attack. Moreover, he had passed through a minefield and dug in positions which surrounded Benghazi ; and when he was inside the town he had been in-formed that the ships had left the port, and that aircraft were using only one airfield which was strongly guarded. Further, the standing garrison was expecting to be reinforced by five thousand Italians from scattered camps in the surrounding area.

David digested this unhappy news in silence for a moment or two, then he turned to Melot. "This Arab is quite reliable, I suppose ? " he questioned.

" I think so," Melot nodded his head in that emphatic way of his. " Oh, yes, I think so. I have often worked with him before. Besides, why should he say these things if they are not true ? What can he gain from it ? If he had *not* told us of them, then it *would* be possible that the Germans were bribing him. But I feel pretty certain that he is all right."

We pieced the information together. It was evident that the enemy knew of our plans and were expecting us. We had lost our most powerful card : that of surprise. Was there now any object in carrying out the raid ? Could our small force do anything against a prepared enemy who was so vastly superior in numbers and equipment ?

In view of this fresh aspect of the situation, our plans would have to be altered, for it was obvious that we would be unable to capture and hold the town in the face of such resistance. The best we could do was to carry out a short, sharp raid and be as destructive as possible ; there would be no likelihood of occupation, and we should retire before daylight. In that case, I reckoned, it would be wiser for the medical aid post to remain outside the minefield ; and eventually it was decided that it should be located near the edge of the escarpment so that any wounded could receive proper attention on the morning after the attack. The men were not informed of the preparedness of the enemy and it cannot be said that our morale fell ; but there were some of us who were quite thoughtful on that evening as we sat round the trucks and considered the possibilities. Paddy scarcely said a word other than remarking that it looked as if there should be some hard scrapping ; and, with a feeling that sufficient unto the day was the evil thereof, we made our way to our jeeps and began to unroll our bedding.

On the next day we left the rendezvous in two separate parties. The first and smaller of these moved off at about midday ; their object was to capture the small fort at the top of the escarpment, for this commanded the pass which was our sole means of approaching Benghazi from the south. The force was made up of about a dozen men, including Johnson, the medical orderly ; Melot and another officer, Longland, were in charge. Having secured the fort, the second party would be able to proceed to the main attack without any risk of interference from their rear.

Consequently we, of the chief raiding force, left the cover of our sheltering bushes early in the afternoon, jogging in single file along the narrow track that wound snake-like round the easy slopes of the hills and followed the valleys along the lengths of their courses. The scene was one of idyllic peace. Native shepherds with their flocks browsing on the hillsides waved to us as we passed. Mothers came from the multi-coloured tents to point us out to their babies as they gazed wide-eyed and vacant ; " Inglees ! " they said, " Inglees, kwayis ketir." They stood watching our procession until we had passed out of their sight. I wondered if they would be telling their children and grandchildren about this in the days to come.

Twice we had to stop for aircraft ; but on neither occasion were they close, nor did they appear to be searching for us. It seemed very strange that they should know of our raid and yet make no effort to attack us as we approached. Perhaps they preferred to lead us on, pretending that they knew nothing, and confident that they would catch us the better by so doing. It was not a very cheering thought ; but anyhow we were one jump ahead of them, for they did not realise that we knew that they were aware of our approach !

Towards early evening we came to a wadi leading away from the track ; and this, it was decided, would be the best site for an advanced rendezvous area and medical aid post. From here, if required, I would be able to reach a casualty from either of the two parties ; but if this eventuality did not arise and if, perchance, the operation should materialise into a holding affair, then this place was easily recognisable and I could be called forward. Ritchie was proceeding as medical orderly to the main party and he and Johnson could be relied upon to get casualties back safely to the medical post. So at this point we drove off the track, halting a short distance from it, to wave farewell to the others as they drove past.

" Oy, Quack ! " It was Bill Cumper of course. " Oy ! Mind you've got yer knives nice and sharp before we're back ! And look 'ere —just you bury yer leg next time you chops it off. See ! Or I'll report you to yer boss when we gets back. You'll 'ave this place looking like a butcher's shop if you don't look out. It's nothing to laugh at ! I'm not joking ! Oh, no ! What ? me ? You've never seen me joke in my life." He turned and watched the French driving noisily past, " Onward—mez amiz," he cried out, striking a gesture as he did so, with one hand pointing towards the sky and the other resting over his heart, " Onward—à la glory." Then he looked back at me, " Well, see you bardin, Doc ; and if I'm eating sphagetti this time to-morrow, give my love to the old dutch. O.K. ? Trezz beans ! "

And with that he revved up and dashed off after the others, with his passengers hanging on for dear life. Soon they had wound up and away over the rounded hill-slope and were lost to our sight.

By now the sun was low in the sky ; so that each valley was filled with a deep violet shadow, and only the caps and the rough shoulders of the hills basked in the glancing rays. We drove up the wadi to a point about a hundred yards from the track, where two bushes arched together, and between them we ran the lorry ; the jeep we hid a little further on. Then we got busy cutting down branches and pulling up the long dry grass to lay over the camouflage nets, until the vehicles were more or less indistinguishable from their surroundings. That completed the hard work, and it gave the three of us the opportunity to linger over our supper, and to lie back and enjoy our cigarettes.

The two drivers made excellent companions, and I knew that they would make very willing helpers if ever I needed them. One of them was Austin who had driven Wilkinson for part of the journey after the latter had been injured. " Any other job," said Austin, " I'd 'ave done and no complaining, but that one was beyond me ! " Dear old Austin ! He was of the salt of the earth and as tender-hearted as a woman towards any one who had been wounded. He and his pal, Hevans, were usually quite inseparable, although on this occasion Hevans had gone on with the main party.

Shaw, the other driver, was the type of person who appeared surly on first impression ; but I preferred them like that ; it was the talkative men who were so trying. And Shaw, like many other reticent people, was as dependable and reliable as any one could be.

We sat there chatting away until it had grown quite late. A pack of jackals could be heard crossing the wadi to one side of us ; their shrill laughter sounded horrible and frightening ; I could feel the hair rising on the back of my neck and almost instinctively found myself wondering where my revolver was. At midnight, we knew, four squadrons of the R.A.F. were going to bomb Benghazi ; and as soon as we heard the first plane droning overhead against the stars we got up and climbed the hill to the north of us, hoping to get a view of the town. But we were not sufficiently near to the escarpment edge to see anything other than the twinkling flashes of the hevay shell-bursts ; while the explosions of the bombs and guns came to us merely as a confused rumble on the soft wind. We made our way down to the valley once more and cast lots to determine the order in which we should keep watch during the night. The luck was with me ; so I decided to take the first spell and, after walking down to the side of the track with my book, a torch and a couple of blankets, I was soon lost once more in the misadventures of poor old Soames Forsyte. I could just picture the unhappy fellow " mousing his way down Cheapside " with everybody's hand, as it must have seemed, raised against him and lifted in protection of Irene. Reading thus I found that time passed quickly, and soon it was two o'clock in the morning. I woke up Shaw and lost no time in making myself comfortable for the night when, just as I was falling asleep, I heard the buzz of a motor in the distance. Almost immediately I felt that something was wrong and lay there, half-awake, half-asleep, listening to the interrupted noise which gradually was growing closer. It sounded as if the driver was uncertain of his way and was exploring each small wadi that branched off the track. I woke Austin and together we walked down to join Shaw, whom we found listening attentively.

" Sounds like a jeep," he remarked, and after a few minutes we could all recognise the familiar chugging of the engine. We signalled our position with the torch and the driver approached us ; it was Robinson, one of the operatives from the first party.

" Mr. Melot's been wounded, sir," he called out.

" Badly ? "

" Pretty fair, I think, sir. In the stomach and legs. He's lost a good bit of blood and we can't bring him back 'cos we've only got jeeps. Mr. Longland's caught it too, but I think they have got a lorry for him."

We walked back to our vehicles and pulled off the camouflage nets. Our previous work in this respect had been a waste of time ;

in removing them we soon had the folds stuck together by the prickly branches and we cursed heartily, knowing very well that it would be at least an hour's work to unravel them again later on. However, there was no time to be wasted, and after bumping our way down to the track, we set off in pursuit of Robinson's jeep.

For the next twenty minutes we drove slowly and without lights, until we had reached a point at which we were signalled off the track by Melot's party. We found him lying on the ground covered by a greatcoat, while the rest stood round in a silent shivering group.

" Hallo, Melot ! " I said, " what's got you ? "

" Oh, hallo, Doc." He looked a lot older, I thought. " There's nothing much the matter with me. Hand-grenade wounds, you know."

" Do you mind if I take a look ? " I asked, kneeling down beside him.

We pulled back his clothing, cutting it away where necessary, and lifted the dressings which Johnson had applied so that we could estimate the severity of his condition. His pulse and general condition were good, whilst a cautious probe inserted into the abdominal wound showed that it was only muscle-deep. That was a relief. But there were multiple leg and thigh wounds, some shallow, others penetrating and making it difficult to assess what damage had been done.

" Well," I remarked after a quick survey, " we'll give you some morphia and a transfusion ; then we'll get you back to the aid-post where we can dress you properly."

" I don't want any morphia, Doc. Thanks all the same."

" But it would be a good thing for you to have some. It would help you for the bumps and jolts on the way back."

" But I'm not in any pain, Doc. I walked most of the way from the fort to here, you know. It's just that I can't walk properly now."

" Yes, I see what you mean. Still, the morphia would do you good." Somehow I felt very foolish in my choice of words.

" Doc, I've never taken any medicine in my life, honestly I haven't. Only some of those chemical tablets which I put in my water to make it fizzy. I've got some here with me now. I'll show you." He began to fumble amongst the pockets of his overcoat.

"Now, look here, Melot, I'm just going to give you a little prick in the arm. So! Now, that's that finished, we'll give you some blood plasma. It won't last very long."

"Well, you know best, I suppose." He shook his head dubiously as he lay there, pretty disgruntled really ; for he was no longer a youngster, and he had formed his own opinions on how to look after himself. The idea of the transfusion did not appeal to him at all ; you could see that from the suspicious expression on his face as he watched the plasma solution dripping slowly from the bottle which Johnson was holding up. Johnson's teeth were chattering hard and in truth it was bitterly cold. I walked over to my jeep to get another blanket.

"Oh . . . I say . . . er, excuse me !" I turned quickly at the sound of this very superior Oxford voice. "Ah ! . . . excuse me . . . do you happen to have seen David Stirling or Bob Melot round here recently ?"

Who in the world is this ? I wondered, as I looked the new-comer up and down. For he seemed to have stepped right out of the heart of nowhere into the lights of my jeep which I had recently switched on in order to examine Melot ; and, if memory serves me aright, he was dressed in a check jacket and a sort of plus-four-cum-leggings outfit, his whole appearance reminding me of a photograph I had once seen of Bernard Shaw as a young man. In his right hand he carried a knobbly walking stick, and this he waved round as he questioned me in order to indicate his lack of knowledge as to their whereabouts.

"Who are you ?" I asked.

"Me ? My name is Farmer. I work round here, you know. But look, old chap, *have* you seen Stirling recently? I want to speak to him."

Somehow the whole situation seemed to be so incongruous that for a moment I was tempted to reply that he had just taken the third turning on the left. However, I thought better of my flippancy and told him instead that Melot was here, that he had been wounded, and that soon we should be taking him back to the medical post.

"Really !" he said with feeling, "I *am* sorry," and with that he strode off towards the others, swinging his stick as he went. He remained with them until we moved off and then disappeared

into the darkness as quickly and mysteriously as he had emerged
from it. Altogether a rather odd little incident, I thought, as we
jogged back along the track. Later, Melot told me that they
had worked together in the past ; and he was highly amused
when I told him of my peculiar meeting with the bearded stranger.

On arrival back at the medical post, we made Melot comfortable beneath a bush and then set to work to untangle the camouflage nets. It was a wearisome job that tried the patience and it
seemed that we would never get it finished. By the time it was
back in position again, a pallor had already begun to creep across
the eastern sky ; the bushes and shrubs stood out with hazy
indistinctness, and the desert larks were uttering their first
monotonous, tuneless notes.

A lorry rumbled slowly down the track and, seeing us wave,
it pulled into the wadi.

" We've brought Mr. Longland along," said the driver.
" He's caught it bad in the chest."

Carefully we lifted him off a lorry and on to a stretcher, and
then bore him laboriously down the wadi towards an irregular
piece of ground where the bushes grew in a cluster. We drew
aside his shirt and examined the wound ; it was very small—little
more than a centimetre across—and there was no apparent
bleeding. But it was situated just above the heart ; the left lung
had collapsed ; he had a sucking pneumothroax and his condition
was serious. In the normal course of events, with early hospital
treatment, he should have recovered ; for there was no evidence
of internal hæmorrhage. Here, however, with a journey of about
eight hundred miles back to Kufra, the future did not look so
good. Even now he was breathless on the slightest exertion. How,
then, could he stand the long bumping journey on the back of a
three-ton lorry ?

We dressed the wound, plugging it firmly, and then propped
him up until he was comfortable ; there was little more that we
could do save to give him adequate fluids and keep him rested.

We wondered how the raid had fared. These men knew
nothing of the main raid, of course, but they had captured the fort
and so allowed the second party to get past. They told us how
they had hidden their transport and then approached the fort on
foot. Mr. Melot had been in front as they climbed the hill!

which it dominated, and by shouting out in Italian that they were Germans who had been sent to relieve the garrison, he managed to get his party almost to within the gates before the Italians had realised their mistake. A short fight ensued in which first Melot and then Longland were wounded ; the remainder of the party quickly captured the fort, and soon the few Italians left alive were grovelling and pleading for mercy.

Having seized the fort, they wrecked the wireless equipment and the barracks, and then, their mission completed, they returned to their trucks. It was at this stage that Melot, who had continued fighting after he had been wounded, found that he could go no further. (In view of later knowledge this was not surprising, since an X-ray showed a fracture of the femur and a veritable snow-storm appearance of foreign bodies in the lower third of the thigh.) Our informants did not know how many Italians had been garrisoning the fort ; but only two were brought back as prisoners and one gained the impression that the fighting had been pitiless.

Our conversation was interrupted by the Rhodesian patrol of the L.R.D.G. returning down the track. They stopped and told us that they had been unsuccessful in their raid ; then they inquired after our news. We gave them such information as we had and recommended that they should begin to search for cover and a hiding-place, for the eastern sky was brightening all too quickly. " We're going on to the rendezvous," they announced ; and as we watched them drive out of sight, I think that we were all dubious whether they would reach it safely.

A minute or two later a Messerschmitt 109 flew straight past us and down the track ; it was about a hundred feet from the ground. We waited in silence, and then it came : the fast crackle of machine-gun fire, sounding hideous and frightening on the chill morning air.

Our day had begun.

CHAPTER SIXTEEN

THE AMBUSH

" Scarce could they hear, or see their foes,
Until at weapon-point they close."
Marmion. SIR WALTER SCOTT.

YES, it was a strange day for us, and throughout the morning we
hid industriously from the aircraft that swooped and circled over
our heads. Indeed, there were few periods when the air was not
throbbing with the noise of planes, and it was alarming the way
they would appear so suddenly over the brow of a hill and with
such little warning. Soon we realised that movement of any
sort could only be carried out with the greatest caution and
accordingly we would bide our time, waiting for a moment of
respite before we moved warily across the open ground to the
next bush. We did, however, have occasional lulls ; and in one
of these we put Melot to sleep, cleaned his wounds—cutting away
the dead tissues—and dressed him properly. Twice we were
interrupted and bent down low, covering the white of the cotton-
wool and bandages and screening any reflection from our instruments. On the second occasion we could hear the plane circling
steadily over us at about two hundred feet from the ground.
Johnson and I crouched down beside Melot who was snoring
away blissfully with his false teeth laid out beside him ; slowly
we moved the stretcher on which he was lying until we had
edged it right under the bush ; then we crawled round the shrub
and hid beneath it on the far side. The plane continued to circle
and then came down lower. Looking between the twigs and
branches of the bush, I could see Johnson blinking at me solemnly
from behind his spectacles and for a moment I wanted to laugh.
Then the plane dived. We heard the engines racing hard as it
flew straight over us and machine-gunned some bushes on the
far side of the wadi. Fortunately there was nobody hiding in
them, and I suppose the Italian felt that he was wasting his
time for he did not return. I prided myself on the way he had

missed the lorry and jeep, and when the noise of his engines had died away we continued with the toilet of Melot's wounds. He recovered consciousness about a quarter of an hour later and was very pleased with life, his words tumbling haphazardly over one another as he swore that the anæsthetic was the best thing he had known for a long time. We left him to sleep off the effects of the pentothal and moved over to some neighbouring bushes.

During the long hot hours of that morning we could hear the shuddering, breaking noise of exploding bombs, interrupted, from time to time, by the brisk staccato of machine-gun fire as the planes searched one wadi after another. The sounds came chiefly from the north and we feared that our main party had been detected, but since movement was impossible we could only pray for their safety.

Lying down there in the shade, and made sleepy by a wakeful night, it was hard to appreciate the reality of the enemy's vigilant pursuit. You saw the planes, sometimes singly, sometimes in groups ; you observed the markings whether Italian or German ; and yet it seemed so strange to think that up there—a few hundred feet over your head—was, say, an Italian farmer or a German clerk. You had never met each other and this was your intro-duction ; with him searching the ground below for the slightest betraying movement, and with you, crouched and huddled, feeling almost that you should be holding your breath and speaking in a hushed whisper.

As you saw these aircraft circle round in constant search, you realised just how much the Italians loved this type of warfare. One thing that distinguished them from the Germans was that, whereas the latter were usually content to machine-gun our trucks, the Italians went for the men. All of which, of course, was perfectly fair and above board ; but one felt that if there was a rotten trick that could be played, then the Italians would waste no time in putting it into practice. From experience in the desert war, one can say that the Italians behaved with all the brutality of cowardice, maltreating our wounded and despoiling our prisoners ; they were treacherous always, and never reliable. The act of surrender to them was not infrequently taken as the opportunity of throwing a grenade or producing a dagger. In their personal habits they were scented and unclean ; their field sanitation was more or less non-existent ; dysentery they accepted as one might a cold in the nose. Child-like they might be ; but that happy smiling nature was only one very small part of the total. What of the cheerful children who used gas against the Abyssinians and boasted that machine-gunning human beings was far better than shooting animals. Of such is the Kingdom of Heaven ?

Yet, despite these facts, if you were to open a current periodical or newspaper you might quite easily see photographs of British girls fraternising with Italian prisoners. On another page you might read of how these prisoners threatened to " strike " if they were not given better facilities, or of how a farmer complained because his " boys " (Italian prisoners !) were not provided with the same comfortable amenities as those of another farmer ; and in later months you would see an article devoted to the protests of the prisoners because they were being subjected to the danger of the flying bomb. They demanded that they should be moved from the southern counties !

The situation was paradoxical. While we in the desert fought and despised the Italians, the people of England quarrelled and wrangled with one another to see who could make the most fuss of them. There was something very pathetic in reading these announcements in the papers. Would British women never learn to hate a foreigner ? Must they always be the ready dupes of a flashing eye and a brilliant smile ? Did they not realise that these were they who were behaving so ignobly towards their own kith and kin abroad ? Could they not understand that these were the men who would draw blood from a stone when they were winning easily, and who would grovel for mercy as soon as they were captured ? Evidently not. The British were trying to fight a war abroad and reconcile the enemy at home ; it was our well-known policy of appeasement, and it gave our men a fine sense of value as to what we were fighting for !

The memory of that morning brings back the picture and the setting. I recall the soft slopes of the hills, the songs of the birds, the aimless flight of the butterflies and the way they opened and closed their wings to the sun. I remember the coloured lizards darting across the ground with quick electric movements, stopping quite still to gaze around with expressionless eyes, cocking their heads from side to side and then scampering off into a thicket.

There was an old chameleon there too. Perhaps he was not so aged really, for even when a chameleon is young he has that " you can't teach me anything " sort of look on his face and somehow manages to appear wise and pompous. This one lay on a branch of a small bush—a dull mottled green and black— with his eyes swivelling slowly this way and that as he contemplated the mysteries of the universe. Directly I moved a finger towards him his throat began to swell and his back to arch up ; fury was written all over his malevolent face and there was a baleful hatred in his eyes. Then, as I left him in peace, he settled down again gradually to the day's routine. Life seemed to move in slow tempo for him ; slow, that is, to all save the unwary fly who just glimpsed a flash of succulent red before he was drawn fast to his doom.

Yes, nature was awake and very busy that morning. Ants were struggling with manifold labours to pull a dead beetle across a little clearing ; messengers ran to and from the main party bearing instructions and preparing the way. It was strange how much of their work seemed purposeless and wasted, how much needless energy they expended in circling round and round a stone, for instance ; or how they would set off with the utmost determination in one particular direction and then appear to forget completely what their object was and wander round in a casual, *laisser faire* sort of way, pausing every now and then to stroke their antennæ as if there was absolutely nothing to do and all day to do it in. If ever there was a case of much ado about next to nothing, I thought, here it was ; and the chances were that they would abandon the beetle in the end !

At midday the planes quite unaccountably ceased their activities, and we emerged from our hiding-places to assess the damage. A jeep appeared over the hillcrest and jolted down the track to give us the news that Dawson, one of our men, had been seriously wounded ; the driver did not know where he was, but wanted me to come in search of him. Loading some of my equipment on to the driver's jeep, we drove towards the encamp-

ment. On our way we passed little groups of men, well dispersed
on either side of the track, with their vehicles camouflaged beneath
the bushes and small shrubs. We stopped to ask directions for
Dawson but, although they knew he had been wounded, none of
them was able to give me any information of his whereabouts.
After a further search we returned to the medical post and I was
happy to discover that no fresh casualties had come in during
my absence.

During the afternoon some jeeps and lorries drove down
the track and dispersed in the rendezvous area. In one such
jeep was Macleod, carried along on top of a camouflage net,
and we used this as a hammock in order to lower him to the
ground.

" 'E's serious, doc," the driver mumbled to me in an aside.
" Arm's broken in two places. 'E wants to have it off."

" Has he been in much pain ? " I asked.

" Yes, very severe. We've given him eight of those morphia
tablets, but they don't seem to 'ave touched 'im some'ow. 'Ope
that was the right thing to do, sir ? "

" Yes, of course it was." For a brief moment I recalled the
attitude of medical headquarters in Cairo : that our men
were too ignorant to be allowed an allotment of morphia
solution for injection in the small phials supplied to R.A.F.
bomber crews—for the R.A.F. were intelligent but the S.A.S.
were made up of hooligans who would not know how to use it ;
that one tablet of morphia per man would be entirely adequate
for our needs.

Poor Macleod ! Every one in the unit knew him, since he
was one of our comedians, and there was always a joke and
a laugh from his quarter. But now it was very different,
his face was contorted and he was almost hysterical with
pain.

I gave him a strong injection of morphia.

" How long will that take to work, Doc ? "

" Three or four minutes."

" Roll on three or four minutes ! Oh, Christ ! " A fresh
spasm of pain shot up his arm as he tried to alter his position
slightly, " Chop off this bloody arm, for God's sake. Take it off,
I tell you." The pain passed away and he turned a pallid face

towards me, " It's bad you know, Doc, I'm not exaggerating. You'll probably have to take it off."

" We'll see, Macleod ; I won't unless I'm forced to. Just you rest now ; that's the main thing."

He rested his head back and soon the expression of suffering had left his face. " It's O.K. now, Doc. Can't feel the pain."

We started him off on a plasma drip, content to leave his wounds until he had recovered from the shock. In the meantime we had the minor casualties to deal with : glancing wounds of the hands, buttocks and legs ; there was nothing to cause any anxiety. While we were dressing them we inquired after the raid. It was pretty obvious that it had not been a success. The men replied in their characteristically candid manner, " We got a pasting all right. . . . Walked right into an ambush. . . . Jeeze ! They had us where they wanted us."

From one source and another we linked the story together. It was by no means as bad as it might have been ; they had given just about as good as they had received in the night action. This was their tale :

After we had dropped out of the convoy, they had driven on towards the escarpment, reaching it just as darkness fell. Here their difficulties had started. Some of them thought the Arab guide had led them down by the wrong track, and were convinced that he was in the pay of the enemy. (I think he was cleared of all these suspicions later on.) But whether or not this was the cause, they experienced great difficulty in getting down the steep, rocky escarpment, and in the end they were obliged to use their lights to avoid accidents. It was quite possible that the enemy could see these lights as they wound their way down the cliff-side. Their descent took far longer than had been intended ; and by the time they had reached the bottom they were well behind the time schedule and still had the plain to cross before they reached Benghazi. They had not gone far when our aircraft began to raid the port. The object of this aerial activity was to divert the enemy's attention and to cover the approach of our ground forces. In fact it did neither ; our men were still some distance away by the time the raid had finished. Not until three o'clock in the morning did they reach the outskirts of the town ; they were

driving in single file down a broad path which was flanked by
ditches and trees, when suddenly they found their way barred
by a wooden, cantilever gate. David Stirling was in the leading
jeep—the only one which had used its lights since reaching the
plain—and he halted the convoy and got out to open the gate.
Finding, however, that it was too stiff for him to manipulate, he
called up Bill Cumper who approached in his usual jaunty
manner and flung it open. Then, turning round and facing the
convoy—standing full in the lights of David's jeep as he did so—
Bill raised one arm in the Fascist salute and cried out loudly in a
Stanley Holloway voice, " Let battle commence ! "

At this particular moment there must have been a number of
Germans and Italians watching the whole scene from their dug-in
positions near the gate. There were more of the enemy hidden
amongst the bushes on either side of the path, and it would be
interesting to know just what they thought of Bill's effort. Did
they imagine that this was an oration to whip up the spirits of
the troops to a fanatical pitch : the prelude to the fray ? What
did they think when they saw this man give their own salute ?
Certainly Bill's words could not have been more appropriate for
hardly had they been uttered than battle did commence, and
with a vengeance. Machine-guns opened fire from either side,
sending coloured streams of tracer criss-crossing over the heads
of the attacking force ; in their excitement the enemy were firing
high. Our men fired back from their jeeps and silenced a number
of the guns. But this could not continue indefinitely, and David
decided that withdrawal was the only possible policy ; it was a
wise resolution but it must have been a difficult one to make for
a man of his calibre. Acting under these orders the jeeps and
lorries slowly backed and turned in the narrow lane. Snipers were
firing on them from the bushes on either side as they did so, but
their answering fire kept this nuisance well in check. Paddy and
Jim Chambers drove up to the head of the column, with their guns
firing long sweeping bursts ; and here they stayed until the
force behind them had driven away. Then they, too, turned and
followed. One jeep was left behind ; it was driven by Sergeant
Almonds, who had been seriously wounded and could not be
rescued.

The next consideration was to reach the cover of the escarpment before it grew light. It was a long drive across that level plain ; a race against time, and against the dawn which was slowly lighting up the sky with such gradual insistence. They raced on as fast as they could ; and by sun-up some of them had reached the top of the escarpment, some were making their way up the pass, while others were waiting at the foot. It was while they were situated thus that the first enemy planes made their attack, flying low over the ground, bombing, and then circling round to machine-gun the vehicles and men. It was an attack which persisted without respite until noon. Each plane flew back to its aerodrome, refuelled, and took off again for another attack. It was easy work for them, with small risk attached to it, for our machine-gun fire appeared to have little effect. At some time during the morning Dawson was wounded ; he was firing from his jeep when a bullet hit him and spun him over as if he had been a child's plaything. Nobody knew of his whereabouts ; most of the men thought he had been brought back to the medical post.

So that was the account of the raid on Benghazi ; an affair in which our casualties appeared to have been relatively light, although there were still quite a number of men who had not been accounted for.

Having finished with the minor wounded we returned once more to Macleod, who by this time was beginning to look a little more like himself and seemed much better for his rest. His arm we dressed cautiously ; the bones were shattered just below the shoulder and again above the wrist, so that he could scarcely tolerate any movement. They were nasty, ugly, perforating wounds, and as we bandaged his arm to the splint I wondered if he would ever be able to use the arm again. It hardly seemed probable. I had decided not to interefere much with the wounds themselves, but to wait until his general condition was better before I did anything in the nature of a debridement. Time, too, was growing short, for by now the sun was dipping down over the hills and throwing long shadows aslant the rounded valleys. An Italian fighter plane was circling round to the north of us ; every now and then it would swoop down, and a few moments later we could hear the dull crackling fire from its guns. Such animosity, somehow, seemed foolish and ineffectual on this still

summer's evening, and it was almost with disinterest that we
watched it head off against the colourful sky towards Benghazi.
Soon the pilot would be stepping out of the plane ; soon he
would be pulling off his flying suit and making his way towards
the mess ; soon he would be laughing and joking with his friends
about the day's sport. . . .

We began to load up our lorries, ready to return to the main
rendezvous. While we had been busy with Macleod, the two
attacking parties had assembled at the bottom of the wadi and
now they were waiting for us. David Stirling and some others
had not yet come back, but we were not unduly perturbed for
we knew that they had remained out to search for and bring back
any stragglers.

That night drive—a mere twenty-five miles or so—was, in all
conscience, a wretched affair : bumping and tumbling about in
the lorry ; pitch blackness all round ; the groans and sudden
sharp cries of the wounded ; the halts to give one of them a jab
of morphia ; the halts because someone had seen a light ahead
and we did not know what it meant ; the interminable, repetitive
halts. Huddled close together, we sat on the ammunition and food
boxes. We half-dozed as we swayed to the movement of the lorry ;
our heads fell low over our chests ; it seemed that our eyelids
could not open. Our minds were half in consciousness and half
outside ; it was a labour to drag the thoughts back to realities ;
it needed a sudden painful effort to pull them over the aching
gulf. Yet we could not rest. There were legs everywhere and no
room for comfort. The wounded lay on stretchers down the centre
floor-boards ; we could smell the stale blood from their wounds.
Asleep ? Awake ? The two had merged together. Someone's boot
was resting on your thigh ; it had become painful ; you tried to
move but your leg was fixed. There was another halt. Voices
in the darkness, grumbling, cursing. The noise of the lorry
grinding and jerking up a hill. Your head fell down once more. . .
it was too much of an effort to raise it. . . .

Eventually we reached the rendezvous. It was about three
o'clock in the morning. Wearily we got out of the lorries. The
wounded were made comfortable. We dragged out our blankets
and threw the camouflage nets loosely over the trucks.

" Home sweet home ! " said a voice in the darkness.

There was a half-hearted attempt at a laugh in response.

" Home sweet —ing home ! " came the rejoinder.

Silence in the wadi. A little breeze that tugged fitfully at the bushes. A deep sigh and a stretch of the legs.

Then sleep, dear God, merciful sleep !

CHAPTER SEVENTEEN

OUR SAD WITHDRAWAL

" The tumult and the shouting dies ;
    The Captains and the Kings depart : "

Recessional.

" The depth and dream of my desire
    The bitter paths wherein I stray—
    Thou knowest Who hast made the Fire,
    Thou knowest Who hast made the Clay."

R. KIPLING.

WE WERE UP AGAIN by six in the morning, wiping the cobwebs from our bleary eyes. Things did not seem to be quite right. There was an atmosphere of apprehension in the camp. What were we going to do now ? How long had we to wait before David Stirling gave us our orders ? Where were the enemy ? Had any ground-forces been sent out after us ? There was a rumour, which was supposed to have originated from the Arab guide, to the effect that we were surrounded by five thousand Italian troops ; they were said to have moved into position while we were pinned down by aerial fire. We thought it over as we ate a meagre breakfast of a little porridge and bacon, our first food for some while. Conversation flagged, for our spirits were not very high.

We posted sentries on the surrounding hill-tops to give warning of the enemy's approach. At any rate we would put up a good fight. Our vehicles were camouflaged more closely, and all the seriously wounded were placed together. There was Wilkinson with his broken thigh, Cox with his amputated leg, Macleod with his useless arm, Longland shot through the lung, and Melot with multiple grenade wounds. We could do little for them in the way of medical treatment other than to make them comfortable, restrict the pain with morphia, encourage them to drink as much as they could, and start them off—Longland and Wilkinson excepted—on courses of sulphonamide by mouth. Longland was looking very fragile. The night journey had upset him and he was getting attacks of shortness of breath with cyanosis. These we relieved with injections of adrenalin ; and with this drug his general condition improved slowly throughout the morning, although, even so, it appeared unlikely that he would survive the journey to Kufra.

There was one other nasty little problem which cropped up at this, of all times. Griffiths, a Welsh driver, had developed a sudden acute tonsillitis with such severe swelling of the tonsils and surrounding tissues that his respiration was becoming embarrassed. It was most unfortunate, and we were obliged to keep a very close and anxious eye on him lest a tracheotomy should become a necessity. Fortunately the condition subsided as quickly as it had arisen. But how I dreaded the thought and the possible consequences of having to use a knife on him !

At about eleven o'clock a jeep drove fast into the wadi, bringing the news that Dawson had been found and brought back a part of the way towards the rendezvous, but that he could be moved no further on account of the pain he was suffering. The driver said he was ready to lead us back to the place where Dawson had been left, so, bidding farewell to the wounded and leaving the medical orderlies in charge, Shaw and I set out to follow the other jeep. Nothing of note occurred during the first few miles, until the erratic behaviour of our jeep told us that one of the wheels was punctured. We shouted and yelled to the jeep in front but were unable to attract their attention. Slowly we fell behind and had the chagrin of watching them draw ahead and out of sight. It was most galling, and pulling up to a halt we jumped out to inspect the flat tyre. It looked like a long delay, but to our surprise another jeep came driving along the track in the opposite direction. It stopped, and after a brief explanation I transferred my equipment—leaving Shaw to mend the puncture —and set off once more towards the scene of the previous day's activities. After a while we caught up with the leading jeep and followed it for some distance before it drew off the track towards a small cluster of scrub. Here, lying in the scanty shade, was Dawson, his healthy bronzed features belying the real gravity of his condition.

" I'm sorry to have given you so much trouble, sir," he said

with a forced grin. Could any words be more typical of the
fortitude of these men ? I wondered, as I made up the pentothal
solution. Could anything more nearly express their spirit ?

Without disturbing him, we injected the anæsthetic, and he
sank back into his first sleep for over forty-eight hours. Examination of his wounds showed that it was necessary to drain the bladder
at once ; a catheter could not be passed so that an abdominal
incision was unavoidable. It was not a pleasant procedure when
one considered the lack of sterility of the conditions under which
we were working. However, there was no other course open to us ;
and as we were proceeding with the operation the familiar drone
of an aeroplane came to our ears and soon afterwards an Italian
bomber flew overhead, describing large circles as it followed the
track towards our rendezvous. We stopped our work until it had
passed over. About five minutes later another plane followed the
first. So they were after us again ! Once or twice we were
obliged to throw a blanket over Dawson and crawl across to some
adjoining bushes, for groups of men were too easily distinguished
at that height. Fortunately the job did not take long, and, by
attaching a clasp-knife over the catheter outlet, we were able to
ensure slow drainage. As I clamped the knife over the tube I was
reminded of the serene words of wisdom that we used to hear as
students on the ward rounds, of the surgeon lolling back in com-
placent self-satisfaction, and of ourselves as we stood round the
foot of the bed wondering who was going to be asked the next
question. No cool green wards now ; no tidy white coats ; no
trim nurses to bear one attendance. Only the green-brown hills
shuddering in the heat haze ; only the hot blue of the sky and
the white of the rocks ; only the thin trickles of sweat running
down our foreheads and flanks.

We loaded Dawson on to the jeep, laying him crosswise on top
of a camouflage net, and then started to drive back slowly towards
the rendezvous. A moment later and we had been forced to move
hurriedly from the track and take cover from an aircraft which
was following the same course. After two minutes' grace we made
another effort, but again we had to chase back towards the sparse
bushes. We gave it up. Aircraft were flying over every other
minute, all leading towards the same quarter. From the direction
of our rendezvous came the familiar sad sound of bombing and

machine-gunning, and looking in that direction we could see a thin dark column of smoke rise lazily heavenward. Through the glasses there was no difficulty in distinguishing the planes as they circled and dived in rotation. Soon another coil of smoke had wreathed up beside its fellow ; we judged our petrol supplies had been hit. Thus it continued throughout the afternoon, with all types of aircraft flying towards those tell-tale pillars of smoke. What could we do ? Plainly it was impossible to move down the track ; yet it was dreadful to have to remain here as helpless spectators. Some of the planes were flying very low and every now and then we would have to hide amongst the scrub. Dawson, at any rate, was happily unconscious of the whole affair ; lying under a small bush he looked as if he would sleep for a century. After a time I began to give up the thought of getting back by jeep. I considered the possibility of walking ; but it was ten miles to go, and with a monkey-box to carry I would not arrive before sundown. I resigned myself to the wait. There was a little water and a piece of cheese in the jeep ; we devoured the latter hungrily ; it tasted wonderful and there was just enough to make our mouths water. Meals were becoming irregular, we remarked, as we lit cigarettes and scanned the skyline once more.

Towards sundown the planes became less frequent, and judging that it was worth our while to try and move, we set off towards the rendezvous. The jolting motion of the jeep woke up Dawson whose dazed movements threatened to unbalance him and spill him off ; it took us a little while to quieten him down. On our way we came upon another jeep, and wishing to get back more quickly I changed my transport. The western sky was a smouldering flame as we rattled busily along the rough surface, and I can picture one lone plane flying slowly back towards Benghazi. To me, at that moment, it seemed that the silhouette of the plane against the sunset glow epitomised our whole suffering and day's travail. The next instant and it was lost against a darker streak of sky. Then came the glimmer of dusk, the uncertainty and haziness of outlines ; it was harder now to follow the track, and by the time we had reached the rendezvous the fires of the burning jeeps and lorries had already begun to stand out clear and red against the gathering darkness. The men were returning over the slopes of the hills whence they had scattered from the air attack. We could hear them calling out to each other as they straggled down.

Further along the wadi we were stopped by Bill Cumper, " 'Ullo, Doc ! " he shook his head appraisingly, " plenty of work for you all right."

" Who's hurt ? " I asked sharply. I was in a very bad humour and felt ready to bite anybody's head off.

He told me ; and as he led the way carefully towards the wounded—for there were several unexploded bombs and anti-personnel devices dropped—I was sorry to see my medical transport ablaze. Nearer to the wounded there was another lorry on fire, with the flames flaring up and down and licking along the metal-work. In the ruddy, fitful light it was plain to see that the wounded had endured a harrowing experience. Unable to move, they had lain there on the stretchers throughout the bombing and strafing ; the two lorries nearby had been set on fire. Several times they had been machine-gunned closely, although Wilkinson was the only one to be wounded ; he had been shot in the leg which had already suffered a fracture. The others, mercifully, had escaped injury. Throughout the afternoon Shotton had stayed beside them, moving from one man to another, and looking after them as best he could. It was a fine example of devotion to duty.

While we were trying to make the wounded comfortable once more, Dawson was brought in on his jeep. He looked terribly tired and weak, and seemed, strangely, to have grown much smaller ; but at any rate he was in less pain than before. Then a lorry rumbled out of the darkness towards us. With much shouting the men inside lowered a body, slung in a blanket, to the ground " One of the French ! " they said. I looked down at the face, white and peaceful ; at the chest which scarcely moved with its quick shallow breathing ; at the fingers as they opened and closed with mechanical lifelessness. It reminded me of the way I had once seen a bird's claws open and close as it died. Poor little Henri ! So this was his last chapter ! No more anger in those brown eyes now ; no more tears for him. Life would no longer be " formidable " ; there would be no more obstacles or trials to be overcome. For now he was mortally hurt, and far beyond any crude help that I could give. Within a few minutes he had died, and we covered him over with his blanket.

Considering the length and intensity of the attack, the number of our casualties had been slight. One or two had been killed outright, but the others had suffered comparatively trivial wounds and did not need to be nursed. This low figure was due to wide dispersal. At first our men had stayed to fire at the planes ; but after a time they had grown discouraged by the apparent lack of effectiveness of their small-arms fire and had scattered to take cover. Actually they had " shot up " one plane to such an extent that it crashed a mile or two away, and several more must have been damaged.

For the next half-hour or so we were kept busy with this impromptu sick-parade, until a messenger came over telling me that David Stirling wished to see me immediately. I walked back the way I had come, past the burning lorries, and found him talking with Paddy and Major Barlow—a recent arrival to the unit, who had helped Shotton to look after the wounded during the day. It was a great tonic to see David back again, even though the circumstances were so adverse. He caught sight of me and smiled ; I found myself grinning back. " Hallo, Malcolm," he said, " you *have* had a busy time ; you must be absolutely exhausted. How are all the wounded ? " He frowned as I told him and hesitated for a moment before he went on, " I'm afraid we have got some very bad news for you. We're moving off in two hours' time, but we simply haven't got enough room to take back the wounded with us. I'm terribly sorry." I looked at him blankly. " We've lost most of our transport, you see," he said, indicating the burning lorries. " We've hardly got enough room for our fit men on what remains ; stretchers are just out of the question."

So it had come at last. Somehow, almost subconsciously, I seemed to have been expecting this news throughout the past two days. It now remained for me to decide on the course of action to be taken with regard to the wounded men. There were six of them all told who needed constant care and nursing ; and of these six it was possible that Melot and Macleod could travel without stretchers ; perhaps they would be all right resting on camouflage nets. With regard to the other four, three of them needed immediate hospital treatment ; while Wilkinson was unfortunate in that, although not really ill, he was unable to travel without a stretcher. It was necessary, then, that we should arrange for these four men to be taken to Benghazi hospital. The question was : how should they make the journey? In this respect we decided to use the two Italian prisoners who had been captured at the fort ; one was a medical orderly—a piece of good fortune for us—and we made the following arrangements :

One of us would remain here with the wounded and, on the following morning, set out for Benghazi with the prisoner as a guide, leaving the Italian medical orderly in charge of the casualties. There would be more than enough water, food and medical supplies to suffice their needs, while an unarmed jeep would be left in which the two men could drive into Benghazi. When these two had reached the town their object would be to contact the hospital, obtain an ambulance and lead it back to collect the wounded ; returning with them to the hospital and being responsible for their disposal.

There was nothing difficult about this plan ; it remained for us to decide who should stay behind. We held a medical conference and talked it over, after which I returned to David requesting that I might stay and see the thing through to my own satisfaction. At the same time I felt that my real duty was to continue with the main fighting force, in case further casualties were sustained. Our present position looked decidedly unpleasant and it appeared likely that there was more fighting to be done. But it was a most unhappy feeling not to know definitely where one's duty lay ; I felt that the best I could do was to offer to remain with the wounded and leave it for others to decide. There was no effort in staying behind—far less in fact, for we were all extremely tired and wanted a rest—whereas the thought of a night drive was pretty cheerless. David and Paddy considered the position and told me that I must remain with the fighting force. So be it. Once more I retraced my steps, and broke the news to the orderlies.

The next problem to be solved was which of the orderlies should be left behind ? It did not seem fair that Shotton should be considered since he was not familiar with the country or the route to Benghazi, whereas Johnson had been to the edge of the escarpment overlooking Benghazi and Ritchie had gone as far as the outskirts of the town itself on the night of the thirteenth. We agreed to leave Shotton out of it and decide on the fate of the other two. By strange chance I discovered a piastre piece in the pocket of my shorts—Heaven knows how it had lingered there !— and by the flickering illumination of the fires I solemnly spun it up into the darkness. " Heads," said Ritchie. We could not be sure for a moment which side up it had landed, until the pale gleam from Shotton's torch showed that Ritchie had called correctly. Johnson did not seem unduly upset. Hunching up his shoulders and blinking seriously at us as was his wont, he resigned himself to his fate. What he really needed, he told us, was a decent Red Cross arm-band ; so we picked the best we had and he fastened it in position. The unarmed jeep was run over to us ; it contained an ample quantity of petrol ; Johnson had a compass ; and it seemed that nothing was lacking as far as planning was concerned.

Perhaps the hardest part of the whole day consisted in informing the wounded of the facts, and in bidding them farewell. It was even worse than I had expected. Dawson was too ill to care much about what happened ; but Longland, despite his condition, found it a bitter pill to have to swallow ; whereas Wilkinson, who was quite comfortable so long as he lay still, swore that he was fit enough to travel. But a stretcher was essential for him ; nor could I take Cox whose general health by now had improved considerably. Melot stated emphatically that he was not going to be left behind, and if necessary he would squeeze up next to the driver on one of the lorries ! Macleod swore by heaven and earth that he would get aboard a truck somehow ; the thought that he might be left behind alarmed him and preyed on his mind. We calmed him down.

In truth, we had all become a little agitated ; probably this was due, in part, to our short sleeping hours over the recent week and the small quantity of food and drink we had taken during the past two days. It was as miserable a moment as I can recall and, strive as I would, I could not help but feel that I was deserting them. After some encouragement and a brief handshake I turned and walked away. What a desolate little scene it was : the blackness of the night broken only by the fires from the burning vehicles ; the smell of burning rubber ; the smoke ; my medical lorry now twisted and almost gutted ; the silhouettes of the men as they sorted out the possessions they had managed to rescue, selecting only those which were absolutely necessary ; the untidy heaps of material that we had been forced to abandon.

I caught sight of Johnson stamping his feet and buttoning up his coat collar, for it was beginning to grow chilly. He had set the two Italians on to laying out a cross in white stones on the hill side, a piece of work into which, in the fawning joy of their release from captivity, they had put their hearts and souls.

" Good-bye, Johnson," I said. " I'm sorry about all this. It's very bad luck."

" Well, someone had to stay, sir."

" Yes." For a moment we stood there in silence watching the crowded jeeps and lorries being lined up ready for departure. " You are quite sure about what you have to do."

" Yes, sir."

" You've got the morphia and syringe ? "

" Yes, sir. Thank you."

" Well ! Good-bye, Johnson. All the best."

" Good-bye, sir."

We shook hands, and I went in search of Shaw and my jeep. He had loaded it up and was ready to move off. " The old jeep had a narrow shave to-day, sir," he remarked, patting it affectionately on the bonnet. " Some time after you'd left me, while I was lying on my back trying to jack it up properly, I suddenly heard a most extraordinary noise—thought a hail storm must have blown over or something. Blime ! It was an aeroplane machine-gunning. You should 'ave seen me move ; Mick the Miller wouldn't 'ave 'ad a look in ! It was a funny thing though 'cos they 'ardly shot at it at all after that ; I reckon they must 'ave thought it was a derelict, seeing the way it was tipped over on one side like. I was watching from the bushes, see ! You won't find me mending a puncture when the bullets are flipping about!"

He went on with the story in his own amusing, jerky manner, but I was too tired to talk, and pulling a blanket over myself, I curled up and fell asleep. There was little peace for me though, and a moment later I was awakened by someone trying to get in on top of me, " Oh, I *am* sorry, sir," came Sergeant Bennett's voice as I rose up in wrath, " I didn't realise you were under the blanket, I could have sworn that seat was empty, definitely I could."

We started off soon afterwards. I could feel the motion of the jeep as I tried to doze off ; the sensation of rising and falling, the bumping, the variation of speed and the gear changing. These items became a part of my dream ; they were woven into the texture of the phantasy. Every now and then I was roused into consciousness with an abrupt start and, peering round into the darkness and at the white gleam of the track we were following, would try and ascertain where we were. Then slowly my eyelids became heavy and more heavy, until I found myself looking distortedly through the merest slits.

" What's that over there ? " I jumped up in my seat as I spoke, blinking and rubbing my eyes.

" Where ? " Shaw's face was turned toward me in surprise.

" Why, straight ahead, of course. How strange ! I could have sworn I saw some men running towards us."

But there was nothing there, nor any need to worry. I lay back and fell asleep again.

" Look out, Shaw, look out—damn you ! You're going to hit the lorry in front. Stop, man, stop. . . . What ? Was I talking ? Sorry. I thought we were going to have a collision. That's all." The muttering sound of the engine continued. By Jove ! It was bitterly cold.

" Did you see that light, then. . . . No ? Probably just my imagination. Don't worry." Confused, frightening thoughts swept across the mind and dropped away into the darkness.

" Where's every one got to ? Hey, Shaw, where is everybody else ? Oh, there they are. . . . Funny thing, I couldn't see them before. . . . How far have we gone ? . . . What's the time ? . . . What are they doing at home now, I wonder ? . . . Bed-time ? . . . God knows ! There's only one time here : sundown. That's the only time that's worth while."

We drove on through the night ; half asleep, half awake ; suddenly terrified, wondering where we might be and what was the cause of all these cheerless halts. Struggling and fighting to keep alert, only to feel that heavy stupor—stronger than any will-power—creep over the mind like a hypnotic drug. We seemed

to halt and keep on halting that night. Once again our old enemy
was catching up with us : just a faint glimmer of lightness in the
east as yet ; just a faint tinge of fear that caught at the throat
and left an unhappy apprehension in its wake. One of our more
poetic drivers put in into words :

"If we don't get a —ing rift on, we've 'ad it, Nobby ! Flat
as a —ing billiard table round 'ere ! No —ing cover nor nothing.
Just the —ing dawn, —ing well stealing across the —ing desert ! "

Remarks sounded clear on the cold night air. It was absolutely
bitter, I thought, as I stretched out my frozen legs and swore I
would not fall asleep again. The wind seemed to penetrate right
through one's clothes, despite the blankets and bedding which we
had wrapped round ourselves. We were depressed. At this hour
our spirits had sunk to their lowest ebb.

Then someone began to play a mouth-organ. The sobbing
notes rose and fell, seemed to draw close and then recede. The
grumbles stopped and the men listened. The tune changed ; it
became more lively with a jig in it. It was a Scottish air, but I
have forgotten the name of the piece. Within a minute the men
had picked it up and were whistling and singing in accompaniment, while heavy boots banged out the time on the floorboards
of the lorries. It became one of those moments that remain
intimately in the memory : our single line of trucks drawn up
along the track ; the bleakness of the open plain, and the dark
flat rim of the horizon ; a paling eastern sky ; the men—dim
figures almost unseen—with their deep voices and tuneful
whistling ; the strange sense of restoration of endeavour that
ensued.

Within an hour we had come to an area of rough ground where
a few bushes were grouped together, and where natural ditches
and a shallow well afforded good cover for the vehicles. We
worked away feverishly with the camouflage ; and even as we
were pulling down the branches and stacking them against the
wheels, two Messerschmitt 109's flew straight past us, slightly to
the north. They looked very ugly and full of spite on that early
morning, and they left behind them their characteristic menacing
whine. Fortunately it was not sufficiently light for them to notice
our movement, and being so low they had passed us almost before
we could hide. We hurried on with the work and, when all was

concealed and not a vehicle could be seen, we hid the wounded away and settled ourselves down to rest.

Although, happily, few of us were aware of it, we were only five miles away from our starting point of the previous night. The rough country marked on the map towards which we had driven had not materialised, and we had been forced to double back on our tracks to the Jebel for the sake of cover. Not infrequently the maps were anything up to five miles in error on a feature or a landmark, and that was the cause of our misfortune. Hence the numerous halts and the long impatient delays.

For September the sixteenth we each had one water-bottle to last throughout the day. We were informed that we should not be having any food until sun-down.

CHAPTER EIGHTEEN

" Yet all experience is an arch where thro'
  Gleams that untravell'd world, whose margin fades
  For ever and for ever when I move."
                                    Ulysses. TENNYSON.

WE DISPERSED WELL, taking cover beneath the small pieces of dry
scrub—those who found bushes were fortunate—and making the
best of the scanty shade they afforded. I slept deeply for about
an hour before the heat of the sun and the curiosity of the flies
wakened me to realities. Besides my water-bottle I had brought
up a Penguin edition of *Further Experiences of an Irish R.M.*, but I
could not enter into the spirit or humour of the thing, and did not
find it as absorbing as the family affairs of the Forsytes. My train
of thought was interrupted too frequently by the drone of aircraft,
and every now and then one would be obliged to curl up and try
and disappear beneath the sparse camel-thorn. It was one of
those occasions, as the men would say, when you made a noise
like a pebble ! But descriptions of these aircraft have grown
wearisome ; sufficient it is to say that throughout the day the
enemy were in search of us ; sometimes low enough for one to
be able to distinguish the pilot's head as a dark ball in the semi-
circle of the cockpit ; sometimes so high that the plane looked as
pale as a gull while it circled round steadily, waiting to detect
the slightest movement.

It was a tedious day. As the sun grew higher in the heavens
the shade from the patchwork of scrub became ineffectual. The
heat struck directly down upon us ; the hours lingered and
crawled past ; more aircraft came over. The sun was a little
over to the west now—the time should be about two o'clock. It
was definitely over now, and still no planes had caught us. They
were becoming less frequent and operating singly. The sun began
to approach the horizon ; the water in our bottles was lukewarm.
Shortly before sundown I walked down to my jeep, collected

some medical kit, and made my way over to Macleod. He soon lost consciousness under the pentothal and we had sufficient time to cut away the dead tissues and dress and splint his arm properly. It looked as if both his wounds had been caused by explosive bullets for they were ragged and destructive. As we were dressing him, a bomber flew past to the east of us ; in the rosy evening sunlight it looked almost peaceful as it winged its way home. Then Macleod began to wake up. " Don't leave me ! " he cried. " Let me come with you ! Oh, please don't leave me ! " He was weeping hysterically, re-enacting, in his anæsthetic delusions, the incidents of the previous evening. Finally we pacified him and carried him down on a stretcher to his lorry, where we made him comfortable on top of a camouflage net.

In the cooler air of the evening we sat round the cook's three-ton lorry and, with watering mouths watched our porridge being prepared. I looked round for Paddy Mayne but could not see him ; it was only then that I discovered that we had split up into two parties during the previous night, each of which was to make its way back to Kufra independently. By so doing it was reckoned that we were less likely to be detected. Major Barlow was in charge of our convoy, while Paddy was leading the other ; David Stirling had remained behind in the Jebel with three jeeps —including a wircless jeep—to make sure that any stragglers, not yet accounted for, should be picked up.

It seemed strange to be eating again ; the small helping of porridge and the hot black tea cheered us up considerably. The cigarettes, too, tasted quite fresh after the heat of the day, but our supplies of them were running short and we had to ration ourselves severely. By the time darkness had fallen we were ready to move off in our crocodile procession. Mike Sadler was navigating for us ; he drove in the leading jeep, using his lights in case of any obstructions or anti-personnel devices on the track. In all probability he was the best navigator in the Middle East, having worked with the L.R.D.G. until quite recently, when he had transferred and been commissioned in the S.A.S. Certainly he had seen as much action as any one and this was merely another job for him. Before the war he had left England to farm in Rhodesia, and it was through him that many of us became familiar with some of the fine men one met at the Rhodesian Club.

Mike was one of those engaging people who was clever without showing it ; a rare accomplishment and, with his boyish enthusiasm, he accepted responsibilities as they came : leading us off on this drive, for instance, and looking very much as if it was all part of an interesting game.

During the night we covered a good deal of ground, and throughout the next day it was our great pleasure not to sight a single aircraft. On again the following night and day, until the afternoon of September the eighteenth found us heading back along our own tracks between Jalo and the Sand Sea. Here we were in a quandary, for, according to our plan of action, Jalo should have been captured by the Sudanese Defence Force ; yet as we drew near, we could hear the sound of artillery and occasionally the more shuddering explosions of bomb bursts. Evidently the battle was still in progress ; a matter which concerned us deeply because we had expected to get our further supplies of petrol from the Sudanese Defence Force. Most of our petrol had been lost during the bombing at the rendezvous and what remained had only just allowed us to come this far. We waited for a while, listening to the thud and boom of cannon and wondering which was the correct portion of the oasis to approach. Eventually it was decided to send Maclean and Sandy Scratchley with two trucks to investigate the situation, and to try and obtain sufficient petrol to get us back the remaining four hundred miles to Kufra. Away they went and were soon lost to sight. We wheeled in the opposite direction towards some close-growing clusters of vegetation and stunted palms ; and here we hid the vehicles, ate our solitary meal of the day, and prepared ourselves for a welcome night's rest.

The next morning dawned fresh and clear, and we relaxed in languid ease until the gathering heat had made us cast off our blankets. There was nothing for us to do, but rest. Each man had his water-bottle to last the day ; there was nothing to eat until sundown, so we might as well lie back and read. By now we had finished our cigarettes ; some of the men tried crushing up the vegetation from the dried palm fronds, rolling it in cigarette paper and smoking it ; but the result did not justify the effort.

What had happened to Maclean and Sandy ? Their prolonged

absence grew more and more worrying as the hours went by. From the direction of Kufra came the intermittent rumble of battle and once during the day a plane flew straight over us. The time passed slowly and we began to wonder whether we should have to restrict our food and water more drastically. The wounded were in good heart, except that Melot was being pestered by biting ants which appeared to have been attracted by his stale blood. They were very small in size and it was almost impossible to rid him of the nuisance. Apart from this, however, there was nothing very outstanding about the day. I wondered how my parents would be spending the time at home for to-day was my father's birthday. I tried to imagine what they would be doing by way of a birthday treat ; often they went to the cinema if there was a good picture showing. What were his presents this year, I wondered ? Gramophone records ? We were always adding to our collection and by now it must have grown to impressive dimensions. Or so it seemed to me on that hot afternoon as I lay back and stared at the never-ending blueness of the sky and thought how marvellous it would be if, just for an hour or two, I was allowed the bitter-sweetness of being at home.

During the evening we sent Bill Fraser into Jalo with two more jeeps ; it was essential for us to know our exact position so that we could act accordingly. Already some of the men were beginning to look a bit exhausted, and the uncertainty of waiting was not good for the morale. Judge then our happiness when Bill returned about three hours after darkness had fallen, with the news that he had contacted the S.D.F., and from them had obtained the necessary petrol which was waiting to be collected. The S.D.F. were withdrawing from their attack during the night and would be retiring south to Kufra, Sandy Scratchley and Maclean were safe but they had driven into the oasis only to find themselves between the S.D.F. and Italian forces ! Consequently they had had a rather harassing time of it, and their prolonged inactivity was more a matter of compulsion than volition. Poor old Sandy ! You couldn't help laughing about it afterwards.

Well, this news was wonderful ! It seemed that our difficulties were over, and Bill, having showered some Jalo dates upon us, disappeared once more with a three-ton lorry to collect the petrol. He returned the next morning with Sandy, and it was decided to continue to hide up throughout the day and make our get-away during the night. Accordingly we set off just before sundown and drove hard along the flat, beaconed track, which we had used for our northward drive. On again the next morning, averaging between thirty and forty miles an hour, and with the ground so even that the wounded were not upset by the speed, until at last we had reached Bir Zighen. Here a well had been sunk by the L.R.D.G. while nearby was a good-sized food-dump. I fear we all made pigs of ourselves : drinking just for the pleasure of drinking, and eating until we felt our bellies grow heavy and swollen. The satisfaction of knowing that there was more food and water at hand, and that we could not exhaust our supplies however much we ate, was too wonderful and complete to be described.

At Bir Zighen we linked up with the S.D.F. whose doctor informed me that they had suffered several casualties during the recent fighting ; and that they were waiting here for a day or two in the hope that a plane would come and transport their wounded the remaining distance to Kufra and thence to Cairo. They had, indeed, been wirelessing Kufra frequently on this point, but as yet had received no signal in reply. I asked if I could leave my wounded with them and thus save Melot and Macleod the distress of crossing the Sand Sea ; their doctor agreed readily, and in any case, as he pointed out, even if they could not obtain a transport plane, the wounded would be far more comfortable travelling in the Sudanese hooded-lorries than in our own open three-tonners ; they would at least obtain shade and protection from the sun.

Accordingly on the next morning we re-dressed the patients' wounds, made them comfortable and bade them farewell. Then away over the ridged Sand Sea once more, with its fierce white glare, its cruel slopes of soft sinking sands, its back-breaking toil and heartaches ; away over the desolate undulating wastes until at last we came to the rugged country beyond. Rugged and beautiful, it seemed, as we jogged along steadily in the evening light. For the rocks and hills were tinted with fine pinks and mauves which gave way gradually to the softer shades of distance. Surely this was a fitting framework for one of Grimm's fairy stories ! And from these barren hills, turned to an icy blueness by the evening light, one could well imagine that some dragon would emerge at any minute. Or might not some huge giant suddenly show his head above these turreted battlements and, with a shake of a knobbly club, emit a roar which would shake the very earth? Yes, it was through such country as this that we, a small weary procession, threaded our way; and there was considerable happiness in our hearts when one morning we caught sight of the dirty green of the Kufra oasis shuddering in the heat-haze of the hollow before us. Our convoy was drawn up beside the old Italian fort at the northern edge of the oasis, and we were waiting to go down the road in single file.

"Home at last!" said Shaw with a cheerful nod of his turbanned head.

I turned and watched him as he sat there, with a little smile on his lips, beating out a jazz tune with his fingers on the driving-wheel of the jeep.

"Do you remember when you said that last?" I asked.

Slowly the smile became a grin, which spread over his face. Then "Aiewa!" he remarked sagaciously. "But not to worry this time!"

As it turned out he was wrong again, for two days after our arrival we were attacked by eight Heinkels. They came in from the north, flying low over the oasis and strafing the place pretty thoroughly. Their two main objectives were the airfield and the fort; on the former they destroyed several of our aircraft, while some lives were lost up in the Italian barracks. Crouching down among the palm-trees, we never had a clear idea of what was happening. It was very different from the desert, for here our visibility was limited to a hundred yards or so. From time to time the planes would roar over, spraying the palms with machine-gun fire. The whole thing lasted only about forty minutes, and I think I am correct in saying the gunners shot down four out of the eight planes—a very creditable performance.

We waited anxiously for David Stirling to turn up, wondering, as day succeeded day, whatever could have delayed him so long. When someone is late for an appointment your mind runs riot with the various ideas and possibilities which might account for it, and you tend to oscillate between optimism and extreme pessimism. So it was with us; and one day a rumour circulated through the camp to the effect that David had been captured ; somebody had heard a German broadcast which announced that the daring Colonel Stirling was now a prisoner-of-war in Germany. Like most rumours it was impossible to trace it to its origin and its veracity was disproved soon afterwards by David, himself, turning up with his jeeps. Although he had remained in the Jebel for several days after our departure he had not picked up any stragglers. His party, however, said they had seen an Italian ambulance on its way to our rendezvous to pick up our wounded ; so that, at any rate, was a comfort.[1]

Looking back on it now, one can sum up the results of these September raids. I am afraid they do not make impressive reading. Firstly our own raid had been a complete failure owing to the lack of surprise. Evidently the enemy had been informed by agents in Egypt or—and this was less likely—in Kufra. Arab spies, complete with transmitting wireless sets, had been discovered in the oasis. With regard to our losses, I did not find out what the exact figures were, but I doubt if they were high : say twenty or thirty men out of an attacking force of about a hundred.

The lack of success of our raid was in part offset by the New Zealand patrol of the L.R.D.G. who, with great dash, had raided Barce and destroyed about twenty-five planes on the airfield.

The Rhodesian patrol, who were attacking objectives in the Benghazi area, had suffered the same misfortune as ourselves, while the Tobruk and Matruh raids also were failures. One could, of course, say that such and such a gun position was destroyed or that so many enemy troops were annihilated, but that does not alter the main fact : the raids did not achieve their objects.

The Sudanese Defence Force had found Jalo a more difficult proposition than they had expected, and had been ordered to call off their attack. Some reports stated that, after a few days of confused fighting, both the S.D.F. and the Italians had withdrawn on the same night, leaving the possession of the oasis to the surprised native inhabitants ; but I do not know if there is any truth in this.

[1] I have since learned, with deep sorrow, that the British party who were left behind at Benghazi, died later as a result of their wounds. I can understand why Dawson died ; the outlook for Longland was uncertain ; Cox, I had expected to recover ; while the cause of Wilkinson's death must remain a mystery. Finally, Johnson, the medical orderly who accompanied them, also died some eighteen months later, although no reason is known for this.

So much, then, for those unhappy days. Yet David Stirling's enthusiasm was by no means damped. He had no harsh criticisms to make. On the contrary his view was that, since the enemy had known of our raid, none of us could be blamed for what had taken place. " The raid simply wasn't on ! " But now, he continued, looking round at us eagerly, there was an easy target we ought to be getting busy on : the railway line from Tobruk to Alamein. That should make a lovely objective, and there should be no difficulty in blowing it up at more or less regular intervals and thus restricting its use to a minimum.

In addition David had some fresh ideas concerning the future of the Special Air Service. He wanted it divided into two squadrons which, by relieving one another, could constantly maintain a force in the rear of the enemy. Sooner or later the Eighth Army would be attacking from Alamein, and then the two squadrons could leap-frog one another as the enemy's line withdrew. Paddy, now promoted to a major, would be in command of the squadron which would be operating during the next month or two. The railway line would make an ideal target for tip-and-run raids, and other objectives could easily be signalled from headquarters. I think Paddy was happy to be in charge of a squadron ; he picked out fifty of the men he knew best ; while I, for my part, counted myself fortunate in being able to join in with him.

First, however, we should have to refit—that glorious word !— and we waited impatiently for the aircraft to arrive at Kufra and fly us back so that we could collect fresh vehicles and stores. These days of waiting seemed very drawn out. There were flies everywhere and they allowed us no rest ; it was simply a case of maintaining a constant fanning movement with the hand. By night the mosquitoes and ants pestered us. We had no nets with which to protect ourselves against the former, and each man worked out his own salvation against the latter. I recall that I laid out a rectangle of empty petrol tins for use as a bed ; this defeated the ants all right, but each time I turned over it was to a musical clanking accompaniment, whereas the slightest movement produced some sort of metallic response. The only way I could avoid the mosquitoes was by completely covering myself with a blanket, yet the nights were too humid and hot to allow this. In fact, looking back on it now, it is a bit of a mystery how any of us ever got to sleep ; and when we did it was to the irritating whine of a mosquito which hovered not far away. . . .

Our main relaxation consisted of a visit to the salt-lake or a swim in the circular pool. The lake was by no means easy to find since it was almost completely surrounded by palm-trees, and on several occasions we drove straight past the depression. It was situated about three miles away from our camp ; and in order to reach it we were obliged to wend our way through the palm-trees and round the occasional mud buildings—startling the goats and chickens with our unexpected appearances—until the ground became less fertile, and more hummocky and open. The sloping banks of the lake were white with crystalline salt, while the water itself was similar to the Dead Sea, being very harsh to the mucous membranes and of a density that made it impossible to swim with any ease. Here, lying in the shade of the trees, we would munch away at the dates, reading whatever book we had brought along, and rejoicing in our escape from the maddening flies. In the late afternoon we would return to camp in time for the call " grub up " and with the unhappy realisation that another night of fitful wakefulness lay ahead of us.

One afternoon we toured the neighbouring oases to select a camp site, for David had informed us that we were to make our winter-quarters in the neighbourhood. So away we went, bumping over the soft hummocky ground that separated one clear-cut palm-fringed oasis from the next. The sharp definition between desert and fertile cultivation was quite remarkable ; we passed straight from the white glare of the one into the green shadow of the other. Each little oasis had its group of families, its farms of dates, olives and maize ; each had its headman who was responsible to the main oasis for the maintenance of order and discipline. At each one we found a deep well, with walls built of palm-wood, whose contents could be drawn up by using a dried goatskin as a container ; we tasted the water and found it as cold as a mountain stream and beautifully fresh. Sometimes the natives had formed little irrigation channels leading away from the wells, and these they would flood during the day and so manage to keep the land fertile. Then another of their peculiarities was the manner in which scarecrows were constructed. These were made from dried asses' skins and could be seen, propped up on a pole, in a good number of the plots. The wild life of Kufra was quite considerable, but why a bird should be frightened by a stationary ass was a point that defeated me completely !

Soon afterwards we left for base in the old trustworthy Bombays, striking east to Wadi Halfa where we refuelled ; and then flying northwards, following the sinuous course of the Nile, until we had reached the Australian squadron's airport at Halwaan. Here we landed and were entertained most generously.

" Well," said David looking round at the Australians, " thank you so much for all the help you chaps have given us, especially you, Ginger," he added, turning to Shaw. " Now that you have got to know us so well, you simply *must* come with us on our next raid."

" What ! " exclaimed Ginger in that very genuine way of his. " What ! Come on the next raid ? Not —— likely ! "

Poor old Digger Shaw ! As it happened he was killed in an aircraft accident soon afterward ; but he only lost his life because he was trying to pull someone else out of the blazing plane. And, for my part, I shall never forget the way he came to my aid on that hot September morning about forty miles south of the rendezvous, when death itself had seemed to elbow its way in and keep us quiet company.

CHAPTER NINETEEN

LIFE IN THE SAND SEA

" There is silence where hath been no sound,
   There is a silence where no sound may be,
   In the cold grave—under the deep deep sea,
   Or in the wide desert where no life is found."
                 Sonnet : Silence. THOMAS HOOD.

ALTHOUGH WE, that is to say, A Squadron or Paddy Mayne's squadron, set up our winter quarters in one of the Kufra oases—a complete little camp with its own reed huts, quartermaster's stores and even a miniature officer's mess—our advanced headquarters was situated in the heart of the Sand Sea. This locality had been chosen because it was practically inaccessible to the enemy ; indeed it was hard enough for us to drive up the narrow spit of comparatively firm sand from the south, and we knew that it would be a great deal harder for the enemy to try and approach through the softer sand to the north. It was said, too, that no planes flew over the Sand Sea, that a forced landing in such a lifeless waste meant almost certain death for its occupants. Whether there was any truth in this I would not care to say, but certainly we were never troubled by aircraft.

It was here, then, that we lived throughout October and November ; and during these months patrols were driving up north to attack the railway line with persistent regularity. Our dwelling-place was clean and very isolated ; for we were tucked away in a deep hollow, and all around the tumbling sand-dunes encompassed us about. The soft beauty of their symmetrical curves, and the sinuous outlines, accentuated as they were at morning and evening by the glancing rays of the sun, provided an artistry one could not readily forget ; and I shall long remember the delicate rosy flush, reflected for a moment from the smooth sand-surfaces, as the radiance of the sunset dwindled and died like a funeral pyre. Frequently in the evenings I would climb up the steep, moulded slopes, my feet sinking deeply with each step I took, until I had reached a summit from which I could watch the colours live and tremble and die. The solitude was most impressive ; and the sight of the crested dunes mounting one behind the other as far as the eye could see, conveyed a sense of restful eternity. It was beautiful to watch the lines grow more distinct as the sun drew low in the sky ; to see the shadows falling down the slopes and filling the smooth hollows below ; the effect of continual change ; the gradual creeping movement of light and darkness. As I walked over the even slopes, leaving my footprints behind me and noting the geometrical precision of the little wind-blown wrinkles and wavelets, I found myself wondering if I was the first person to trace his mark across this particular piece of ground, and considering the possibility that nobody would follow in my footsteps until the world had come to an end. How quiet it was ! The mind had soon put aside the war and realities to embark upon its own flights of fancy.

In the Sand Sea we were about one hundred and eighty miles south of the coast at Tobruk, and our patrols would allow two or three days in which to approach their targets. Jim Chambers had only recently returned from a raid when I arrived at the rendezvous, and I was struck immediately by the change in him. He was suffering from very bad desert sores ; not of the usual type, but deeply ulcerating and heavily infected ; and with this complaint he had lost all his usual boyish enthusiasm and cheerful vigour. He was plainly unwell ; you could tell that by the lassitude and apathy which dogged him. He was depressed, too, about his raid because he had not been able to confirm the results. He described to me how they had buried the charges beneath the track and then waited nearby to watch the next train blow up. When, however, a locomotive did come puffing along the line, nothing happened ; the train receded into the distance. They decided that it was due to the dampness of the soil, for the weather had been very bad in the coastal belt and the " boggy " nature of the ground had made their progress difficult. So they laid another charge using a different technique ; but even as they were thus employed an enemy party detected them and attacked. In the mêlée that ensued, Sillito, their navigator, was lost. Fortunately, however, there was a happy conclusion to the story, for Sillito, himself, trudged in to the rendezvous, footsore and.

weary, some eight days later ; and this was the tale he had to tell :

When, quite suddenly, he had found himself completely alone in the vicinity of Tobruk, he squatted down for a minute to reckon out what his next move should be. He had neither food nor water —only a compass and a revolver. He considered what he should do. He could march northwards and give himself up to the enemy ; he could start heading east towards Alamein keeping well within the coastal belt, where the Arabs might help him, where an occasional bir would provide him with water, and where derelict trucks and lorries might well contain something in the way of necessities ; or finally he could walk due south, away from the life of the coastal belt, through the arid desert where there was next to no chance of meeting any form of life or water, and where a mistake in direction meant a certain and unpleasant death. It was the final alternative that he chose—a lonely march of nearly two hundred miles towards that little hollow, in the middle of the Sand Sea which we had chosen for our rendezvous.

Off he set, trudging steadily southwards and apparently not worrying much about the distance at first. On account of the recent rains he was able to drink from the puddles whenever he felt thirsty ; but as he progressed the ground became dry and more stony, and it was imperative for him to make each mouthful of water last. The skies became pitilessly blue and unchanging ; he took to resting during the real heat of the day, continuing with his march only when it had grown cooler and when the glare and shudder of the skyline had disappeared.

Imagine the loneliness of this ! Day after day with the sun arching up over him ; without a soul to whom he could voice his thoughts ; with a flat landscape that stretched on and on in front of him ; with no indication of his whereabouts nor how far he had travelled. Just the day and night to show how time was passing ; and the conviction that he was correct in his compass-course to give him encouragement.

On the second day the water gave out, and from then on he stored his urine in an old bully-beef tin that he found lying on the ground—but, he said, the urine became more and more con-centrated. The contents of the tin he threw away, for the bully beef was too hard to masticate : it formed a sticky bolus in the mouth which was hard to swallow. To lie down and rest could not have been an easy decision, for it must have seemed that an hour without advancement was an hour wasted ; yet it was the only logical way by which he could reach his goal. The fourth day passed, then the fifth, and his progress began to slow down. His feet were sore, cut and blistered ; it became a question of determination and staying power. He continued on his course— a lone figure trudging for mile. after barren mile across the vast emptiness of the desert.

On the sixth day he saw some dots on the skyline. Can the reader imagine his feelings when he saw that they were moving ? Were they real ? he wondered. Was this a trick of the eyes ? Was it the heat haze ? No, they actually were vehicles. They were coming towards him. On their present bearing they would pass by him a little to the west. Yes, they were jeeps ! He could see them quite clearly now ; he could make out the machine-gun mountings. Almost beside himself with joy, he waved and waved and tried to shout. But they were going on as if they had not seen him ! Surely that was not possible ! Suddenly an idea occurred to him, and tearing off his shirt he rummaged in his pockets and found some matches. In a moment he had set fire to his shirt and was waving it slowly backwards and forwards over his head. It burned with a smouldering flame and the smoke faded readily on the hot air. With something akin to despair he watched the jeeps drive past. They became distorted shapes in the heat haze, then they were dots, then they had vanished completely. He was alone once more with the heat, the sweat, and his thoughts. He turned and went on.

It was on the eighth day that first he sighted the white pointed slopes of the Sand Sea as it lay sprawled out in front of him, extending about a hundred miles to the east and west. Somewhere along this northern border there might be a few jeeps which were preparing to go out on a raid or had just returned from one ; he was dependent upon his own navigational judgment and the entrance and exit tracks of the vehicles for finding the exact location ; and if the jeeps were not there he would be forced to cross another forty miles of soft, sinking sand dunes before he reached the advanced rendezvous. It is doubtful whether he could have achieved this extra march, but luckily it was not necessary as he found the tracks and soon afterwards came upon a small patrol. In this, fortune was with him ; for the men would have left on the previous day had not one of the jeeps broken down and their departure been thus delayed.

Soon after his arrival he was sent back to Kufra and thence to base for some leave. His feet were being dressed daily ; and even when he had been with us for a week he still found it painful to hobble about. But that was all he had to show for his experience ; that and a hesitancy of manner and an expression in the eyes that told their own story of mental strain and physical hardship.

I hope I do not exaggerate or over-emphasise the various points of this story. Yet I think it would be difficult to do so, for I can remember one brief hour when I had foolishly lost myself ; that dreadful feeling, like a shocking stab at the heart, when all of a sudden I realised that I had no idea where anybody else was. It seemed a long while that I searched for the rendezvous on that occasion, realising, as I did so, that each step I took might be leading me away from the others.

I was worried about Jim Chambers. His sores were not responding to treatment and I was glad when I heard that a convoy was soon returning to Kufra, for the Sand Sea was no place for him in his present condition. Indeed it was hard to realise that this was the Jim Chambers who had encouraged his men on from one effort to another as they brought their lorries through the long patches of soft sand ; or that this was he who had been only too happy to drive up and give the answering fire at the Benghazi ambush in order that the others might withdraw.

" You know, doc," he said one evening, " I can't make it out at all, but I don't seem to have the same keenness or enthusiasm these days. It's not like the old times, when it was such terrific fun digging out the trucks, swearing away and ragging like hell all the time. Didn't you reckon that was good sport ? "

" Sometimes." I nodded.

We were sitting at the foot of a huge dune that rose steeply above us in the darkness. It was some time since we had had our cocoa, and soon we would be tucking ourselves up in our blankets and wriggling into a groove in the soft sand. Most of the men had

already gone to bed, but we could still hear the mumbles of
some voices.

" Now," Jim was saying, " all that enjoyment seems to have
gone. Now it is just so much hard work."

" Well, damn it all, man ! " I replied emphatically, " you're
not up to the mark to start off with."

" No, I suppose not."

" Don't you worry ! Soon you'll be in the mess at
camp. There'll be Eric Parten and Bobby Dodds and Corporal
Leitch to see that you put away more grub than you can cope
with. Why ! You'll be as fit as a flea and hopping all over the
place ! "

But he was not very convinced, and I knew why. Like quite
a number of soldiers he hated " going sick " and being sent to
base on medical grounds. His conscience troubled him and he
wondered if he was " letting the squadron down." He was
worried, too, that his health should give way like this, that he was
not desert-worthy ; and he was terribly anxious to return to us
as soon as possible.

" I wish I'd done something really good before going away,"
he remarked after a pause, " just something to prove myself, you
know. Not that I want any gongs or anything like that, but just
for the mental satisfaction of the thing."

" Now, don't you be silly, Jim ! This last raid of yours was
all right."

" Well, maybe. But we didn't have any definite proof. I
suppose the trouble is that you start getting depressed when you
compare yourself with people like Jock Lewis or Paddy or
Sergeant Almonds. You see there's such the hell of a standard
to live up to, isn't there ? Look at Jock Lewis and the name he's
got in the unit ! He never earned any official sort of recognition,
but just you listen to some of the men talking about him. Any one
would think he was a sort of God ! *His* influence has lasted on in
this unit all right. If it hadn't been for him, none of us would
be here now."

It was rather strange looking at the matter in that light, and I
wondered what Jock Lewis would have thought if he could have
seen us here. For as Jim had said, it was entirely due to his training
of the unit—the way he had led the early marches on a water-

bottle a day, the lying up in the sun, the night attacks on dummy objectives—it was entirely through *his* preparations that we had reached our present position. David had been the man with ideas; while Jock Lewis and Paddy were those whose efforts had helped to make them practicable and successful. They had worked in a sort of mutual symbiosis. And here we were now : Paddy with his own squadron in operation and reports being wirelessed back to base :

"Railway line destroyed at —— Station. Offices and sidings blown up." or "Road mined at ——. Telegraph lines demolished."

It had been the growth of a unit.

"Well," I said finally, " I know you haven't got anything to worry about, Jim, and I know the men think the same."

At that he grinned rather sheepishly, and soon afterwards we had both retired to bed and fallen asleep.

He was off the next morning, and we stood round the lorry while they loaded it up with rations and stores. We passed away the time of waiting with the usual flippant phrases, and it was not long before the men were ready and the driver had started up the engine.

"O.K., Miller ? Ready to go ? " Jim was standing in that characteristic way of his ; with feet apart and hands on hips.

"O.K., sir."

"Good ! " He turned round to us. " Well, so long, boys. Good-bye, Paddy," he put out his hand and then looked ruefully down at the bandages and shook his head. " I've got all your Christmas mail. 'Bye, Sandy, I'll remember those books. Cheerio, Doc, I won't forget your films." He forced a little smile. " Don't worry, I'll soon be back."

"Good-bye, Jim," we said.

He clambered up painfully and nodded to the driver. We could see him waving to us as the lorry grew smaller and smaller, until at last it had become just an ungainly smudge against the vast expanse of sand.

It was several weeks later, almost Christmas in fact, when we heard the news that he had died in hospital as a result of the diphtheritic infection of his sores.

CHAPTER TWENTY

THE STORY TELLERS

"Telling a tale not too importunate
To those who in the sleepy region stay,
Lulled by the singer of an empty day."
WILLIAM MORRIS.

THE DAYS at the Sand Sea rendezvous passed pleasantly enough; they were long lazy days with nothing much to do except to talk, read and eat. Sick parades were brief affairs. We were not short of food or water; the company was good; we lacked nothing. Paddy had enlisted several newcomers into the squadron of which Bill Fraser was second in command. Harry Poat, who quickly grew an attractive Santa Claus beard; Johnny Wiseman, who on occasions would give us lessons in European history; Sandy Wilson, young and eager; Berneville Clay, the incurable optimist; McDermott, a fair-headed North Irishman; and McDonald, a Scot, were amongst their number. Mike Sadler, who was a navigator-cum-operative, now boasted two pips, while Sandy Scratchley held a sort of roving commission with us. These, then, were the officers of our squadron, although there would always be a number of them out on raids at any particular time.

The other ranks, too, were very happy here, enjoying their periods of rest in between the raids. Sergeant Rose had now become the squadron sergeant-major, and a fine job he made of it. As for Sergeant Bennett, I shall never forget the horror in his voice when I suggested that he would be just the man to look after the sanitation side of things for the squadron. It had become obvious that the number of flies in the camp were on the increase, so we shifted our rendezvous area to another position about five miles away and settled ourselves down to a strict regime in field hygiene. It was at this juncture that I had voiced my opinion concerning Sergeant Bennett's capabilities.

"Sanitation! Wot! Me, sir?" He laughed mirthlessly.

" Why, I don't even know the difference between a fly-trap and
a . . . er . . . well . . . a refuse-pit," he finished lamely.

" Then, Sergeant Bennett, this is just your chance to find out.
It isn't often we get the opportunity of being paid to learn something fresh. You should seize it gladly and with both hands."

" Well ! Wot d'yer make of that," we could hear his indignant
tones a few minutes later as he talked it over with some of his
sympathetic mates. " Sanitation ! I ask you ! Who'd 'ave
thought I'd 'ave dropped to that ! "

However, we soon had him busy, and he certainly did appear
to take an interest in the work, although you never could tell for
certain, as he was such a perfect actor. One minute he would be
looking so worried, with a deep frown on his forehead, and the
next he would be laughing away as if he had never known a care
in the world. Between us we started to construct a fly-trap ; and
soon the idea had caught on amongst the men, with the result
that all sorts of quaint variations of the original model of the
" Trap, fly, pattern, field," might have been seen decorating the
sunlit slopes of the sand-dunes. Sergeant Bennett had his own
speciality with a little bit of treacle inside ; Downes and Adamson
—two of our operatives—were busy putting their theories with
sardines into practice ; and eventually we had about a dozen fly-
traps decorating our camp area. But if ever flies had been known
to take a hearty dislike to a nice tasty piece of rotting sardine or a
lovely sticky bit of jam, then this was the occasion. They shunned
those traps as if each one had contained a spider instead of some
tempting morsel.

Sergeant Bennett shook his head in perplexity while he sat
watching his trap and giving a running commentary on the
progress made :

" One fly's landed on the outside. He's going to walk in now.
Yes, definitely he is. . . . He can smell the jam that's wot it is. . . .
Go on, walk in, you silly. . . . Ah ! I see wot it is. . . . He doesn't
know where the entrance is. . . . That's wot it is. . . . Definitely ! "

Then there would be a brooding silence for a minute or two as
events moved to an ominous climax in Sergeant Bennett's direction, until finally the sound of a vicious swipe with a fly-swat told
us that another little drama had just been concluded. If you were
near enough you might hear his angry mutterings :

" That's the way in . . . there ! . . . See ! . . . You silly little—— ! " And then he would settle down once more and resume his vigil for the next unwary fly.

In this way an amateur fly-trap competition sprang up, although, needless to say, our fly-swats claimed many more victims than all the traps put together. Then, too, one must confess to the very childish but amusing folly of placing little odds and ends of dismembered flies in Sergeant Bennett's trap when he wasn't looking, and then accusing him of cheating when we came to add up at the end of the day. That expression of righteous indignation which came upon his countenance, and the grievous hurt in the tones of his voice as he disclaimed any knowledge whatsoever of such and such a mangled fly, were perfect representations of injured innocence.

Yet there was far more common sense in his make-up than you might, at first, suspect. For he was one of our oldest operatives, and you could bet your bottom dollar that he would not still have been with the unit if he had not had a pretty good head on his shoulders. In fact he had been on so many raids, one way and another, that he tended to get his details mixed up when he came to tell you about them afterwards. This always struck me as being strange for when your life is in danger you do not, as a rule, forget about the incidents afterwards ! Rather, the converse holds true. But Sergeant Bennett would start off : " Ah, yes ! I remember, sir. That was on the Tamet job. Now, wait a minute ! No, it was at Mersa Brega . . . definitely ! . . . Yes, that's right. Mersa Brega. Well, we was walkin' along the track—it was pitch black, mind you, no stars or nothing—and Mr. Stirling says as how we ought to separate into two patrols of two men each. So we did as he said, and away he went with Sergeant-major Riley. Well, we were going along towards the road when suddenly we hears voices over on the right—or was it the left now ? Anyway it doesn't matter much, but we think that's pretty funny—hearing voices, I mean—and we reckoned we'd better find out about them. So we crouched down and stalked over ; Lilley and me was together. No. Let me see ! It wasn't Lilley, it was Kershaw. Lilley had been with me on the job before. Or was it Phillips ? . . . Oh, I forget now, but anyhow we was creeping along when Kershaw whispers over to me that there were some chaps *behind* us. *Behind*,

mind you ! So I says, ' Are you sure ? ' And he says definitely he
is. Well, for the next quarter of an hour we goes stalking round
and round to try and get behind *them*, see, and find out who *they*
are ! Then, all of a sudden, a voice comes out of the darkness, ' Is
that Sergeant Bennett ? ' So I says, ' Definitely it is ! ' And he
says, ' Well, this is Sergeant-major Riley, blast yer ! ' Oh, dear !
Was Major Stirling wild ? 'Cos our two patrols had been stalking
each other round an enemy airfield, yer see. Makes yer laugh,
don't it ? But we weren't laughing then I can tell you. Never felt
such fools in our lives ! I think it was the Mersa Brega job."

In the good old days of peace, Sergeant Bennett told me, he
used to live at Oxford ; and, from what I could make out, he
lived for one thing alone—the students' rags. It appeared that
there were a number of policemen at Oxford who seemed to
" have got it into their silly chumps " that Sergeant Bennett, of
all people, was the sort of chap who would do such a foolish thing
as to " kick a copper up the backside while he wasn't looking and
then leg it fast." As if Sergeant Bennett would ever dream of
doing anything like that ! The fact that you could be put in jug
on so remote a suspicion just went to show how little truth there
was in all this talk about liberty. Liberty indeed ! Why, the very
word was foreign wasn't it ? Ah, but the students' rags ! A smile
of happy reminiscence lit up the usual rather sad expression on
Sergeant Bennett's features. " The stoodents' rags ! You could
get a bit of yer own back on the cops then all right ! Nice little
haul of Bobbys' caps you could make if you went about it the
right way. They didn't stand much chance of getting you in *that*
crowd. 'Sides, 'ave yer ever seen a copper without his 'elmet ?
He don't look properly dressed like, does 'e ? Sort of naked
somewhere. Coppers don't arf look embarrassed without their
'ats, yer know. Oh, yes ! You could pay back a few old scores in
those rags, definitely you could."

I remember, too, his indignation when we were listening to the
wireless one evening. We had a captured Italian set with us and
Sergeant Bennett had appointed himself to do the manipulating.
I think it was some item after the news that was on at the time,
and the suave voice of the announcer was speaking with patronising pride of the fine parachute boys in England. Why, he
remarked as he described a recent visit to their camp, these lads

were so tough that one of them had even played some tunes on his mouth-organ as he parachuted down to earth. At once a look of ferocious indignation spread over Sergeant Bennett's lank features. " D'yer hear that ! " he cried aghast. " Tough indeed ! Why, we was playin' mouth-organs and things, takin' photographs, makin' jokes and doin' all sorts when we were parachuting two years ago ; but we didn't 'ave any nice little announcers to come along and say sweet things about us. Oh, no ! It's the lovely clean boys who sit on their backsides at home that get the write-ups. Why, they're so tough at home that they 'ave to ask for comforts for the poor soldiers stuck out in the wilds of Yorkshire. The wilds of Yorkshire ! " You should have heard the anger in that voice ; it would have made a tragedian jealous. " All the blinking B.B.C. can do is to say how blinking tough they are at 'ome. Well, I don't know wot the world's coming to. It's deadly, that's wot it is, definitely deadly ! " And with a resigned shake of his head he returned to his book once more.

If you did not know Sergeant Bennett you might have thought that he was deeply upset by these worldly injustices ; but when you came to understand him better you realised that they were really his joy of living. And when, a moment or two later, you heard his merry laugh ringing out among the sand-dunes as he chased after a battered old football, well, you could imagine just how much he must have enjoyed those rags at Oxford.

It was blowing a sand storm ; and the white grit as it swept, whistled and eddied round the trucks, sought out each one of us, stinging and biting and blinding. Earlier in the morning the breeze had played over the summits of the dunes, giving them accompanying wisps of fleecy white, so that they looked like snow-capped mountains ; and the sand, falling with a soft hissing, had drawn sinuous patterns on the downward slopes. Then the breeze had become a crying wind, flinging up the grains with joyful gusts so that the world became smaller and smaller, so that the jeeps and lorries disappeared from sight ; and we were living in our little circle of dirty grey.

We crawled under the tarpaulin that was slung over from one side of a lorry, leaning back against it and sitting on the loose flaps to keep them in position. Every now and then a vicious flurry of

sand whisked through a hidden gap in the canvas and set us all
blinking and rubbing our eyes. It was impossible to read, so we
lay and talked, shading our faces with our hands when we heard
the drive of the hissing sand coming towards us.

"Thank God we haven't got to travel in this !" muttered
Sergeant Lilley. "It reminds me of the day we left to attack
Berka drome. We only managed to drive about forty miles and
the truck got so hot that we had to keep on changing our positions."

I looked across at him, with his curly black hair, and his dark
eyes with the little furrows and wrinkles round them. I could not
help wondering why he had taken up this form of life ; for he was
getting on for forty, and had a wife and family to look after at
home. I suppose it must have been the individuality of the work
that appealed to him ; certainly he had learned to depend upon
himself right from the earliest days, and as a result he had learned
a straightforward and sound philosophy of life. Never hilarious and
never downhearted, he always maintained a steady level of good
humour as if life could not spring any surprises on him.

"Did you have any luck on the raid ?" I asked.

"Well, in a way, yes, and in a way, no, as you might say. The
job was unsuccessful 'cos we didn't get anything ; but on the
other hand we were mighty fortunate to get away. The L.R.D.G.
took us there—G patrol, it was—and they dropped us off about
thirty miles east of Berka. There was four of us, all told : Major
Mayne," he jerked his thumb in the direction of Paddy's jeep,
"and three of us corporals—I was a corporal then, you see, Doc ;
and each of us carried twenty-four bombs, some in our haversacks
and some slung from our belts. Well, it seemed the devil of a long
walk, that did, what with the darkness and our loads getting
heavier and heavier all the time—it was hard work and no
mistake ! But by the next morning we had reached a little Arab
camp, so we lay up all that day with the goats and the chickens.
They smelt pretty high !" he grinned, "You ever slept with
chickens, Doc ?"

I nodded.

"Good for you ! Those wretched things just can't leave a chap
alone. They were pecking and chirping round us the whole
blasted time. Still, we were too tired to worry about 'em and we
slept like logs. That evening we had a good meal with the Arabs,

but we pushed off early 'cos we wanted to get to the Berka airfield by midnight. Well, everything went all right, and we was just getting on to the drome when—would you believe it?—our blinkng Air Force has to come over and raid the place. There was shrapnel and bombs flying about all over the place—clink, clink and swish, swish ; and every now and then a terrific boomp ! By Joe ! We make some hefty bombs, you know ! I often wonder what the Itis would have thought if they had found some of us dead on their airfield the next morning ! Well, after a bit it got quiet, and Major Mayne sent me off to put a bomb on the first plane—we could just see it in the darkness. So I started crawling along the ground, and I'd just got within about ten yards of it when suddenly a sentry shouted out a challenge. Now, Major Mayne acts fast yer know, and I couldn't rightly say what happened next in this particular case, but I reckon he must have thrown a grenade as quick as a flash 'cos all I could see was a couple of Italians parting in mid air. That gave the alarm, worse luck, and things began to get pretty hot, with the sentries firing at us from all sides of the drome. The stuff was whistling over our heads this way and that, and I can tell you we weren't feeling so good."

A sudden gust of wind hit the tarpaulin, billowing it out like a sail, and passed on leaving us coughing and spitting out the dust. Sergeant Lilley wiped the back of his hand across his mouth and continued :

" As I say it weren't too comfortable on that drome and we decided it was a good thing to get away while we could. They had our range more than once as we ducked and ran for it, so Major Mayne shouted out to us to split up into two groups and find some place to hide. I was with Corporal Parker, I remember, and we managed to get through the guards, and found a house with a decent-sized garden which had a hedge running round it. We were only just in time though, 'cos a minute later some lorries— Lancias they were—began rolling up to the house and unloading Iti soldiers. From where we'd hidden ourselves in the hedge we could see them patrolling all around the place. Parker crawled over beside me and whispered that we ought to beat it ; but I was too lazy—just like I am now, Doc, you know ; I don't get moving unless I have to—and I told him to go to sleep. As a matter of fact I was so blinking tired that I dropped off straightaway and didn't wake up until soon after six o'clock when it was beginning to get light. I could see a couple of Iti sentries talking their heads off a few yards away from where I was, and I s'pose it was their voices that must have woken me up. I looked round for Corporal Parker but he'd gone. We never saw him again."

He paused a minute, licking the grit from his cracked lips before he went on.

" Well, this garden wasn't my idea of a health resort as maybe you can guess, so I crawled over very quietly to where I reckoned Major Mayne would be hidden—but he'd gone too. It looked as if I was in a tight spot. I was hiding under a bush, you see, and from it I had a pretty good view of a couple of Iti girls—not bad lookers either—walking round the garden with an Alsatian dog. I watched 'em as they came right past me and you can guess that my heart was beating mighty fast. They came so close that if it had been some other time or some other place—oh, well ! What the hell ! " He rolled over and laughed. " Still, I didn't 'ave any time to let my mind wander, 'cos darn me if that blasted Alsatian didn't find me. A friendly sort of cuss he was, and hard as I tried I couldn't prevent 'im from licking my face. The girls stopped a little farther down the path wondering what was the matter, and started calling to the animal. I gave him a smack on the nose that sent him away at a trot, and the girls gave him another smack when he got to them, so I reckon he caught it at both ends. Now I could see I was going to get nabbed if I stayed there any longer ; there seemed to be nothing else to do so I got out of the bush, stood up, and started to saunter off. You see it would 'ave been stupid to try and crawl away in the open. Well, I reckon that was the longest walk I've ever done. There were Itis here and Itis there—I seemed to be walking past them for the next five miles. I s'pose they took me for a Jerry or one of their own chaps 'cos I was only dressed in shorts and a shirt."

" After a while I reached the railway line and there one Italian did stop me. Dark, swarthy little devil, he was—I reckon he couldn't 'ave been more than twenty. We were neither of us armed, but he started to make out that I was his prisoner and tried to force me to go back to the camp with him. Now I don't like Itis, doc, and this chap was no exception. So I had to strangle him. Funny, killing a chap with yer own hands, Doc ! I can still see his white face and dark brown eyes quite clearly. His cap had toppled off in the struggle so I put it back over his head to make 'im look more natural.

"Well, I left him lying there sprawled out and looking up at the sun, and I pushed on as fast as I could till I came to an Arab camp. The Arabs gave me some food and hid me away in a corner of one of their tents, and I went to sleep. By Joe, there were plenty of fleas there all right! You know, I reckon those Arabs get so used to fleas that they begin to think there's something the matter with 'em if they stop scratching for awhile.

"I can't say rightly how long I slept there; but it hardly seemed any time at all before the Arabs were shaking me and waking me up. They pointed out through an opening in the tent, and who should I see but Major Mayne and Corporal Storey walking back. By Joe! I felt a lot better for that. We all had a good bite of grub and then we walked over to the rendezvous where we met the L.R.D.G. patrol; and that, Doc, was the end of that."

"Well, you were lucky all right," I commented.

"Yes, in a way," old Sergeant Lilley would never commit himself, "but we didn't do any damage, you see. Still it wasn't so bad for an old 'un like me. I showed 'em I could still beat an Iti when it came to the point," he gave a grunt of approval. "That was the best part of that trip, I guess."

Beside us, as he was speaking, the tarpaulin had been waving and flapping like a live thing; and all the time we could hear the sound of that steady, driving hiss outside.

"You enjoyed it, did you?" I asked.

"It's all right now, Doc—to look back on, you know!"

"But don't you prefer the successful raids?"

"Yes," he thought for a moment, uncertain. "Yes, I s'pose so. There's that feeling of satisfaction. But they aren't so thrilling when you come to think about 'em afterwards. There was that time when Major Mayne's patrol got over fifty planes in one week. We've called that airfield 'Paddy's Own!' ever since then. You ask Sergeant Bennett; he'll tell you all about it. It's good now to think that the Italians were phoning and wirelessing to Benghazi and Tripoli, saying that they were surrounded by overwhelming British forces and couldn't hold out much longer. There was only five of us there, you know ! " He smiled, " Yes, and it was good lying outside the airfield and watching them firing off their flak, thinking they were being bombed as one plane after another blew up with a bang. You certainly feel you have done your job all right. Yes, I s'pose those are the best raids."

He lifted a flap of the tarpaulin and peered out. From where we were, we could see the flying sand turned to a murky, swirling red by the light of the setting sun.

" Pity the poor sailors on a night like this ! " said Sergeant Lilley as he crawled back to his place.

I see that I have referred to the officers and sergeants, but have made little reference to the men, who were, of course, the core of the unit. The names come back to me as I write ; and even now in imagination I can see their dark, tanned bodies, the rough, tousled hair and beards ; can picture them lining up for their meal with clinking mess-tins, and can almost hear their jokes and sallies being thrown backwards and forwards. O'Dowd, Evans, Austin, Downes, Robinson, Miller, Cunningham, Shaw and many others. They would be busy at work on the jeeps and lorries, looking after the maintenance, cleaning the guns and testing them out, checking up the stores and equipment and learning navigation. And the cooks—little Paddy Allan who was killed not long afterwards, and Hammond who joined us from the R.A.S.C.— always seemed to have a full day as they did their utmost to disguise the bully and biscuits. Then there was Shotton who had become the squadron's medical orderly ; you could not have asked for a better man. Between us we had managed to get an Indian-pattern ambulance as far as the Sand Sea ; no mean feat, when all is considered, for they were not strongly constructed. This vehicle had been especially fitted with several gadgets inside, and consequently we took a little pride in its upkeep. We had felt that something of this nature was very necessary to the unit, but now that we had got it, there seemed to be very few casualties. Our most severe loss occurred when one of the returning patrols drove over some mines : one officer and three men were killed outright. Nevertheless the ambulance was very useful as a resting place for any one with a fever ; and Robinson, I remember, took refuge there during his attack of otitis media.

Once inside, they were sheltered from both sun and flies ; moreover, a point I may as well emphasise, they were not disturbed by their friends.

It is quite remarkable, sometimes, how callous soldiers are towards their friends. I can recall an occasion when I went into one of the wards of the underground hospital at Mersa Matruh. The atmosphere was shocking. It was difficult to see the far end of the ward on account of the haze of cigarette smoke. There was the continuous noise and babble of men shouting out to one another ; while, above the din, the wireless blared away and grated out its music. The man I had come to visit was dangerously ill from his wounds—too ill to be moved. Several other men were present whose condition was extremely grave. Their companions must have been aware of this but they seemed to take no notice. If you had questioned one of them, he would probably have shaken his head and, with an impressive display of concern upon his features, replied " Yes. I reckon that chap in the corner must be pretty bad. Just lies there and don't say nothing. It's that gas gangrene they talk about. That's wot he's got, I believe." And the next minute he would be shouting out at the top of his voice if any one wanted a " buckshee V cigarette." Quietness is seldom appreciated by a soldier until he is ill, and then he is not allowed it. That appears to be one of the circumstances that is bred of war.

During this time in the Sand Sea we blew up the Tobruk-Matruh railway line seven times. I will only mention two of these raids. The first was led by McDermott who, with his patrol of three jeeps, drove up by night to the railway line and camped down near the station. His intention was to blow up the first train that halted there ; but unfortunately the next goods train that came rattling along blew a loud blast on its whistle and went straight through. There was no further traffic on the line ; the sky slowly lightened, and realising that there was no time to be lost, the patrol drove into the station. The Italians who were supposed to be on duty, and those who were roughly awakened from their sleep, received a most unhappy surprise. No shots were fired—there seldom were on a successful raid—the shivering Romans, with their hands held high above their heads, being concerned only with their own immediate welfare. Two Germans, also, like good industrious early birds, were discovered at the top of a telegraph pole busily engaged on mending the line. In this precarious position they found it hard to understand who these bearded people were on the ground below, but once they had done so, they showed a commendable speed in making their descent. All the prisoners were then herded together by one man, while the rest worked fast placing the bombs, laying the fuses, and destroying the place systematically. One rather amusing incident occurred when a charge had been laid : apparently the fuse was very short and necessitated a fast withdrawal once it had been lighted. Consequently a jeep, with its engine running, was driven into position nearby ; as soon as the fuse had been lit, Corporal O'Dowd, the man who had fired it, jumped on to the jeep and the driver promptly accelerated away. The driver, however, was just a little too prompt and he moved off with such a jerk that O'Dowd was somersaulted off the back of the jeep. It was typical of the enemy that, whereas the Germans laughed heartily at this mishap—which, incidentally, resulted in no injury —the Italians were too occupied in cowering in sheer terror to be able to appreciate it.

The other raid did not really materialise ; but Sandy Scratchley, who had been pining for action, was selected as a likely candidate to blow up an oil-dump just behind the enemy's lines : that is to say between Daba and Alamein. This, naturally enough, was an extremely difficult target, if only on account of the numbers of enemy troops in the area ; and I am afraid we all had a bit of a laugh over it, especially when Sandy, with his quaint humour and odd Damon Runyan expressions, worked out a plan of " jumpin' a train " at Matruh and " ridin' the rods " as far as El Daba. Taken as a general rule one may say that the more closely a target was situated to the enemy's fighting line, the harder it was to approach ; so that it was with sincere wishes of good luck and God-speed that we saw Sandy jog away northwards one morning across the Sand Sea. I cannot say for certain what happened to him except to mention that, after a series of startling experiences, he discovered that he had penetrated our own as well as the enemy's lines ! He was making good progress for his target, apparently, just when the Eighth Army broke through the enemy's defences ; and for the next few days he spent a lively time bobbing up and down behind pieces of camel-thorn while battles were waged about him, and while mixed forces swept past him on every side. But he looked just as cool and debonair when next I saw him in Shepheards. It was simply another story to him, and not a bad one at that !

The Eighth Army did not take long to advance from Alamein to Tobruk and beyond, and by that time our position in the Sand Sea had become valueless for we were no longer behind the enemy's lines. It was obvious, then, that we should have to make a fresh rendezvous ; and with this object in mind we began to pack up our stores and get ready to move.

CHAPTER TWENTY-ONE

" Growth is the only evidence of life."
                                    CARDINAL NEWMAN.

" Makes mighty things from small beginnings grow."
                                    DRYDEN.

THERE WAS something almost sad in leaving the Sand Sea with its
memories, its associations and its comradeship ; and it was with
a certain sense of regret that I watched it sink away into the heat-
haze. Our course took us over flat, uneventful country where
mirages lay like silent pools against the horizon and vanished
quietly at our approach. Skirting a limb of migrant sand-dunes
we came to our first rock features—mushroom-rock[1] and sugar-
loaf hill—strange freaks of wind erosion and weathering from
which we took the next bearing that brought us to the more rugged
scenery in the neighbourhood of needle-rock. At this stage of the
journey I found myself trying to judge how close we could get to
a mirage before it disappeared ; close enough, I found to recognise
the trembling reflections of conical hills or jagged stony outcrops.
It was not difficult to understand how, after several days of thirst
and fatigue, a traveller might mistake these shapes for sailing
ships, palm-trees, or any other objects of his desire ; nor, from the
tales of the survivors, how such strange legends must surely have
arisen. Even as I was considering the point I could see the jeep
in front of me heading for a mirage, apparently " taking off " when
it reached the " water's edge " and flying through the air.

Rather less than a hundred miles to the north-east of Kufra we
came to two Blenheim aircraft which had force-landed some time
previously. Beside them were the graves of their crews who had
perished from exhaustion and thirst. About fifty miles away, I was
told, was another Blenheim, also with its little group of graves.

[1] Rocks which had been weathered into a mushroom-like shape were not uncommon in the desert and made good landmarks.

302

Only one man from the crews of these three planes had survived the ordeal of waiting for rescue in the loneliness and heat of the desert. This tragedy was due to a slight error in navigation ; but the most trivial mistake in the desert can result in a complete loss of one's sense of position, and a man may die on his own doorstep without knowing it. The reader may get a clearer mental picture of the circumstances if he imagines Kufra oasis as a small island set in a large sea, with no other islands situated within four hundred miles. It can be appreciated, then, that only the closest accuracy will bring a person back to the exact point from which he has started ; and landmarks are often more deceptive and unreliable than otherwise. As I sat in the cockpit of one of the Blenheims and read the rough " log " notes jotted down in pencil —the mileage on such-and-such a bearing, the wind variance, and the weather conditions—I could almost visualise from these little scraps of paper just how this dreadful thing had come about. Outside, the hot wind was moaning round the wire struts ; it had been the self-same wind which had blown up a sand-storm when the aircraft were grounded, blanketing over them in all its yellow fierceness and delaying the rescue of their crews by both land and air patrols. As I say, they were less than a hundred miles from Kufra—three days' march—and when they were found, only one of the party was alive.

After a couple of days at Kufra we set off for our next rendezvous which was to be situated at Bir Zalten, a spot about eighty miles south of El Agheila. Here we met David Stirling, who had brought B squadron with him along the coastal road to Agedabia before striking south-west into the desert. He was not looking too fit, I thought, for he had only just been discharged from hospital where he had been undergoing treatment for desert sores, and now he had conjunctivitis and was obliged to wear dark glasses. However, he seemed far too interested in the next series of operations to let this worry him much ; and I have a strong suspicion that the eye-baths I ordered for him were not taken with any regularity !

David's schemes were as follows :

A squadron (Paddy Mayne's squadron) should cover an area as far as Misurata, while B squadron proceeded further west and raided targets up to Tripoli and the country immediately beyond.

(At this time, which was early in December, the front had been stabilised to the east of El Agheila, and it will be remembered that the First Army had landed in North-West Africa and was making slow progress towards Tunisia.) These squadron operations were to extend over December and January and were timed to work in conjunction with the attack of the Eighth Army. The targets consisted chiefly of enemy encampments which were to be attacked frequently, and the coastal road which could be mined and demolished sufficiently to hold up enemy traffic.

In addition to these plans, David, himself, wished to contact the First Army by driving straight across to the south of the fighting zone from one front to the other. On his way he would do what damage he could with explosives and strafing, while the journey would give him a good idea of the nature of the country for future operations. For this job he required Mike Sadler as navigator and, in all, I think his patrol was made up of twenty to thirty men.

I will not go into the results of these raids in detail but will merely remark that A squadron enjoyed considerable success and few casualties. B squadron, however, was working in more cultivated and less open territory ; moreover the Arabs of this part of Tripolitania were hostile to the British. Consequently their losses were relatively heavy, and the effectiveness of their raids was not so easy to assess. Possibly, too, their results may have been dependent upon the relatively large number of fresh operatives in " B " squadron ; for, without a doubt, experience and seasoning in this sort of work were more important than zeal and valour. Not for a long time did we hear what had happened to David's men. A mysterious silence closed down upon them and we became anxious for their safety. Eventually Mike Sadler and two sergeants returned to our camp and told us the full story.

Everything had gone pretty well with them until they came to the Gabes Gap, where they had been forced to pass through a small bottle-neck in order to continue on their course. It would seem that their presence had previously been disclosed by the Arabs ; for the Germans had sent out both aircraft and ground patrols in search of them. It was in this gap, then, that they were caught early one morning while they were resting ; the speed and weight of the attack soon put an end to their resistance, and only

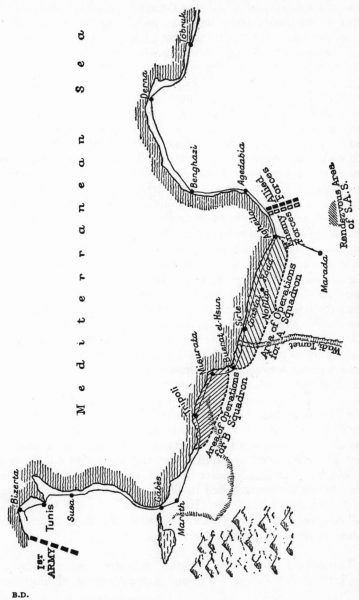

AREAS OF OPERATIONS OF A. AND B. SQUADRONS. DECEMBER, 1942 AND JANUARY, 1943.

a few of them were able to make their escape. This they did by hiding in the bushes and rough grass, while the Germans walked all round them, machine-gunning each likely hiding place. It was not a pleasant experience. When the Germans had left, they lost no time in getting away. There were four of them : Mike Sadler, Sergeant Seekings, Sergeant Cooper and a French sergeant—all of them old operatives. Keeping together, they set out to walk the remaining distance of a hundred miles or so to the First Army. More than once they were surrounded by Arabs who attacked them—manhandling them, tearing their clothes, beating them with sticks and stoning them as they tried to get away. Each time they were stopped by a native band they were forced to parley and appear friendly, for the very smallness of their numbers forbade any attempt at force. On one occasion, Sergeant Cooper was struck on the forehead by a flying stone which cut a gash over his eyes. The blood running down his face blinded him, so that two of the others had to grasp him by the hands and lead him as fast as they could through the gauntlet of thrown missiles. There is something very Biblical about the scene ; and one is reminded of the hard fate dealt out to those who appeared to offend the law of the Pharisees. Certainly Mike Sadler considered it a far more harrowing experience than anything he had suffered at the hands of the Germans. But by dint of hard marching, and by avoiding as much trouble as they could, they reached, at last, the lines of the Americans in Tunisia. They were footsore, weary, and must have looked like nothing on earth ; hence they were sent straight to prison. But they were not detained long ; soon their identities had been established and they were forced to repeat their story over and over again to their incredulous listeners. In conclusion I should say that, although David Stirling never saw this patrol accomplish its mission, yet his efforts were not wasted. For Mike Sadler had hardly arrived with the First Army before he was recalled to Eighth Army headquarters and asked to help navigate the New Zealand division round the southern end of the Mareth Line and along the same course that he had so recently trodden.

Throughout these two months, A squadron's rendezvous remained at Bir Zalten. We had hoped to establish ourselves further to the west, but at the last moment David had taken our petrol for his operation and we were obliged to remain where we were ; and although our site was now of no value as a rendezvous, since returning patrols made their way back via the Eighth Army, yet it did, at any rate, serve as a half-way station for convoys bearing supplies from Benghazi to B squadron's rendezvous. As a habitat the area was perfect ; and we were very happily situated amongst the broken outcrops of chalk and sandstone cliffs ; while the shallow caves which had been hollowed out at ground level provided us with handsome sleeping quarters. They afforded us protection, too, from the rain—unless the wind was blowing into the entrance—although, in this connection, they were not as safe as they might have been. For here, in the coastal belt, grey-clouded, rainy days were by no means uncommon and were more in the nature of prolonged cloud-bursts. In a comparatively short time the moisture had soaked through the upper strata of the cliffs, and as you lay sheltering in your cave below, you could hear heavy thuds as sodden chunks of the cliff-face dropped off and landed within a foot or two of your resting place. This gave rise to a sense of insecurity which was not lessened by noting places where other cliff-faces had plainly collapsed *en masse*. In this respect the advantage of a low-lying cave with no high cliff-face above it, was considerably offset by the fact that the rain quickly soaked through ; and looking back on it now I am inclined to wonder how many of us earned the legacy of a good dose of rheumatism for our later years. Once the rain had started to cascade over the cliff-face like a miniature waterfall, then you certainly did have to keep a sharp look-out ; and there was nothing unusual in seeing torches flashing through the darkness on some wet night and showing up the diagonal lines of driving rain, as some little party hurriedly decamped from their flooded sleeping quarters. I can remember one evening when I had walked over to Sergeant Lilley's cave to enjoy an hour or two at some innocent game of cards, how a sudden, violent storm broke over us, and, by its very severity, prevented us from returning. After waiting an hour for the rain to abate, two of us set off for our caves, squelching and splashing our way through mud and puddles, until, of course, the inevitable occurred and we lost our way. Both of us were under the impression that we were perfectly familiar with our camp surroundings, yet in was half an hour later before we had discovered our whereabouts and had returned, drenched and ill-tempered, to our respective abodes !

Our wireless set was invaluable ; and here, as in the Sand Sea, I found myself wondering at the sense of strange isolation which was provoked by the strains of dance music which came drifting over the desert air at night. All that life that once we had known at home was now something that belonged to a different world. It was apart and remote from us ; it no longer belonged to us ; it was unreal. Did it make us bitter, as we huddled round and listened to the gusty laughter of the music-hall concerts ? Were we envious as we thought of the cosy warmth inside the hall, and pictured the clean, colourful dresses of the girls on the stage ? Perhaps we were a little ; for everything from England sounded so smug and so superbly self-satisfied. Then, too, there was the poor type of humour exercised by so many of the entertainers : the patronising sentiment given to " *our* men " and " *our* boys " ; and the routine, coarse jokes concerning the relations between the wives that had been left behind and the lodgers in the homes. Doubtless the people in England appreciated this brilliant form of wit ; the soldiers abroad did not. It was too true and too tragic to be comical.

What was funny, however, was the great competition that took place amongst the British stage and radio " artists " after the African campaign had ended : the rush to see who could tour the Middle East first, in as short a time as possible, and get back to the microphone—the finishing post—to announce what they had just done.[1] In the days after any enemy threat to Africa had been eliminated, these " stars " were fairly crowding out to see the " boys of the Middle East "—provided, of course, that their other engagements allowed them to do so. With electrifying rapidity one name followed another in this remarkable effort to entertain the forces.

It was interesting, too, to note which of our great " stars " had sufficient time to spare—from their contracts, presumably—to visit the soldiers who had been wounded, some of them maimed and disfigured for life, and who lay at the near-by hospitals. Very

[1] These remarks do not apply to ENSA concert parties, many of which remained abroad for considerable periods of time.

few did this ! Very few could be bothered ! Very few could set aside the extra hour or two in their hectic rush from one crowded, clapping hall to the next ! And in passing one might as well mention that the front seats of these halls were reserved for the worthy gentlemen who fulfilled their various staff appointments with such verve and audacity. After the soldiers had been queueing up for several hours in order to hear a concert they had the pleasure of witnessing, from their back seats, the local gentry— excellently clad, wined and fed—as they made their martial way to the orchestra stalls. Sometimes the soldiers found they had wasted their time in waiting outside and that there were not enough seats for them—dash it all, you couldn't expect an artist to make more than one appearance in a dreadful place like Malta ! —and then their pleasure at seeing the staff officers was not quite so marked.

As I have said, one felt a curious sense of detachment in listening to some of these wireless programmes : it was like tuning in to life in a different world ; something that we had known in the past but dared not recall too closely in the full poignancy of the memory ; a life that was so different and so distinctly defined from our present way of living that it might have been cut out with a pair of scissors, so sharp was it. I can still remember with a smile the incongruousness of seeing Sandy Scratchley and Digger Shaw, one night of our journey through the Sand Sea on the way to Benghazi, perform the Big Apple to the strains of some London band that was swinging it hot ! We laughed until our sides ached as we watched them going through the weird antics in this vast and vacant setting. The men were very funny too, in the way they used to dance round in the sand with an invisible partner for company. They loved Bing Crosby ; Vera Lynn came too seldom for their tastes, while Jimmy O'Dea, as I remember, was the favourite of the Irish contingent.

Classical music, on the other hand, was unpopular in our company, and no sooner had the theme of some symphony come stealing melodiously forth, than it was a case of, " Take 'er away, Nobby ! " or " Get somethin' wiv a kick in it, Chalky ! " In the world of music it seemed that poor old Beethoven and Wagner had fallen somewhat from grace ; presumably these Germanic airs would have upset our fighting spirit. Mendelssohn and Chopin

passed out with flying colours ; both of them being Jews, one took
it for granted that their music was banned from the German
stations. Slowly the musicians had assumed their different sides
in this world conflict ; and when Russia entered the fray we
immediately found much fresh talent at our command, while
many a composer who had once been looked upon askance,
now came fully into his own. Tchaikowsky for example ; and I
find it hard to believe that there is any radio listener who cannot
whistle his Nutcracker Suite or the first movement of his first piano
concerto perfectly and with consummate ease.

I hope that such criticisms or complaints as I may have had
to offer in the past few pages have not been too wearisome to the
reader. It should be borne in mind that it is the privilege of the
British soldier to be allowed to grumble ; and I well remember
Robin Gurdon informing me of this once when I told him how
depressing it was to hear all the grumbling that went on in the
regiment. " But it's their very life-blood, Doc," he had replied.
" You mustn't take that seriously ! Why, they couldn't live
without grumbling ! "

During our brief visit to base after the Benghazi raid, I had
managed, by dint of much hard work, to obtain a puppy. It was a
lady, I'm afraid, coal-black all over and with a querulous curl of
the tail which pronounced it to be, beyond all doubt, a pie-dog.
Thinking, in my innocence, that I should have a faithful old bitch
to follow my footsteps in later years, I took her down to Kufra and
thence to the Sand Sea. But I was soon to be disappointed. For
if ever an animal picked up bad manners more quickly than
H.M.S. Saunders—for she was named after her camp of origin—I
have yet to hear of it. Within a week she had learned to respond
to all sorts of names which the men considered to be adequately
descriptive ; while any whistle that might herald food in the
offing brought her panting across the sand as fast as her short,
squat legs would carry her. Indeed it was her belly that was the
ruin of her—that and the men—nor was it long before she had
utterly forsaken me for the happy, easy-going life of the cook-
house, where food of some description or other was available at
almost any hour of the day. Moreover it was at the cook-house
that she built up her rather uncertain " pie-doggish " friendship

with another bitch that had recently been captured, together with a couple of disreputable looking Italians, by one of our fighting patrols.

Nevertheless, despite these canine failings, she was an attractive little thing ; and I can see her, even now, jogging along the crest of a sand-dune, silhouetted out with startling blackness against the hot blue of the sky, and with her tail curled up in beautifully symmetrical spirals over her hind-quarters. As a matter of fact the Sand Sea mystified her considerably. The silence of those dunes was something she could not understand ; there were times when she would stand barking at them for almost half an hour at a time as if expecting some rabbit to pop out and scamper away ; at others she would be suddenly startled by the echo of her own yelp and become furious with this hidden, insolent stranger who mocked her very voice ; while at others again she would become well-nigh mad with insatiable curiosity as she burrowed away hard into the sliding sand with her fore-paws, yet found herself unable to discover any bottom or foundation to it. I remember, too, that she would get frightened if I took her walking some distance away from the rendezvous. At first she would be all a-bustle with her ears cocking this way and that and her tail bobbing along behind in cheerful company. But after we had gone for half a mile or so she felt she had had enough ; her tail would begin to droop and she would look back longingly in the direction from which she had come as if to say : " Where *has* everybody else got to ? How very oppressive this silence is ! What about turning back now ? " Slowly she would fall behind, and then, when she thought I was not looking, would turn round and desert me completely. It was interesting to note the way she sniffed her way back ; the idea of following our tracks never occurred to her. And how her spirits picked up when at last she did sight the rendezvous and cookhouse once more ! In a flurry of sand and in a wild din of happy barking she would scamper straight for home.

Soon she had developed a friendly little trick of crawling in under my blankets with me at night ; and then, for reasons of her own, she would leave me at about three o'clock in the morning and snuggle in with somebody else. There was nothing snobbish about H.M.S. Saunders ! I think she slept with every man in the

camp on more than one occasion. And she could make such
endearing, throaty and human sounds of satisfaction as she curled
up beside you, that no one could deny her entrance to bed or cave.
She was no longer my dog ; she had become " A " squadron's
mascot.

In this way life continued smoothly for H.M.S. Saunders
until we came to leave the rendezvous at Bir Zalten. Then, just
at the moment of our departure, she must have gone jogging
casually over to one of the caves to see if Jeffs or Austin or Sergeant
Lilley was at home, for when we halted for our midday meal some
fifty miles away there was no H.M.S. Saunders with her curly tail
to be seen anywhere. After some argument it was decided that
the convoy should wait while some of us, in a couple of lorries,
returned to the rendezvous. The journey took us a good two
hours, and when we got there we could see no sign of Saunders
at first. Then we caught sight of her, watching us furtively from
behind a rock and trying to decide just what sort of a reception
she was going to receive at our hands.

" Saunders ! " we cried, and our voices echoed back in hollow
resonance from the empty caves around, " Saunders, come here!"

At that she crept towards us for about five yards and·then,
suddenly taking fright and fearful of a beating, she turned tail
and disappeared once more behind her rock.

" Saunders ! " we called out reproachfully, " Saunders, old
chap ! What's the matter, old boy ? Come along, there's a good
fellow." With sweet, persuasive tones we endeavoured to wheedle
her from her hiding-place ; and all the while, under our breath,
we were cursing her to the blackest depths of hell ! Imagine for
yourself the picture of half a dozen bearded men holding out their
hands and chirruping to this wretched creature who came
towards us every now and again with feebly wagging tail, only to
tear away as soon as she thought we had approached too closely.
We made a dash for her once but found ourselves no match for her
nimble speed, and it took us another ten minutes before we gained
her confidence again sufficiently to draw close. But eventually
we caught her ; and by the time we had driven back to the others
it had grown dark, and most of the men had got to bed and were
in little mood to appreciate either her happy barkings or the way
her swishing tail nearly shook her hind legs off the ground. The

rescue of H.M.S. Saunders had not been a very dramatic event.

We paused for a day at Benghazi before we continued our drive ; and it was here, on a dull, drizzling morning that Griffiths, our grey-haired retainer, informed me : " Saunders has been served, sir ! A big dark dog it was with a piece bitten out of one ear—something in the nature of a retriever I think it was, sir." which was his way of saying that it was a black pie-dog. But that was not the only romance in her life. Later on (in this short history of H.M.S. Saunders) when we went up to the ski-school in the Lebanon we took her with us. What a dainty little figure she cut as she pranced along delicately in the snow ! And soon it was evident that we were not the only ones to notice it. For the ski-school boasted a magnificent Alsatian whose dignified mien had earned him the name of Rex. He bore us, the ski-students, an aloof good-will so long as we were inside the building ; but outside in the snow he had learned various antics, such as pretending to attack as we learned to ski down inclines, which put us completely off our balance. Yes, he was a fine dog with plenty of spirit and, believe it or not, he fell madly in love with our jaunty little H.M.S. Saunders, despite her disreputable pie-ard strains and her diminutive size. There was something quite touching in the way he would meekly follow her around, ready to fall in with her every wish ; the way he would get out of the most comfortable chair when Saunders, and Saunders alone, entered the room. And there was something very amusing, too, in the way in which she took all these favours for granted and scarcely threw a glance in Rex's direction ; in the way she scarcely acknowledged his presence, far less his faithful doggy love. But I dare say he got over it all right after we had left the ski-school ; probably it was just one of those fleeting romances of the wild ; for surely nature could never have intended that Rex and H.M.S. Saunders should be united in holy wedlock.

Despite our comparative inactivity at the Bir Zalten rendez-vous, the time passed very quickly. Away to the north of us we could hear the intermittent mutter and rumble of the heavy artillery of the Eighth Army ; on a cold winter's night, when we had thrown our greatcoats over our blankets, we would listen to the distant sounds and pity the poor gunners their lack of sleep.

Then came the deep silence as the sounds of battle passed away to the west ; and we began to feel that our position was no longer essential. Being in wireless contact with the others, however, we were always ready to join in any raids if called upon to do so.

Here we passed Christmas and New Year's Day ; and I can remember how depressed I felt when I heard the familiar Christmas carols coming over the wireless. They sounded so sad and plaintive out there, bringing with them, as they did, the memories of previous Christmases at home : the crackers and the coloured paper ; the cheerful fireside and the chestnuts popping out on to the hearth ; the way we would listen to the King's speech in the afternoon ; and a picture of my mother holding up some piece of clothing to the light and, with mingled pleasure and reproach, telling my aunt that she really ought *not* to have gone to so much trouble and expense to get it. Peace and goodwill, with Europe yet to be conquered ! I can picture us now as we squatted round on the ground, scooping up the food from off our plates : we were bearded, dirty and dishevelled ; we were wearing the same clothes that we had worn for the past six weeks as we listened to an English choir singing, " God rest you Merry Gentlemen, let nothing you dismay ! " But perhaps we were lucky to have venison for our dinner. Sergeant Phillips was really responsible for this and claimed to have shot the deer ; but on tasting the flesh it was generally agreed that the animal must have laid down and died somewhere and that Sergeant Phillips had just happened to pass that way. Certainly the cooks deserved full credit for their Yuletide efforts ; yet, even so, I could not help feeling downcast.

We had a party on Christmas evening. The fire drew us together in a large noisy circle ; while the red light flickering over our faces made each man look alive, animated, quiet, thoughtful or apostolic as it caught and held his expression for a sharp instant. There was Paddy, with his bushy beard and massive shoulders, giving way to the mood of the moment and joining in with his strange unmusical singing to each song in turn. But he refused to sing a solo, contenting himself instead with reciting some of French's poems and becoming so enrapt with their spirit that, even as he did so, his brogue became marked enough for us to find the verses hard to follow. He showed an easy tolerance of sentimental jazz songs ; and in reply to my criticism he pointed across at Shotton and said, " Look at him ! He's singing his heart out. Don't you see, he's as happy as a skylark. Och, never you mind, Malcolm, we'll have you singing ' Macnamarra's Band ' yet ! " Yes, Paddy was Irish all right ; Irish from top to toe ; from the lazy eyes that could light into anger so quickly, to the quiet voice and its intonation. Northern Irish, mind you, and he regarded all Southerners with true native caution. But he had Southern Irishmen in his Irish patrol—they all had shamrocks painted on their jeeps—and I know he was proud of them ; he never grew tired of quoting the reply given by one of the Southerners in answer to the question : why was he fighting in the war : " Why ? " he had replied. " Of course it's for the independence of the small countries ! "

There was something very rugged and forceful about Paddy's leadership. Although he lived and slept with the men, queued up behind them as he waited his turn for food, and ate with them, yet no one would dare to overstep the mark and become too familiar with him. For he could silence a man with a glance, could cut him short without a word ; while every one held a considerable respect for his physical capabilities. And yet despite, or together with, these characteristics, he would be the first man to come up and try to discover why you were depressed at Christmas time. Such were a few of the qualities that made him so successful as a commander.

When the Eighth Army had swept right on and it became obvious that our position was of little value, we packed up our goods and belongings and made our departure. This then, was the end of our campaigning in Africa, and now we might bid farewell to the desert ; the desert with its strange appeal, with its miles of monotonous uniformity and yet its continuous subtle changing. The moods of the desert : the loneliness, the solace, and the clean sterility. Here, in these little cliffs and caves that had been our hiding-places, we had left our mark : the sign of human habitation. In a few weeks it would be erased by wind and sand. So, too, would our tracks ; and those deep furrows that our lorries left behind them would soon be covered and swept clean. We could take our place for a little while, we could make our stand and the desert would hold us to her ; but of memory there would not be left a trace. The desert was too vast ; our fading marks could not long defy her immensity. But as for us— we always had our recollections. Happy they might be or bitter as gall, but they remained and could not be touched. And with us we took our memories of heat and cold ; of early dawn, fresh as the dew on a petal ; of the glory and splendour of many tinted sunsets. Memories of evenings when we had driven hard across the flat sand, as it stretched out towards the sky-line ablaze with reflected golds and reds ; of little clouds, lit and bedecked with colour, standing out like lanterns against the fading light ; of the flower blue, the soft amber, and the fresh green of the sky before it grew dark and the first stars looked down upon our wanderings.

Here we had learned to navigate, to plot our course, and to mark our position ; here we had learned the names of stars and constellations as nightly they wheeled over our heads ; and here we had grown wise, becoming self-reliant and tolerant of the humours of others, taking pleasure in little things, and learning from the examples of our fellows. Our time had not been wasted ; for we had gained resourcefulness and knowledge from our own haphazard and natural way of living, and we realised the true worth of our own insignificance. In this way we had matured, we had known a greater mental sufficiency, had discovered our fears and reactions to danger, and had tried to overcome them. We had become familiar with hardship and with the submission of the body to a rigid control, so that it became at last a mere disciple of the mind.

This was the bequest of the desert ; and, in some ways, we regretted our departure from the land that had taught us these things. As we drove back fast towards Kabrit, we passed those places with which many of us had become all too well acquainted in the past. Here was Tobruk, bleak and desolate, with an icy wind blowing over the bare rocks, and the harbour looking the very picture of lifelessness ; there was Capuzzo and Sidi Rezech with the dust sweeping low, as usual, across the ground, concealing imperfectly the burned-out trucks, the trackless, blackened tanks, and the significant clusters of wooden graves that served to mark a former battlefield ; and there was Halfaya Pass with the flat plain below that a number of us knew closely from earlier fighting and unsuccessful attacks. So perhaps it was as well that the desert war was ending ; we had enough sad memories to keep us company.

But what of the unit, now that David Stirling was a prisoner and this phase of operations had been concluded. The Special Air Service was too highly trained and held too fine a record to be put lightly on one side. Already a third squadron, C squadron, was specialising in fol-boat work under the direction of Jellicoe and Sutherland for tip-and-run raids on the enemy coast ; while during the months of February and March A squadron repaired to the ski-school in the Lebanon for a fittening-up course in case they should become involved in mountain warfare. Although the unit had greatly increased in size, some of the old operatives were no longer with us. Bobby Dodds, Eric Parten and Peter Warr had either left or were in the process of doing so ; while Bill Cumper's movements had become very uncertain—he was now employed largely as an instructor to outside units—and we saw little of him. I missed the old faces and the old atmosphere ; I was very depressed by the loss of Jim Chambers, and, having completed the training parachute jumps for my own moral satisfaction, I decided that it would be wise for me, also, to bid my farewell. It was not a case of leaving a weakening unit ; rather, the reverse held good ; and before we had gone we could see the firm foundations of the new S.A.S.

Certainly my departure was no loss from a medical point of view, for Philip Gunn—the best doctor I had met in the desert— had recently joined us. In addition there was another doctor procured by Maclean, who would be attached to Jellicoe's squadron. So it was with an easy mind that I handed over the medical equipment and made my preparations to go.

Under the fresh organisation there were two sub-units each made up of about two hundred men ; one was led by Paddy Mayne, being trained hard both in parachuting and sea-landing exercises to become a sort of super-commando ; while the other, under Jellicoe, continued its training for smaller and more widely dispersed raids. In order to become more acclimatised to European conditions the camp at Kabrit was broken and the S.A.S. moved north to Palestine.

At this point my story of the desert adventures of the Special Air Service comes to an end. In writing it I have endeavoured to break away from the cold facts of results achieved, and have striven to show the sort of family life—if you can describe it thus—that went on inside the unit. The S.A.S. was made up of such a fine group of men that even now I find it difficult not to " day-dream " about past experiences ; and sometimes I find the pen has lingered while the fancy has flown back to recapture those moments of good fellowship. But perhaps the critical reader will ask exactly what the S.A.S. did achieve in the desert. " All this is very interesting," he may say, " It is most diverting to read of the way you dashed about the desert in your jeeps like a crowd of over-grown schoolboys. But what precisely *were* your results ? " So to them, and to those who love statistics, I can only quote the following figures : We destroyed a total of approximately four hundred enemy aircraft in the desert ; A squadron, during the autumn of 1942, demolished the enemy railway line on seven occasions ; while between September, 1942 and February, 1943, forty-three successful attacks were made against German key positions and communications. Our raids, then, were more than mere pin-pricks ; and there were occasions when we must have diverted enemy forces and upset their road convoy system con-siderably ; while the steady drain on their aircraft probably exercised an influence on the course of the desert war. As I have remarked before, the Special Air Service made a rule of under-stating its results for fear that it might be suspected of exaggera-tion ; in writing this account I have endeavoured to do the same.

With such leadership as that exercised by Mayne and Jellicoe, the continued success of the Special Air Service was never in doubt. Of C squadron I can say nothing, in all probability their results will one day receive the public's attention. On the other hand news kept coming to me of Paddy Mayne's Unit and, by all accounts, its desert reputation was more than justified by its deeds in Europe. I trust I shall be forgiven if I quote the press concerning his command : " The S.A.S. started the invasion of Sicily . . . and made what is believed to be the first daylight opposed assault landing of the war with the capture of Augusta." From Sicily they moved to Italy and at this time I received one of Paddy's rare communications : " We have done four sea-borne operations," he wrote, " and the Unit has done smashingly well. General Dempsey, the Corps Commander, paid us what, I imagine, were the highest compliments paid to any unit. Among other things he said we were the best crowd he had ever had under his command. I think he is right, too ; the lads have done well ! "

A month or two later I received another letter : " Poor old Sandy Wilson was killed in our last operation and Bill Fraser was wounded. I had a letter from Bill to-day saying he was much better, so I am glad about that. Bob Melot also had a bullet into his chest and out somewhere round his back. With a bit of trouble we managed to get him to go to hospital, but he came back after a couple of days with a card to say he was fit for full duty ! "

" Bob Lilley, Rose and Sgt. Bennett are the steadiest of the old hands. All our officers have been really good. Phil Gunn has done some grand work ; he is just what I expected him to be. I have heard that Sgt. Almonds—you remember he was captured in the Benghazi raid—has got through to our side ; I am trying to meet him. . . . Our future I believe is pretty rosy. I think the chaps will get what they deserve—they don't know it and I don't think they are worrying."

By the spring of 1944 the Special Air Service had reached brigade strength and was training in England for further operations. Long before the Normandy landings were made they had parachuted down at scattered points throughout France, wreaking havoc with enemy railways, blowing up goods trains, and continually harassing the main thoroughfares. Working on much the same principles as they had done in the desert, each patrol kept in touch with the squadron headquarters which in turn wirelessed back its information to the regiment. Their jeeps and equipment were dropped to them by the Air Force ; and many a German guard must have been just as surprised to see them driving along the little French country lanes as were the Italian sentries on the dusty tracks in the old Libyan days.

As the continental offensive developed and gained weight, so the S.A.S. probed deeper and deeper into the enemy lines. By attacking strong points here and there, and acting in co-ordination all the time ; by raiding and wrecking the main supply lines ; and by sending back information about good bombing targets for the Air Force, they assisted materially in the rapid advance of the

Allied armies. From France to Belgium, and then beyond into Holland and Germany ; each raid added a fresh tale of bluff and daring ; of encounters with an enemy whose great superiority in numbers was offset by his lack of preparedness ; of successes which look mundane and uninteresting in cold print.

These, then, were the achievements that Stirling and Lewis foresaw in 1941 : these were the results of their continued effort and toil at times when the very future of the unit appeared to be at stake. This is what Mayne laboured for and helped to make practicable : a unit that was founded on comradeship and high endeavour. I only hope that, in writing this book, I have helped to portray that spirit so that you, the reader at home, may know what manner of men they were in the Special Air Service.

THE END

POSTSCRIPT

So what happened after my time with L detachments SAS? When I left it in 1943 there were still two years of the war to run and, for me, another forty years of medical service. From the desert, I was posted to 64 General Hospital in Cairo. Here, however, there was little useful work for a rusty general duties officer, and so I was not sorry when I was moved on to Malta.

Malta in 1943 was very pleasant. The officers in the Field Ambulance to which I was attached went out of their way to make me comfortable, and it seemed very strange to live in a house. The bomb damage in the harbour area was considerable, rather like the east end of London on a large scale. But once you were away from Valetta and the air force landing base some villages seemed almost untouched. Food rationing had been very severe and, unlike Cairo, Malta had taken the full brunt of the war. After a short spell, I was transferred to the military hospital in the centre of the island. We were responsible for British and Maltese service personnel, together with their families, the casualties evacuated from Italy, and young people of both sexes from Tito's forces in Yugoslavia.

I was fortunate enough to be taken under the wing of Bob Nevin, the senior surgical consultant, who trained me as his anaesthetist, and who later became Dean of St Thomas's Hospital. Everyone was very patient with me, as I tried to cope with this new work. However the recurrent abdominal pains that I had suffered in the desert while I was medical officer to the 3rd Battalion Coldstream Guards caught up with me. At that time I had been whisked off to Cairo where despite my doubts over diagnosis my appendix was whipped out. Now in Malta, I found I was right — it was a gastric ulcer and I was advised to take up work with more regular hours in future both in the Army and at home. It was at this time, isolated in a side ward of the hospital, that I wrote this book, while the events of the desert war were still fresh in my mind. The ulcer took a long while to heal, and I was invalided home exactly four years after my departure.

England seemed another civilisation, however, and I felt an alien, totally out of place in this new environment. I married the girl I had left behind me in 1940, and my wife and our families helped me readjust. I still found myself avoiding social gatherings for some years after that, however, perhaps because of the cumulation of my earlier traumatic experiences as a ship's doctor in Dunkirk harbour, evacuating the wounded from the British Expeditionary Force, then in Tobruk the following year with the Coldstream Guards and the SAS following that, or perhaps because of my isolation in the hospital in Malta.

In England, after more hospital investigation and sick leave, I was given administrative duties in Sussex and finally demobilised at the end of 1945. Mindful of the advice I had been given in Malta I decided to take up public health, a subject about which I then knew absolutely nothing. I obtained two higher medical degrees in infectious diseases and public health, and put them to use in a variety of county appointments. It was interesting work, supervising the health of the public from the cradle to the grave. With the dissolution of the County Health services in 1974, I became occupational health doctor for the county services, developing a high regard for the Fire Service's courage and determination. Now my life has come full circle. I am retired, and am out of doors as much as possible, either in the garden or walking by the river. In the good company of the trees and clouds. I can sense again the wide sweeps of desert, in which I used to commune with the universe and tell the time by the sun by day and the stars by night.

During the war I carried a camera with me, and the photographs I then took, together with my weekly letters home and my war diary, I have donated to the Imperial War Museum. *Born of the Desert* was first published in 1945, at a time when the use of my real name would not hae been appropriate as I was active in the medical world. Malcolm James are my Christian names. Now, however, circumstances have changed, and I can sign this postscript with my full name.

Oxford, 1991.   Malcolm James Pleydell.

NOTES TO NEW EDITION
Compiled by David List

"On 14 September 1942 1st Special Air Service Regiment raided Benghasi and then withdrew to the escarpment East of the town. During the next two days it was extremely dangerous to move by day owing to the Italian and German aircraft which were searching the area bombing and machine-gunning anything seen. Captain M. J. Pleydell, RAMC, the Medical Officer attached, attended to the wounded without any thought of his own safety. On one occasion while he was removing a bullet from Captain R. M. E. Melot's thigh a German plane was circling overhead. On being told that Corporal A. Drongin, who had been wounded in the stomach, was too ill to be moved he drove five miles to him and operated. On the 15th at 1400 hours the main body of the Regiment was discovered by the enemy airforce in a narrow wadi. From then until dusk they were bombed and machine-gunned incessantly. Doctor Pleydell was not in the wadi when they were discovered but on hearing the bombs and seeing what had happened, he drove back. In the wadi he moved around the twelve wounded giving morphia and dressing their wounds, paying no attention to the bombs or bullets. Being as he was, 500 miles from the nearest Advanced Dressing Station, he undoubtedly saved many lives by his bravery and skill. Note: This officer has carried out consistent good work on three other operations.

> Lieutenant-Colonel H. J. Cator, MC
> Commanding, 1st Special Air Service Regiment"

So runs the unpublished and corrected citation for the Military Cross awarded for Operation Bigamy to the author of this work. Doctor Pleydell gave pseudonyms to every man either killed or wounded featuring in this account of his time with the special service unit raised by the late Sir David Stirling, Scots Guards (15 November 1915 – 4 November 1990) and christened for deception purposes as 'L Detachment' to go with the preceding 'J' and 'K' Detachments of the mythical 'Special Air Service Brigade' created by Lieutenant-Colonel Dudley Clarke, Royal Artillery, Wavell's Intelligence Officer (Special Duties) and a founder of the Commandos.

Malcolm Pleydell arrived at the L Detachment camp on 6 June 1942 as an experienced medical practitioner who had served as a ship's doctor during the evacuation of the BEF from Dunkirk and then with 3 Coldstream Guards in the early desert campaigns and was posted out of the unit (as from 21 September 1942 a fully fledged, albeit, hostilities only, regiment of the British Army in the Middle East) on 29 March 1943. His description of these formative years of Britain's elite Special Forces regiment is a valuable mixture of direct, personal experience and the memories he collected and recorded of the officers and men he served with. Whilst recuperating in hospital on Malta, Pleydell wrote from memory and used his own, now lost, war diary, letters and Press clippings. Subject to official censorship, and without access to the official record, his narrative necessarily contains some slips in the spelling of personal names and errors of fact which are now rectified here. Compiling these notes was a task that could not have been attempted with any degree of confidence before the arrival of the Internet and the widespread availability of electronic finding aids to trace United Kingdom public records.

The 'Lewis' of his account of the Detachment's early training and disastrous first operation is actually John Steele 'Jock' Lewes, Welsh Guards (killed on operations 30 December 1941). On the night of 16/17 November 1941 five Bombays of 216 Squadron, RAF, departed the airstrip near 8th Army's forward headquarters carrying fifty-five officers and men. The names of the casualties from that drop and the two men killed previously in parachute training – before Pleydell arrived with the unit – are shown in the Roll of Honour which now appears at the end of this book. Contrary to his belief no men of the, by then, real Special Air Service Brigade landed in France prior to the Normandy landings on 5/6 June 1944 although six men from 1st SAS, reformed in the United Kingdom under the command of Blair 'Paddy' Mayne, were amongst the first British troops to parachute into France on that night on Operation Titanic.

The personalities of the men in the SAS make up the heart of Pleydell's writing. Of the NCOs he describes 'Bob' Bennett and 'Johnny' Rose were from the Grenadier Guards; 'Pat' Riley, the Coldstream Guards; 'Johnny' Cooper, the Scots Guards; 'Tate' (actually 'Bob' Tait, MM from the London Scottish and designer of the original 'Excalibur' sword of freedom badge of the Regiment) and Edward McDonald from the Cameron Highlanders; 'Reg' Seekings from the Cambridgeshire Regiment were all on the first, and only, parachute operation. 'Dave' Kershaw from the Grenadier Guards, also on that operation, lost a leg when serving with the Parachute Regiment at Arnhem. ('Bobby Dodds'; actually R. W. Dodd, also transferred to the Parachute Regiment and died at Arnhem on 20 September 1944 whilst serving with 10 Para. Peter Warr from the East Surrey Regiment, the first Ringway trained Parachute Jump Instructor attached to L Detachment from 6 November 1941 to 5 January 1943, also served with 10 Para at Arnhem and was decorated for this.) 'Bob' Lilley and 'Jim' Almonds from the Coldstream Guards; 'Paddy' O'Dowd from the Irish Guards (later killed on Operation Devon at Termoli, Italy, 5 October 1943 as was 'Sandy' Wilson who was A. M. 'Sandy' Wilson from the Gordons (killed the following day on the same operation.); 'Ted' Badger and Derek Miller from the Royal Artillery; 'Cantell' (actually Syd Cattell, 1 East Surrey Regiment); John Cunningham from the Royal Sussex Regiment; Arthur Phillips from the Royal Warwickshire Regiment, 'Jack' Sillito from the Staffordshire Yeomanry and Fred 'Chalky' White from the Loyals were all decorated for actions when with the Regiment.

'Sergeant Sculthorpe', described as being later commissioned has not yet been identified. 'Mike' Sadler, MM, 4 Rhodesian Anti-Tank Battery – the Detachment's original Corporal desert navigator on loan from S Patrol of the Long Range Desert Group – was commissioned into the SAS, most irregularly 'in the field' by David Stirling himself and was subsequently decorated again for actions with the Regiment. To CSM 'Pat' Riley (who was an American citizen) and Sergeant 'Johnny' Cooper, noted by the author as both later commissioned into the Regiment, should be added 'Ted' Badger, Edward McDonald and also 'Jim' Almonds after his escape from Italy – having been taken prisoner on the Benghasi raid – and the Canadian 'Bill' Deakins of the Royal Engineers who was one of Captain 'Bill' Cumper's men.

Of the officers, 'Bill' Cumper, commissioned from the ranks into the Royal Engineers, was ex-143 Field Park Squadron, 7 Armoured Division and was decorated for his part in Operation Bigamy, the Benghasi raid, which is so vividly described by Pleydell in Chapters 14–18. George Jellicoe was The Earl Jellicoe, son of the famous British admiral and from the Coldstream Guards. When Pleydell arrived at Kabrit he was planning, with *Capitaine* Georges Bergé, MC, Chef of the Free French *Infanterie de l'Air* detachment in the Middle East, Operation Anglo against Heraklion airfield on Crete to disrupt the German air effort against a Malta bound convoy. The other French officers he alludes to were actually *soldats* Jacques Mouhot, Sibard and Pierre Leostic. The last named was to die on the operation which landed from HMS/M *Triton* on the night of 13/14 June 1942. It was David Sutherland, from the Black Watch and Special Boat Section, heading for another airfield target on the same island who landed with his team from the Greek submarine *Papa Nikolas* on the same night. Bergé (who died 17 September 1997) and Mouhot were both captured (Mouhot later escaping and being decorated for this). Jellicoe later rose to command the Special Boat Squadron, 1 SAS (subsequently the Special Boat Service) and was finally succeeded by David Sutherland. Both these officers were decorated for this and other operations. The Detachment Adjutant Eric 'Parten' or 'Parent' was actually E. G. Parton and Bernard Schott was from the General List (formerly King's African Rifles) and ex-G (Raiding) branch of GHQ, Middle East. 'Bill' Fraser was from the Gordons, commanded the ground RV party in the first parachute operation (due to injuries received in training for this) and was first decorated for the Operation Green Room raids in July 1942. On the same operation were Gordon Alston from the Royal Artillery and Special Boat Section (later Intelligence Officer, 1 SAS), Fitzroy Maclean from the Cameron Highlanders and Randolph Churchill from 4 QORH (these latter two were both Members of Parliament at one time or another and Churchill was, of course, the son of the Prime Minister of the day). Pleydell's replacement RMOs were J. R. Macintyre and Philip Gunn, RAMC (who was also to be decorated whilst serving with the Special Raiding Squadron, 1 SAS, and was sadly killed in a road traffic accident in December 1944). Colonel Buttle, RAMC was awarded the OBE and was at 15th (Scottish) General Hospital. His RADC colleagues nicknamed 'Fangs' and 'Forceps' have not been identified.

Of the remaining SAS officers Barlow was V. W. Barlow from the KSLI; McDermott was H. M. C. MacDermot, MC from the

Royal Artillery; Harry Poat was H. W. Poat from the KOSB; Johnny Wiseman was J. M. 'Johnny' Wiseman from the DCLI; and Sandy Scratchley was A. J. 'Sandy' Scratchley from 4 CLY. (These last three officers were all decorated for actions with the SAS in later campaigns.) Berneville Claye was D. W. St Aubyn Berneville-Claye from the West Yorkshires. He was also known as 'Lord Charlesworth' and when captured in 1943 and held in Campo 38 in Italy (and later Oflag 79 in Germany with many of the other SAS officer prisoners of war) was known as Bournville Clay or Berneville-Glaye or, during a short period of absence from the camps, as *Hauptsturmführer* Belleville-Clave, Coldstream Guards, Britische Freikorps, having gone over to the enemy and enrolled in the Waffen SS. Not mentioned by name as such in Chapter 8, but present with the author at the rendezvous at Bir el Quseir were Stephen Hastings from the Scots Guards and Carol Mather from the Welsh Guards (both were later decorated for their wartime service and the latter became a Member of Parliament, post war).

Pleydell frequently mentions and describes the men of the Free French *Infanterie de l'Air* detachment in the Middle East but none are mentioned by name except 'Jacques' who was *Aspirant* Jacques Martin (later killed on operations in France) and 'Henri', 'Henry' or ''Enry' who was *Aspirant* Germain Guerpillon killed on Operation Bigamy. In Chapter 6 he describes the raids on Fuka airfield in July 1942 and *Aspirant* André Zirnheld was killed on this operation. His men Jean Bouard (wounded across a finger) and Philippe Fauquet were later decorated by the French, whilst Jean Le Gall and Victor Ituria (killed later on operations in France) were decorated by both the French and British governments for their SAS service. *Aspirants* Klein and Michel Legrand and *Soldat* Jean Roquemaure were the French wounded and sick referred to in Chapter 8 along with the LRDG's M. B. P. Fraser, MM of the Scots Guards. Both Legrand and Roquemaure also received French decorations with Legrand also being decorated, twice, by the British for western desert and later operations. Sgt Taxis was the French operative who accompanied the first SAS patrol to make the link-up between the 8th and 1st Armies mentioned in Chapter 21. Aimé Gillet, Henri James, Emile Logeais, the brothers Georges and Jean Royer and Jean Tourneret, taken prisoner on an earlier airfield raid against Martuba in June 1942 – betrayed by a Ger-

man, ex-French Foreign Legion and 361 Afrika Regiment –
member of the Special Interrogation Group (raised by Captain
Herbert Buck, MC, 3/1 Punjabis, who was to die in the United
Kingdom whilst serving in the SAS) were killed when the *Nino
Bixio* taking them to long-term prisoner of war camps in Italy was
torpedoed by a British submarine. Other German-speaking personnel who were trained to operate as members of the German
Army in Buck's SIG sub-unit of 51 (Middle East) Commando
served with distinction attached to, or later in, L Detachment, then
the Special Boat Squadron of 1 SAS and latterly the Special Boat
Service in the Middle East and Mediterranean theatres. Of these
Pleydell refers to two Palestinians 'Karl' and 'Joseph'. 'Joseph' has
yet to be identified with any certainty but 'Karl' was Karl Kahane,
a German Jew, decorated with the EKII for service with the Kai-
ser's forces in World War I, who transferred from Sutherland's SBS
to the RAF Regiment, 1328 Wing at the end of the war with
Germany.

Pleydell's active service account commences with Chapter 5 and
the July 1942 raiding programme – with attached RAF Ground
Liaison Officers – which commenced with the experienced G1, G2
and Y2 Patrols of the Long Range Desert Group under Stirling's
command for the first time and was subsequently joined by their
R1 Patrol. His 'Arthur Sharpe' was Flying Officer D. L. Rawnsley,
RAFVR, from 204 Group, RAF (who subsequently died on 22
February 1943) and 'Ginger', 'Sandy' or 'Digger Shaw' was Flying
Officer 'Laurie' Pyke, RAAF, of 'Two-Sixteen' Squadron, RAF
who died in an aircraft accident on 5 November 1942. Robin
Gurdon was The Honourable R. B. Gurdon of the Coldstream
Guards commanding G2 Patrol and he and the author both served
in 3 Coldstream Guards prior to transfer into special service.
Gurdon died of wounds on 13 July 1942 having commanded his
Guards patrol since 27 February 1942. His soldier/servant was
Vaughan of the same Regiment and his original Patrol Sergeant
was James Wilson of the Scots Guards and a decorated LRDG
soldier. His wounded 'Corporal Preston' was Serjeant J. P.
Stocker, RTR who was decorated for the actions described and
'Parker' was Guardsman Murray of the same Patrol who had been
wounded in the left elbow and arm and taken two bullets in his
right thigh in the same air attack. Confusingly Pleydell has 'Bob'

Lilley referring to 'Corporal Parker' in Chapter 20 when telling his story of the attack on Berka Satellite airfield on 12/13 June 1942 when this was actually Corporal A. Warburton from the Welsh Guards who was taken prisoner after that raid. A typographic error would seem to account for his having 'Johnny' Rose refer to the death of 'Arthur Morton' of the Daily Telegraph when he was actually Arthur Merton, OBE who died on 28 May 1942 after the road traffic accident described.

'Rowlands' killed on the Sidi Haneish airfield raid of 27 July 1942, described in Chapter 9, was Lance Bombardier J. W. R. Robson of the Royal Artillery and opens the list of SAS dead mentioned by the author, most of them sustained on Operation Bigamy and cared for by him in the Wadi Ftilia. Almost all can now be identified with certainty, although, sadly, despite many years of effort, two of the men supposedly killed outright in the Sand Sea together with Lieutenant D. S. Kennedy (of A Squadron, 1 SAS, originally from 169 (8/Gordons) Battery, 100 LAA/AT Regiment, RA) and Corporal Allan Sharman, 6 RTR on 20 November 1942 mentioned in Chapter 20 cannot; although this is possibly because the author's account is faulty. Similarly 'Don Pettit', described as died in the Sand Sea on the way to Benghasi, would actually appear to be R. H. Shorten, General List, who died a month later on 19 October 1942 when his jeep rolled over.

Of the men 'Cox' was either Driver William Marlow, RASC or Serjeant J. W. Webster of 1/4 Essex Regiment; 'Dawson' was Corporal A. Drongin of 2 Scots Guards; and 'Wilkinson' was AQMS E. A. N. Sque, REME from 4 Base Workshop. The badly wounded 'Macleod' was man named Laird and he would appear to have survived his journey back with the SDF.

The officers were 'Longland', actually C. S. Bailey from 4 QORH and 'Bob Melot' from GHQ, ME, G (Raiding) branch was R. M. E. 'Bob' Melot, General List, who was subsequently decorated and died serving with 1st SAS on 1 November 1944. The cook 'Paddy' Allan was P. J. Allan 87 HAA Regiment, RA killed on 5 December 1942 during Operation Palmyra.

In Chapter 14 Pleydell conceals the presence of men from the Royal Navy on the operation. The death on 12 September 1942 of the Assistant Harbourmaster, Haifa, Lieutenant-Commander R. A. B. Ardley, RNR of HMS Stag is alluded to under the guise of the loss of a 'gunner officer' instead of that of Ardley, the veteran holder of the Polar Medal in Bronze with clasp 'Antarctic 1929–33'. In a footnote Pleydell records that 'Johnson' his Medical Orderly, who remained behind with the wounded after the unsuccessful raid on Benghasi, died some eighteen months after the operation. In fact 'Razor Blade' A. Johnson is now known not to have done so and 'Shotton', actually also a real name, survived too. It therefore appears that 'Ritchie' is a real name, that he was an ex-Commando Regimental Medical Orderly and it was this man who went into captivity and subsequently died and the author has confused the names.

A number of other SAS soldiers appear in Pleydell's narrative, amongst them is 'Hevans' who was R. E. 'Bob' Heavens from the Royal Artillery, who was executed 7 July 1944 under the infamous 'Kommandobefehl' on Operation Bulbasket with 1st SAS in the Bois de Guron, Forêt de Saint-Sauvant by Radfahrschwadron des Korpstabes LXXX Armee Korps and now lies buried in Rom Cemetery, Deux-Sevres, France. Other readily identifiable men are 'Storey' who was 'Jimmy' Storie of the Royal Scots Fusiliers and one of Stirling's original men as was J. Leitch, of the Scots Guards, the mess steward.

Pleydell mentions an unnamed USA Army officer in Chapter 13 who was probably David Lair and in Chapter 15 gives the name 'Farmer' to A. S. Lyle-Smythe of the Secret Intelligence Service (known in the Middle East theatre as the Inter Services Liaison Department) who operated in the Benghasi area in 1942. His account in Chapter 11 of Jellicoe's recovery of twelve escaped prisoners of war conceals the crew of 104 Squadron, RAF, Wellington II 'B' Z8509 (Sgt A. J. Willis, New Zealand Sgt J. L. Joyce, PO H. J. King, Sgt J. C. Weston and the wounded rear-gunner J. C. Barr) together with Lieut D. A. G. Allen and Sappers Frearson, Smithson and Driver Goddard (all Royal Engineers of 1 Field Squadron, 1 Armoured Division), Witham of the Durban LI, McGarvin of the HLI and one other unnamed soldier who all flew out with the SAS in Bombays from LG 64 on the night of 4/5 August 1942. Jellicoe and his men were hunting the German doctor and his pilot who were captured by T1 Patrol of the LRDG and who feature in Chapter 10. This was Surgeon Captain Baron von Lutteroti, (subsequently awarded the EKII) of 580 Aufklärungs Abteilung and his Luftwaffe NCO pilot who both escaped from the SAS on the night of 2/3 August 1942. They then walked some 60 miles to their own forces and reported the presence of Major Stirling with British, New Zealand, Free French and Free German troops who were promptly sought out by his unit. Strangely enough, this German doctor was met with again by the SAS when he also treated some of their men on operations in Germany at the end of the war. Contrary to Pleydell's account in Chapter 6 and Chapter 7, Jellicoe had previously only captured two men: a driver and a mechanic of Gerast. Afrika on 7 July 1942.

Pleydell's account of the incident where David Stirling, 'Paddy' Mayne, 'Johnny' Cooper and Karl Kahane were nearly all lost to posterity by the premature initiation of a time-pencil occurred in a Chevrolet truck borrowed from Robin Gurdon, who would himself have transferred to the SAS on return from the operation on which he was killed.

Finally, it is worth recording that General Dempsey, the Corps commander quoted with approval by 'Paddy' Mayne in Chapter 21, at the conclusion of this book, subsequently became Sir Miles Dempsey and the first Colonel Commandant of the Special Air Service Regiment when it was reformed after the war.

David List, 2001

APPENDIX
by David Buxton

ROLL OF HONOUR

The Roll was compiled from a variety of sources held in public records, and registers published by the Commonwealth War Graves Commission. It is as complete as it can be with the evidence available. Pleydell uses pseudonyms for several of the casualties, such as 'Dawson' for Cpl Drongin, and others he does not identify by name. Even using a variety of searches, several remain unidentified.

The personnel are either buried in cemeteries or commemorated on the Alamein Memorial, and all were honoured in 1998 by the SAS Regimental Association. This project aimed to identify all the wartime dead and both veterans and volunteers alike visited fifteen countries to lay wreaths in 63 cemeteries and on 10 memorials that honoured the SAS casualties of World War II.

An additional product of this commemoration was the compilation of the first official Roll of Honour remembrance book for the Special Air Service Regiment, to be dedicated at a future date.

'L DETACHMENT, SAS BRIGADE' July 1941–August 1942, and 1 SAS REGIMENT September 1942–May 1943

1610059	Gnr	Patrick Joseph Allen	RA	05.12.42[1]
141129	Capt	Christopher Sidney Bailey	4 Hrs, RAC	15.09.42[1]
2696934	Gdsm	Stanley Bolland	Scots Gds	20.11.41[1]
5437777	Cpl	Leslie Jock Brown	DCLI	15–18.01.43[6]
IA/1013	Capt	Terence Frederick Thomas Chambers		
			5/Mahratta LI	04.12.42[2]
2876138	Sjt	John Cheyne	Gordons 16.11.41–27.12.41[1]	
2695218	Cpl	Anthony Drongin	Scots Gds	16–19.09.42[1]
3318385	Pte	Joseph Aloysius Duffy	Seaforths	16.10.41[2]
	Sgt	Aimé Gillet	French Det	17.08.42[8]
	Asp	Germain Guerpillon	French Det	16.09.42[8]
3657806	L/Cpl	Sydney James Hildreth	S Lan Regt	19.11.41[1]
55987	Capt	the Hon Alexander Hardinge Patrick Hore-Ruthven		
			R Bde	24.12.42[5]
	Sdt	Henri James	French Det	17.08.42[8]
	Sgt	Isodore Jouanny	French Det	17.08.42[8]

2882330	Pte	Douglas Keith	Gordons	09.12.41[1]
557709	Tpr	Stanley Vincent Kendall	Warwick Yeo, RAC	30.10.42[1]
106690	Lieut	Douglas Stewart Kennedy	RA	20.11.42[1]
2696787	WOII	David Lambie	Scots Gds	18.01.43[1]
	Sdt	Pierre Leostic	French Det	14.06.42[8]
65419	Lieut	John Steel Lewes	Welsh Gds	30.12.41[1]
	Sdt	Emile Logeais	French Det	17.08.42[8]
3651857	Sjt	John Joseph Mannion	S Lan Regt	14.02.42[7]
T/119344	Dvr	William Marlow	RASC	15.09.42[1]
97290	Lieut	Eoin Christopher McGonigal	RUR	18.11.41[1]
IA/664	Capt	Denis Luke Maurice Murphy	CIH, IAC	15–18.01.43[6]
3056939	Pte	Malvern Nixon	R Scots	15–18.01.43[6]
831653	Gnr	Frank William Rawlinson	RA	11.03.43[2]
886920	L/Bdr	John William Robert Robson	RA	27.07.42[1]
	Cpl	Georges Royer	French Det	17.08.42[8]
	Sdt	Jean Royer	French Det	17.08.42[8]
2696965	Sjt	Fred Senior	Scots Gds	15–18.01.43[6]
7887122	Cpl	Allan Sharman	6RTR, RAC	20.11.42[4]
163658	Lieut	Raymond Herbert Shorten	G List	19.10.42[1]
5672780	Pte	Thomas John Sillett	Somerset L I	31.10.42[1]
2087918	WOII	Eustace Arthur Nicol Sque	REME	19.10.42[1]
2692673	Sjt	Sidney James Stone	Scots Gds	05.12.41[3]
	Cpl	Jean Tourneret	French Det	17.08.42[8]
2821591	Pte	Kenneth Warburton	Seaforths	16.10.41[2]
6012106	Sjt	James Walter Webster	Essex Regt	16.09.42[1]
	Asp	André Zirnheld	French Det	27.07.42[8]

Key to burials/commemorations:
[1] Alamein Memorial, Egypt
[2] Fayid War Cemetery, Egypt
[3] Benghazi War Cemetery, Libya
[4] Knightsbridge War Cemetery, Libya
[5] Tripoli War Cemetery, Libya
[6] Enfidaville War Cemetery, Tunisia
[7] Freetown Cemetery, Sierra Leone
[8] SAS War Memorial, Sennecey le Grand, France

The following members who are mentioned in the text were subsequently killed:

128655	Major	Philip McLean Gunn	RAMC & MC MB ChB	
			HQ SAS Bde	09.09.44
820065	Sjt	Robert Eric Heavens	R A & 1st SAS	07.07.44
2719054	Sjt	Christopher O'Dowd MM	Irish Gds & 1 SAS	05.10.43

163579   Major Robert Marie Emanuel Melot MC

                                          G List & 1st SAS   01.11.44

203919   Lieut   Alexander Melville Wilson   Gordons & 1 SAS   06.10.43

HONOURS AND AWARDS

Following the success of the early raids both David Stirling and 'Paddy' Mayne were made Companions of the Distinguished Service Order, an award usually reserved for officers of much higher rank, but showed how the army high command appreciated their services.

Lieutenant Colonel David Stirling was captured in January 1943 but was later awarded an OBE to go with his DSO for his bravery whilst a prisoner of war, and on repatriation became Deputy Commander of the SAS Brigade in the United Kingdom during the four months prior to its disbandment. 'Paddy' Mayne was to command the Special Raiding Squadron, 1 SAS Regiment on its reorganisation under Lieutenant Colonel H. W. Cator MC. The Squadron then returned to the United Kingdom in 1944 and expanded into a new 1st SAS Regiment under Mayne's command.

The Military Cross awards were for acts of bravery such as 'Bill' Cumper's actions at the Benghazi road block; 'Bill' Fraser's destruction of aircraft and Malcolm Pleydell's conduct tending wounded under fire.

The Distinguished Conduct Medal and the Military Medal were given for a variety of acts of bravery or service on a number of raids. Some of these stand out, such as the DCM to 'Johnny' Cooper after he countered an enemy ambush on the way back from a raid, having already thirteen raids under his belt; John Sillito's 'long walk' (it was thought he had perished following signals referring to T. J. Silett being initially misinterpreted); and 'Jim' Almonds' gallantry after taking over his party after his officer 'Jock' Lewes had been killed.

Honours and Awards to 'L Detachment, SAS Brigade' July 1941–August 1942 and 1 SAS Regiment September 1942–May 1943

2655648   Sjt   John Edward Almonds   3/C Gds   MM

898919   Sjt   Edward Aitchison Badger   RA   MM

2617533	Sjt	Robert Bennett	6/Gren Gds	MM
2695138	Sjt	William Gordon Brough	2/S Gds	MM
2060658	Cpl	John Vincent Byrne	Gordons	DCM
6141548	Cpl	Charles Sidney Cattell	1/E Surrey R	MM
2698113	Sjt	John Murdoch Cooper	2/S Gds	DCM
202597	Capt	William John Cumper	RE	MC
6400007	Pte	John Cunningham	R Sussex R	MM
2695796	Cpl	Geoffrey Downes	S Gds	MM
2885910	Sjt	Jeffrey DuVivier	Gordons	MM
132513	Lieut	William Fraser	Gordons	MC
53282	Sgt	Victor Iturria	French Det	MM
124546	Capt	The Earl Jellicoe	C Gds	DSO
40067	Lieut	Augustin Jordan	French Det	MC
320025	Cpl	William Faa Blythe Kennedy	Greys, RAC	MM
4121633	Sjt	David Kershaw	6/Gren Gds	MM
52297	Cpl	Jean Le Gall	French Det	MM
40102	Asp.	Michel Legrand	French Det	MC
2660913	Sjt	Ernest Thomas Lilley	C Gds	MM
2660913	CQMS	Ernest Thomas Lilley	C Gds	MID
124488	Capt	David Carol MacDonell Mather	W Gds	MID
87306	Lieut	Robert Blair Mayne	R U Rif	DSO
87306	Lieut	Robert Blair Mayne	R U Rif	MID
2928608	Sjt	Edward McDonald	Camerons	DCM
56634	Capt	P. S. Morris-Keating	Rifle Bde	MID
2719054	Sjt	Christopher O'Dowd	I Gds	MM
97456	Major	Peter Carlton Oldfield	Warwick Yeo	MID
5107891	Sjt	Arthur Phillips	R War R	MM
133658	Capt	Malcolm James Pleydell, MB	RAMC	MC
2656281	CSM	Charles George Gibson Riley	C Gds	DCM
2617725	Sjt	Graham Rose	6/Gren Gds	MM
2617725	SSM	Graham Rose	6/Gren Gds	Bar to MM
35050	Lieut	Alexander James Scratchley	4 C Lon Yeo	MID
5933155	Sjt	Albert Reginald Seekings	Camb R	DCM
324811	Tpr	John William Sillito	Staffs Yeo	MM
72647	Capt	Archibald David Stirling	S Gds	DSO
72647	Capt	Archibald David Stirling	S Gds	twice MID
108190	Lieut	David George Carr Sutherland	Black Watch	MC
2888673	Sjt	Duncan Robert Tait, MM	Gordons	Bar to MM
187052	Capt	Peter Esmond Warr	E Surrey R	MBE
3535141	Cpl	Frederick Henry White	Loyals	MM
154976	Cpl	Harold White	RASC	MM

The following personnel mentioned in the text were also subsequently decorated whilst serving with SAS in the later campaigns:

2655648	Sjt	John Edward Almonds, MM	C Gds	Bar to MM
28655	Capt	Philip McLean Gunn, MB	RAMC	MC
328084	Sjt	John Arthur Holmes	1st SAS	MM
87306	Major	Robert Blair Mayne, DSO	R U Rif	3 bars to DSO, CdeG

(France)—from Jan 1944 to Oct 1945 he commanded 1st SAS Regiment

123359	Capt	Harry Wall Poat	KOSB	MC
282465	Capt	Willis Michael Sadler, MM	1st SAS R	MC
35050	Major	Alexander James Scratchley	4 C Lon Yeo	MC
5933155	Sjt	Albert Reginald Seekings, DCM	Camb R	MM
324811	Cpl			
	(A/Sjt)	John William Sillito, MM	Staffs Yeo	Bar to MM
256809	Lieut	John Martin Wiseman	DCLI	MC

David Buxton, 2001